Keith Martin on

COLLECTING
JAGUAR

Keith Martin on

COLLECTING
JAGUAR

Keith Martin's
Sports Car Market
The Insider's Guide to Collecting, Investing, Values and Trends

MOTORBOOKS
INTERNATIONAL

This edition first published in 2004 by Motorbooks International, an imprint of MBI Publishing Company, Galtier Plaza, Suite 200, 380 Jackson Street, St. Paul, MN 55101-3885 USA

The information in this book is true and complete to the best of our knowledge. All recommendations are made without any guarantee on the part of the author or Publisher, who also disclaim any liability incurred in connection with the use of this data or specific details.

We recognize that some words, model names and designations, for example, mentioned herein are the property of the trademark holder. We use them for identification purposes only. This is not an official publication.

Motorbooks International titles are also available at discounts in bulk quantity for industrial or sales-promotional use. For details write to Special Sales Manager at Motorbooks International Wholesalers & Distributors, Galtier Plaza, Suite 200, 380 Jackson Street, St. Paul, MN 55101-3885 USA.

ISBN 0-7603-2070-5

Front cover: 2005 XKR by Jeff Dorgay

Designed by Susan Bard

Printed in China

Jaguars As a Way of Life

The Mille Miglia retrospective has become my favorite classic car event. I have done it six times, first in 1999 in my XK-SS and subsequently in my D-type. In May 2004 I drove my 1955 D-type (XKD530) and finished 78th overall and 2nd among the American teams.

The pace this year from the Futa Pass to Brescia on Saturday evening was slower than the previous days, and remarkably stress-free. Cruising along in the D-type through that starlit night, I thought about how fortunate I was to be competing in this famous Italian event, in one of the world's greatest cars. My thoughts turned to how a significant part of my professional career has centered around one marque—Jaguar.

Gary Bartlett and wife Kathy, with their Jaguar XK-SS.

This fascination with Jaguars started at Christmas in 1960, when I found a four-lane Aurora slot car track under the tree. I can't remember what the other three cars were—I was piloting the D-type. This fascination struck again when my wife of 32 years (then girlfriend) Kathy and I went in 1969 to the Delaware Cinema in Muncie to see "M.A.S.H." Parked in the "No Parking" fire lane was a 1965 Carmen Red E-type fixed-head coupe, with the English registration plate DWK825C. I could not take my eyes off of it. I thought it was the most beautiful car in the world.

Subscribers to *Sports Car Market* will understand that something forever changed the way I look at cars that night. I traced the E-type to a surgeon in Anderson, Indiana, and pestered him until he sold it to me a month later for $2,500.

The day after I bought it, I drove it from Muncie to North Carolina and from there to Tampa and back. Although after buying the car I had about $250 to my name, I felt like a king. I even loved washing it. Somehow it felt good just to touch its curves.

Jaguar maintenance in Muncie in 1969 was limited to the local Jaguar dealer, McClelland Company, which I couldn't afford, or "Shorty" at Yingling Gulf. I decided to work on it myself at my dad and uncle's tire and battery store. Other Jaguar owners noticed the Jag's frequently raised bonnet, and as a result soon there were more customers wanting a Jag tuneup than needing Prime batteries and Kelly-Springfield tires.

By 1975, I had moved on to a 1971 XJ6. In between, I had owned an XK 120 OTS, an XK 150 FHC and a 1969 E FHC. About the time I got the XJ6 my dad, getting tired of all of the Jaguars parked at his tire shop not needing tires, told me that it was time to take the Jaguars elsewhere. I left and started G.W. Bartlett Company. The new Jaguar business took off immediately and we worked hard to develop a reputation for quality, service and value.

In 1980 while searching for an "as original" interior for an E-type in England I struck up a deal with the owner of a Jaguar upholstery business to become the US importer for his British produced interiors. Eventually, we had to learn how to manufacture these parts in Muncie; the British firm simply could not keep up with the demand in the US and Europe. It's odd how a career evolves—who would have thought that so many classic Jaguars all over the world would end up with interiors made in America's heartland?

In 1983, my company formed a relationship with BLE Ltd. in Birmingham, England to sell performance parts for the XJ-S. When BLE ran into difficulties, I purchased the rights to various parts and manufactured them in the USA. We then developed and sold about 250 versions of the Lister XJS to Jaguar dealers around the world.

In the '80s, prices of collectible cars including Jaguars were booming, and G.W. Bartlett Company was in overdrive trying to keep up with the orders. *Sports Car Market* devotees will recall that the end of the torrid market was near. For me it ended at a classic car auction at the N.E.C. in Birmingham, England in 1990. The auction failed to find a buyer for a single car.

I knew that my business in Muncie would be affected. Fortunately workforce in Muncie was very skilled, and transitioned into producing interior components for the automotive industry in the US and Europe.

When the XJ 220 was previewed in 1987, I thought it was fantastic. However, in 1989, when the price was announced at £290,000 (more than $450,000), and considering the fact that they would not be EPA or DOT legal, I never thought owning one would ever be possible. But thanks to the "Show and Display" legislation championed by Bill Gates, ownership became a reality.

Mike Beasley (Managing Director of Jaguar in 1998) told me one afternoon in 1998 that Jaguar had 14 new XJ 220s in a "deep sleep" at Brown's Lane. Aware of the new legislation, he asked me if I had an interest in buying one to make them USA legal. We agreed and completed the paperwork at the Goodwood Festival of Speed two weeks later.

My XJ 220 was the first car to be approved by the DOT under the new legislation, permit number 00-001. In some ways, being behind the wheel of the XJ 220 offered the same types of thrills and excitement that driving the E-type in 1969 had.

Keith Martin and I first met in Soragna, Italy, some years ago. He had just finished a stint in the Tour Auto driving an Alfa GT Junior, and was getting ready to pilot a three-window Alfa 1900CSS in the Mille Miglia.

I recall that we had a long talk about C- and D-types, and the necessity of proper recordkeeping so that real and "less-real" ones could always be separated, at least in the marketplace.

Thumbing through the pages of *Keith Martin on Collecting Jaguar*, I find that each article gives me some new bit of information about the marque, and increases my appreciation of Jaguar and their incredible heritage. Of course, as a lover of Jaguars, having a book full of stories only about Jaguars is about as close as it gets to a perfect read!

There are many marques and models of cars, and we each find our own way to the one that is special for us. For me it is Jaguar. I've enjoyed my ride so far, and I look forward to putting many more miles under my tires in years to come. —*Gary W. Bartlett*◆

Contents

Section IV: Ultra-Exotics

Part V: Concours, the Mille Miglia & Insurance

Jeff Dorgay

Leaping Cats, Leaping Writers

Just as a Jaguar is made up of thousands of moving parts, *Keith Martin on Collecting Jaguars* is made up of hundreds of contributions by scores of enthusiasts.

Sports Car Market Magazine (the source of most of the information here) is written by enthusiasts for enthusiasts. And the same goes for this book.

Each author has more than his share of time spent behind the wheel (or underneath!) of Jaguars, from early SS 100s to XJ220s to the latest XKRs.

The profiles here follow the *Sports Car Market* approach, with an introductory section about a car that was offered at auction, and an analysis of the amount it sold for by one of our experts.

Profile authors include *SCM*'s Senior Contributing Editor Dave Brownell, who can been seen piloting his very own 3-Liter Bentley along the back roads of Vermont. Gary Anderson, formerly publisher of *British Car Magazine* and a good friend, has made some typically insightful comments in both the profiles and in his own column, *Cat Q & A*. Steve Cram, Bill Neill and Brian Rabold also added their pithy insights.

Michael Duffey, formerly *SCM*'s popular Mr. Kerb, chimes in with some of his own Q & A.

Setting this book apart from our previous efforts, *Keith Martin on Collecting Porsche* and *Keith Martin on Collecting Ferrari,* is material unique to the Jaguar book that has not appeared before in *SCM*.

The contributors of those articles are Ron Avery, Martin Emmison, Cameron Sheahan, Richard Griot, and Phil Weeden. Gary Bartlett, a long-time *SCM* subscriber, offers a thoughtful look back at his life with Jaguar in the Foreword, taking us from his very first E-type, through his XK-SS and D-type, and ending with the XJ220s he federalized and serviced.

Thanks to Dutch Mandel, Associate Publisher at *AutoWeek*, for making available several informative reviews of modern Jags by Kevin Wilson as well as Dutch himself. And thanks to Phil Wheeden and *Jaguar World Monthly* for the great piece on the Mille Miglia. Cars of Particular Interest (CPI) has graciously provided the information we use in the 20 Year Picture price graphs.

The regular *SCM* gang has beavered away, burning the midnight oil (scraped off the garage floor from under the *SCM* E-type, no doubt) to write and copy edit this book. Yeoman duty was done by Kathleen Karapondo, who edited every piece here, picked out all the pull quotes and headlines, and wrote whatever was necessary to mold ten years of articles by different authors into one harmonious style, which reflects our own *SCM* voice.

New to *SCM* is designer Susan Bard, a Portlander who has done a terrific job taking our already-established format

and giving a fresh, light look. David Slama, the *SCM* Production Manager, has shepherded the entire project from start to finish, the most thankless job of all. David, joined by Susan and Kathleen, make a formidable artistic, editorial and production team, and it's been a pleasure to work with all of them.

Jeff Dorgay is the photographer for our cover shot, and Monte and Neil Shelton graciously made both their dealership and the shiny black XKR available to us for it.

Other photos in this book were provided by the following auction companies and we thank them: Barrett-Jackson, Bonhams, Christie's, Coys, and RM Auctions.

The heart of *SCM* is its auction reporting, and you'll find the reports in this book enlightening as well. The auction reporters pull no punches, calling a beauty queen a beauty queen, and a fright pig a fright pig. Nearly every weekend, there's an *SCM* analyst at an auction somewhere, working away to provide you with the insights that will help you become a more proficient collector. Analysts included in this book are Richard Hudson-Evans, David Kinney, John Clucas, Scott Featherman, Carl Bomstead, Dan Grunwald, B. Mitchell Carlson and the ubiquitous David Slama.

We highly appreciate the cooperation of the auction companies as they let our experts prowl around the cars they are offering; included here are reports about cars from Artcurial, Barrett-Jackson, Bonhams, Bonhams & Butterfields, CCI (Branson), Christie's, Coys, H&H Auctions, Kensington, Kruse International, McCormick, Mecum, RM Auctions, Russo and Steele, Shannons and Silver.

MBI Publishing Co. has continued to cajole me in a friendly way to keep this book on track, and Tim Parker and Zack Miller have been instrumental in providing advice based on their many collective years in the book business.

I'd like to dedicate this book to my 13-year-old daughter, Alexandra, who learned to drive a manual-shift car last summer on the beaches of Cape Kiwanda, OR and tells me she thinks an E-type will make a perfect first car for her in a couple of years.

In all, this book really does represent the efforts of a bunch of enthusiasts, people just like you whom I happened to rope into the task at hand: putting together the best of *SCM* on Jaguars. I do appreciate their efforts, and I'm sure that by the time you've read from the first page to the last, you'll do a much better job when you pick out your next, or your first, Jaguar.

If there are any errors or omissions in this book, they are mine alone. Now, pour yourself a glass of good warm English beer, sit back into a comfortable chair, and enjoy the read.
—*Keith Martin* ◆

An Insider's Guide to Collecting Jaguar

I was just outside Baker City, Oregon, when the rotor on my 1967 E-type coupe exploded. One minute, I was cruising along at an indicated 120 mph, the next, I was coasting silently to the side of the road.

After I pried the distributor cap off, I saw that the Asian-manufactured rotor was built to improper specs, and was hitting the contacts in the cap. While I was waiting for the tow truck, I went across the road and looked back at the white coupe, sitting silently, in the middle of the forest.

Now this wasn't exactly the way I would have chosen to admire the graceful lines of the car. And as the event I was on was a Porsche Club–sponsored rally, the failure of the Jaguar made me the subject of many pointed comments that evening about the relative reliability of German versus English cars.

But soon enough, a tow truck arrived and another rallyist (a decent enough fellow even if he was driving a bright red 2004 Boxster S with red-painted brake calipers) located a proper English-made rotor at the local NAPA store. In the parking lot outside the historic Geiser Hotel, it was just a matter of a few minutes to install the new rotor, and the next morning we were back on the road, where Jaguars like to be.

In *Keith Martin on Collecting Jaguar*, we take a look at this illustrious English marque from the very first SS cars to the latest XKRs. We examine both the glorious successes of the lightweight factory E-type racers and the sad XJS models of the late '70s, when Jaguar simply didn't have the resources to meet US smog and safety regs and maintain the performance and reliability of their cars. On these pages, we'll introduce you to some very adaptable cats, from the 1937 Jaguar SS 100 that for years doubled as a gentleman farmer's tractor, to the series I E-type roadster proclaimed by one British journalist to be "the finest crumpet catcher ever devised." You'll also nod your head in recognition of the unruly passion that compels seemingly sensible human beings to sink more cash into restoring their Jags than they can ever hope to recoup. But that's the effect these felines have over mere mortals.

Of course, it's the XK series that most collectors are familiar with. The 120s, 140s and 150s were revolutionary in their time, offering surprising performance, groundbreaking styling and a relatively affordable price. The E-type, of course, rewrote the rules once again about how sexy-looking and fast a GT car could be. I've owned a variety of E-types over the years, and the two-seat coupe is still my favorite. The cockpit, with the

additional storage space under the fastback hatch, is simply perfectly sized for two people, their overnight stuff, and a little cooler for drinks and snacks.

You'll find lots of first-hand observations about finding, buying, owning, restoring and selling these models inside this book. But we don't stop there; insights about the very latest XKR models, along with the supercars like the XJ 220, are here as well.

The current chapter for Jaguar is a happy one, as since Ford's purchase of the marque in 1989, the cars have gotten progressively more competent and easier to live with. The S-type has been a great success, and each year seems to bring us a better and faster XK model.

As with all the books in this series, including *Keith Martin on Collecting Porsche* and *Keith Martin on Collecting Ferrari*, the information is provided buffet-style, rather than as a fixed-price/multi-course dinner. Open the book to any page, in any section, and just start reading. I guarantee that you will find something informative and entertaining at every turn.—*Keith Martin* ◆

Section 1

SS & Classic XKs

The 120s, 140s and 150s were revolutionary in their time, offering surprising performance, ground-breaking styling and a relatively affordable price. With the XK 120 (whose very name was a numerical guarantee of its top speed), $4,000 got an enthusiast a racy-looking roadster with a 3.4-liter double overhead cam straight-six that put out 160 horsepower.

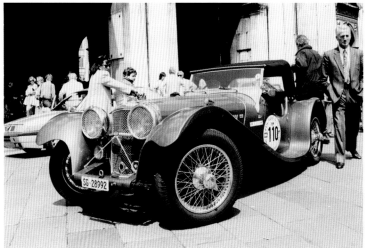

The first Jaguar I owned was an Olde English White XK 120SE, with painted wire wheels and dual exhausts. I remember two things about the car, first, how impossibly close the large steering wheel seemed to my chest the first time I got behind it, and second, how I forgot everything else in the world when I revved it up and set off down the road.

I'm sure by modern standards its brakes were horrible, handling worse, and it probably had barely enough horsepower to keep up with a Honda Accord. But to a sports car enthusiast, the feeling of the road rushing under those long sweeping fenders, the pavement being so close by my left elbow, and the view through the classic two-piece windshield made me feel like I was in the most wonderful car in the world. And at that moment, I was.

I don't think I ever put the top up on that car; in fact, I'm not even sure it had a top. I've owned 140s too, and enjoyed their clearly superior handling due to the placement of the engine further back in the chassis. I've always felt a little sorry for the XK 150s, as they had neither truly classic styling nor, with the exception of the 3.8S, the performance that was about to be unveiled.

But neither model strikes the chord that the 120 does, with its pure lines, primitive interior and uncompromising approach to the English definition of what a sports car truly should be.—*Keith Martin* ◆

1936 SS 100 Two-Seater Sports Roadster

Devastatingly handsome, rakishly low, and exuding more than its share of visual panache, the SS 100 is *the* classic pre-war Jaguar

by Keith Martin

Chassis number: 18031
Engine number: 259843

Labor of love: "Best Owner Restored Car" award is well deserved.

When the young William Lyons introduced his devastatingly handsome SS Jaguar 100 sports two-seater in the fall of 1935, it was viewed with some skepticism by the rather conservative English sporting motorists of the day. Rakishly low, with over 90 mph readily available and acceleration to match, it was well-equipped and finished, yet cost a mere £398. Surely there was a catch somewhere? Time has shown there was, indeed, no catch. With its long, many-louvered hood, its open cockpit with cutaway sides and its arching fenders, the SS Jaguar 100 symbolizes traditional 1930s sports car design, just as its brilliant successors, the Jaguar XK 120 roadster and the Jaguar E-type coupe represent the 1940s and 1960s.

William Lyons' masterstroke was to make use of existing well-tried components from the multitude of makers surrounding him in Coventry. Steering gear, axles, gearboxes, instruments, even the chassis frame and more, all were "brought in" from the English industry's most reputable companies. The long-lived and powerful overhead-valve engine was evolved by the famed Harry Weslake from a Standard Motor Company unit used in previous SS Jaguar models. Even the striking aluminum fenders were supplied in batches by a specialist, although it must be conceded that each SS Jaguar 100 body was skillfully hand crafted using traditional methods. Brought together by Lyons' young team of gifted engineers, the result was a responsive high-performance car with excellent steering, brakes and gearbox. There was a limited market in Britain in the late 1930s for such a car, even at Lyons' relatively low price. In the few seasons before the war put an end to production, only 190 were sold, plus 118 of the 3.5-liter version introduced in 1937 (though that is a total most of his competitors would have regarded as very satisfactory).

SN 18031 is the last SS built in 1936 and the 31st one produced. It has a documented list of owners since 1946. In the early 1980s, SN 18031 was completely disassembled for restoration. It was sold in pieces to the current owner in 1983 who undertook an exhaustive restoration. He spent hundreds of hours taking notes, carefully examining old photos and seeking the advice of Jaguar experts from as far away as England and South Africa. All the bodywork, painting, chassis, mechanical and assembly was lovingly carried out by the owner, and the car has all-matching numbers to prove it. Whenever original items were missing, such as the top, an original pattern was located to copy exactly.

"With its long, many-louvered hood, its open cockpit with cutaway sides and its arching fenders, the SS Jaguar 100 symbolizes traditional 1930s sports car design."

The final result speaks for itself; SN 18031 competed in four Jaguar Club of North America concours in 1996, scoring four first places, a 99.98, 99.96, 99.96 and 100 points. It has also been awarded the *Best Owner Restored Car* by the Veteran Motor Car Club of America.

This SS 100 sold on August 17, 1997 at Christie's Pebble Beach auction for $156,500. The Price Guide, for 2.5-liter SS 100s, indicates a range of $100,000-$145,000, and the superior condition of this car clearly justifies the premium amount paid.

SS 100s are reliable enough for most vintage events, and certainly exude more than their share of visual panache. The most desirable model is fitted with the 3.5-liter; had this car been so equipped, we wouldn't have been surprised to see it edge near or perhaps past the $200,000 mark.

SS 100s are THE classic pre-war Jaguar, have a dedicated following, and a group of experts such as SCM subscriber Terry Larson of Arizona to help keep them running properly, and make sure that they are restored to original specifications. While not a pure first-tier collectible, nonetheless they will appreciate along with the market in general. This car can be considered well bought.

(Photo and description courtesy of the auction company.)
From the October 1997 issue of *SCM*.◆

Red with black leather interior

Engine: six-cylinders in line, pushrod overhead valves, twin SU carburetors, 2,663cc, 101bhp at 4,600rpm

Gearbox: four-speed manual with remote control and synchromesh

Suspension: semi-elliptic leaf springs front and rear

Brakes: mechanical drums all round

Right hand drive

1937 SS 100 2.5

AUK 634 was last seen being driven between the hop poles on a farm in Kent, touring the fields inspecting hops. The owner found it to be an ideal car for such a job; he said it was just narrow enough to drive through the alleys between the poles

by Keith Martin

Chassis number: 18109

Factory publicity described the sensational new SS 100 as "primarily intended for competition work and sufficiently tractable to use as a fast tourer without modification." The Heynes-designed overhead-valve engine was capable of giving the car genuine 100 mph performance, and the styling of the new sporty two-seater reflected William Lyons' influence at its very best. The cars achieved rally successes in the hands of Tommy Wisdom, Sam Newsome and, later of course, Ian Appleyard, but they also ventured onto the racing circuits, racking up successes on both sides of the Atlantic.

This "barn discovery," registration no. AUK 634, chassis no. 18109, engine no. 253151 and body no. 4833, has a well-recorded history and is a most original car in all respects. A right-hand drive example, it was manufactured June 11, 1937 and supplied to the Wolverhampton dealers, Attwoods. According to records the first recorded owner was a Mr. J. Fellows. Sixteen months later John Montgomery, a farmer from Kent, purchased the car on October 5, 1938, and it remained in his ownership (and subsequently his wife's) until its 1994 sale.

In its heyday, this car was used enthusiastically and was entered into the 1938 Cardiff Welsh Motor Rally, the Coronation Scottish Rally and the 1938 and 1939 Scottish rallies. This is documented through period photographs of the Scottish rallies and dashboard plaques on the car. Subsequently, it was used as an everyday driver until the mid 1960s, when Mr. Montgomery felt it was time to restore his prized possession cosmetically; previous work had already been carried out on the engine as and when necessary.

Last taxed in 1965, the car was laid up in his barn where it remained until July 1994, even outlasting the ravages of a 1988 hurricane, when part of the roof of the barn collapsed; amazingly, the hurricane left only a few dents in the rear nearside windscreen support. Restoration to the bodywork was never carried out, and the car in 1994 still had its original black paint and its original red leather trim and red carpets, although considered beyond saving.

Instrumentation is correct and includes: speedometer, rev counter, oil pressure, amps, petrol and water temperature gauges as well as a Brooklands Motors suppliers plaque on the dashboard.

AUK 634 was last seen being driven by its owner between the hop poles on his Kent farm, touring the fields as he inspected his hops and hop-pickers. It was an ideal car for such a job; John Montgomery was quoted as saying that "the car was narrow

From farm car to barn find: this SS100 now makes hay in the big city.

> "I came along with every intention of buying the car," said the determined man from Hampstead, North London, "although the price I paid was about as much as I would have gone to for it."

enough to drive through the narrow alleys between the poles."

An old green log book, Jaguar-Daimler Heritage Trust certificate, owner's manual and expired tax certificates were available with the car when it came to auction.

Offered at the September 5, 1994 Sotheby's sale, the SS 100 was expected to bring $54,250. However, intense competition between ten telephone bidders and several more would-be buyers in the room saw the price leap to almost double the high estimate, finally selling for a monumental $96,100 including premium.

The successful bidder was businessman Glenn Kalil, from Hampstead, North London, who had come to the auction determined to leave with the prized SS. "I came along with every intention of buying the car, although the price I paid was about as much as I would have gone to for it," he said afterwards.

While SCM doesn't want to be the one to break the news to Mr. Kalil, a more desirable 3.5-liter SS 100, S/N M797E, red over black and in nicely restored condition, sold at the World Classic Auction May 14 and 15, 1994 in Danville, CA, for a mere $90,000.

Top money for a 2.5 is in the $135,000 range, with 3.5s reaching up to $150,000. These are the most collectible of all the Jaguar series, and will appreciate at the front of the market.

(Photo and description courtesy of the auction company.)
From the November 1994 issue of *SCM.*◆

1938 SS 100 Roadster

The first true 100-mph sports car available to the public, the beautifully proportioned SS-100 epitomized power when viewed from any angle; today, they are among the most prized of all prewar sports cars

by Murphy Donohue

Serial number: 39010

These roadsters are among the most prized of all prewar sports cars.

In the early 1930s, William Lyons' design influence began to take its full effect. The Swallow Sidecar Company evolved into Swallow Coachworks, with a highly successful line of Lyons-designed bodies, mostly for the Austin Seven and 6-cylinder Wolseley-Hornet. Swallow's first complete car, the SS-I, based on the Standard (later to become Standard-Triumph) Sixteen (2-liter) and Twenty (2.5-liter) chassis, was introduced in 1931, followed by the SS-II on the Standard Little Nine (1-liter).

SS cars offered value, performance and, most important of all, Lyons' signature long and low look which developed on these cars and became particularly recognized in the SS I Tourer and the later 1935 SS 90. By then the company was SS Cars, Ltd. and motorcycle sidecars were fast becoming a footnote to its history.

In 1936 the first SS 100 was produced, and for the first time the name "Jaguar" was used. (Tradition suggests that the "SS" name wasn't very marketable in mid-'30s England.) The first 126 cars built in the 1936-37 period were equipped with a 2.5-liter engine based on the side-valve Standard engine used in the SS-90, but carrying an overhead-valve cylinder head designed by the legendary Harry Weslake (who would still be developing good breathing engines three decades later for Dan Gurney's Formula One Eagles). Starting in 1938, a 3.5-liter version was adopted. Today these 3.5-liter roadsters are among the most prized of all prewar sports cars.

The 3.5-liter SS 100 pictured here is fully restored and features the bronze competition head. It is fully sorted and ready for vintage competition or touring.

This car sold at the Monterey Sports Car Auction, August 14-15, 1998 for $184,575, including buyers commission. Typically $150-175,000 cars in good older restored condition ($20-30,000 more than 2.5-Liter SS 100s and twice as much as the lackluster side-valve SS 90), this car, having been painstakingly restored and scrupulously maintained, was quite beautifully presented. Along with it came a chronicle of passionate use that confirmed its mechanical steadfastness. This particular car should be considered well bought by the new owner, who paid only a slight bonus for a bit of reassurance; well worth the price for sleeping well at night.

Jaguar SS 100s are esteemed for their unparalleled styling by the gifted Sir William Lyons, as well as powerful performance, which still stands the test of time. The model set the benchmark for all the Jaguars that followed: dashing lines, and awe-inspiring power at an affordable price. By any yardstick, the SS 100 is a breakthrough car and a smart investment, with stunning performance, seductive good looks and affordability. An SS 100 will delight its owner with years of pleasurable driving, and, well maintained, will always bring a good price on the market. Well bought indeed.

(Photo and description courtesy of the auction company.) ◆

> "Jaguar SS 100s are esteemed for their unparalleled styling by the gifted Sir William Lyons, as well as powerful performance, which still stands the test of time. The model set the benchmark for all the Jaguars that followed: dashing lines, and awe-inspiring power at an affordable price"

Years produced: 1938-40
Number produced: 118
SCM Price Guide: $160-$185,000
Tune-up: $200-$250
Interval: 10,000 miles
Distributor cap: $45
Club: Classic Jaguar Association,
Bruce Carnahan,
818.244.9132

1938 SS 100 3.5L

Silkily feline with the grace of a prowling cat, these cars are used and enjoyed by their owners rather than being kept in hermetically-sealed display cases

by Gary Anderson

Chassis number: 39030
Registration number: JSJ 245

I n 1936, only five years after beginning production, SS Cars startled the motoring public with the Jaguar 2.5-liter saloon, the company's first car to feature overhead valves. The engine was the robust seven-bearing, six-cylinder unit built by Standard, but with a new cylinder head designed by Harry Weslake and Bill Heynes. With 104 bhp smoothly delivered, flowing lines, a gearbox which made the best of the power, and a new chassis, it was the model which made the company's reputation. Jaguar was then only a model name, but it was adopted as the company name after "SS" had acquired unfortunate connotations during the war.

If the Jaguar saloon epitomized excitement, it was as nothing compared to the Jaguar SS 100. No sports car better epitomizes the late 1930s, which is why it has been the model for so many modern "nostalgia" cars. It looked right from every angle, and age has not withered its beauty.

Every aspect was in harmony. Stone guards over the large headlights, the long louvered bonnet and large wire wheels were aggressive, yet the flowing lines were silkily feline. It has the grace of a prowling cat. At Brooklands in 1936 a tuned and lightened version lapped at 104.1 mph, but normally owners tended not to race them. Instead they appeared in the rallies, trials and sprints which formed the bulk of British motorsport—and they were successful because of their superb power-to-weight ratio, gearbox, brakes and handling. They were great all-rounders.

Chassis number 39030 was originally dispatched to Glovers, the early SS Jaguar dealers for Ripon on January 13, 1938. The Jaguar Daimler Heritage Trust, who have issued a Heritage Certificate for the car, record that it was originally delivered finished in lavender with blue trim. Purchased from Coys of Kensington in 1975, this beautiful example subsequently spent twenty years with a French enthusiast, before returning to home shores in the late 1990s. During its spell in France it underwent a comprehensive restoration by specialists Le Coq, in which the chassis and fittings were meticulously overhauled. The car comes with its original 3.5-liter engine and gearbox, although it is currently fitted with a competition power unit and uprated gearbox. These items were assembled in the vendor's own workshops specifically for competitive motoring, and detail work included gas flowing of the cylinder head, the fitment of bronze liners to guides and conversion to use unleaded fuel. Further work was subsequently carried out to the suspension and shock absorbers as well as the gearbox by SS Jaguar specialists TRAC at a cost of over $6,400. Much attention was paid to detail, so that components such as the body tub and petrol tank were carefully and discreetly flexibly mounted to avoid damage on the arduous road rallies in which 39030 has become a competitor.

The car, now immaculately finished in traditional British Racing Green, with contrasting black hide, has recently contested such popular and competitive international rallies as the acclaimed Liège-Rome-Liège road rally. Despite this, it remains in the most magnificent condition throughout; and complete with FIVA identity card, UK registration and MO26T certificate it is ready

Labor of love: "Best Owner Restored Car" award is well deserved.

to be entered for any similar international events to be held in this season's calendar of historic motorsports.

This car sold at Barrett-Jackson/ Coys of Kensington's Monaco sale on May 27, 2000 for $183,381.

By any usage, the SS 100 must be considered a true classic. It is rare, lovely, iconic, and best of all, enjoyable. Only 118 of these cars were ever built and yet so many still survive that it is a rare classic car gathering that doesn't have at least one out for the day. Above all, they are cars that are used and enjoyed by their owners rather than being kept in hermetically sealed display cases. And they are practical. Even with the original four-speed gearbox, the seven-bearing engine can stand long distances at modern highway speeds without undue risk. Speeds over 80 mph are not excessive, though one must bear in mind that the car will be brought to a stop with rod-operated drum brakes slowing narrow tires.

This example is not particularly original in its detailing. One specialist noted incorrect chroming used on many pieces and substitutions of modern parts for some components. However, this car was restored to stand up to challenging secondary roads rather than straw-hatted concours scrutineers. The substitution of a competition-built engine (probably from a 3.5-liter Jaguar saloon) and a modern five-speed gearbox are in keeping with this intention, though the original drivetrain was included. If the new owner had the same intention of driving this car hard and enjoying its rugged power, then the price for this attractive, event-proven car was reasonable. It can easily be enjoyed for a season or two of vintage rallying and then cleaned up and sold, with very little net cost to the owner.

(Photo and description courtesy of the auction company.)◆

Years produced: 1935-1939
Number produced:118
Original list price: $1,795
SCM Price Guide: $160,000-$185,000
Tune-up/major service: $400-500
Distributor cap: $60-75
Chassis # : Stamped on right frame rail 9" behind front spring shackle; may be obscured by paint or wear
Engine #: Stamped on raised boss on right rear of block just below head
Club: Classic Jaguar Association, 1754 Hillcrest Ave, Glendale, CA 92669
Web site: www.classicjaguar.org
Alternatives: Bentley 4.5-Liter DHC, LaSalle Series 50 convertible coupe, Mercedes-Benz 500K cabriolet

1949-54 XK 120

If you lived in a major American city in 1949, a new sports car probably caught your eye...it wasn't the first twin cam produced, but it was probably the first one most Americans ever saw

by Michael Duffey

American cars of the late forties were ponderous affairs; overweight, underbraked, softly sprung and technically uninteresting. Some enthusiasts in those days thought a sports car was either a fenderless Ford Model T or maybe an MG. If you lived in a major city in 1949, a new sports car probably caught your eye: it was a Jaguar XK 120.

Though the specifications of this car sound conventional by today's standards, they weren't at all common in the early postwar years. The 120 substructure was loosely based on the MK V saloon having a steel chassis with box section crossmembers, independent front suspension with torsion bar springing and quarter elliptic springs on the live rear axle. Drum brakes provided whatever stopping power they could muster.

The gemstone in this setting was a twin-cam 3.4-liter, 6-cylinder powerplant that produced 160 potent English bhp. While it was hardly the first twin cam produced, it was probably the first one most Americans ever saw.

The skin wrapped around the first 120s was aluminum, it being easier to obtain than steel in postwar England. It also allowed the body panels to be produced in-house. The early bodies were constructed (like all coachbuilt cars of the era) over an ash frame. This was slow work, and on-time delivery of this very popular car suffered as a result. By 1950, steel bodies produced outside the Jaguar factory finally allowed production to keep pace with demand. The doors, boot and bonnet were still made from alloy.

The first fixed-head coupe (FHC) appeared in early 1951. When you sat in the leather seats, similar to ones fitted to the roadster, you were surrounded by lacquered wood, both on the fascia and the door caps. A different door than that of the roadster allowed roll-up side windows. The styling of the disc-wheel 120 coupe was slightly reminiscent of the beloved Bugatti type 57SC coupe.

The final 120 variant was another, more-luxurious convertible, the drophead coupe (DHC). It featured a padded top and wool headliner, along with interior trim similar to that of the coupe.

In addition to the introduction of the coupe and the drophead, the 120 also evolved under the skin. A new model called the SE (or 120M in America) received a boost in horsepower from 160 to 180. This was augmented by stiffer springs, a dual exhaust and most often driving lamps. A change from an E.N.V. back axle to a Salisbury unit allowed the fitment of wire wheels. Later in 120 production, it was possible to order a 120M with close ratio gears and a C-type cylinder head that with the help of 9:1 compression produced 190 bhp.

All of these changes produced a more potent 120 that predictably magnified the weaknesses in the original design. The brakes

A twin cam for the Colonies.

on the original 160-bhp version were marginal in hard usage, and this was in no way helped by the addition of thirty more horsepower. The cooling system might have been adequate for English weather and traffic, but came up short and hot stateside.

Still, if the era that they were conceived is taken into consideration, 120s were standouts in the area of styling and performance; their namesake 120 mph top speed made them one of the fastest production cars available.

If the 120 is your XK of choice, you must still decide which body style and horse-power specification to choose. Between 1949 and 1954, Jaguar built over 11,000 120s, most of them left-hand drive.

If you are a price-shopper, the coupes are always cheaper but are often in worse shape. Not many owners lavished restoration dollars on the FHC. If ease of restoration is your aim, the roadster is the winner. The lack of side window mechanisms, a simpler top and a lack of ornamental woodwork make this a more economical restoration candidate, and they are easier to sell when you decide to move on.

In the cost-is-no-object category resides the early alloy 120. More of a collector's piece than a "driver," they are really not much lighter than a steel car, but if rarity touches your hot button, this is it.

For pure power, a C-type head and a close-ratio-gearbox equipped model is a good bet, though the brakes are really on the edge with this setup. A conservative approach would be a lightly-stressed driver like a disc-wheel roadster with the standard 160 bhp engine, and perhaps an electric cooling fan for the radiator.

The spare, rakish lines of the 120 cause it even today to turn heads wherever it is driven, and it remains an eminently usable and collectible part of automotive history.

From the July 1994 issue of *SCM*. ◆

> "If the era is taken into consideration, 120s were standouts in the area of styling and performance; their namesake 120 mph top speed made them one of the fastest production cars available."

1952 XK 120

The quality of workmanship and the sheer number of man hours spent on this car has given LAB 730 a character and patina rarely found in modern restorations

by Keith Martin

Chassis number: 661032
Engine number: W6275/7

The Jaguar XK 120 caused an absolute sensation when it was launched at the 1948 Motor Show. In the post-war era of rationing and general austerity and hardship it came as a stunning vision of what the future might hold.

It was, without doubt, the most beautiful car in the world, and the fastest unsupercharged production sports model ever made up to that time. Its claimed top speed of 120 mph was so astonishing that to prove it Jaguar took one over to Belgium and clocked an unbelievable 132 mph.

The response from the public at the Motor Show launch on October 20, 1948 caught Jaguar by surprise, and as orders poured in it was immediately obvious that the level of home and export demand could only be satisfied by moving from a lightweight alloy-bodied ash frame construction to tooling up for volume production in steel.

The XK 120 became a colossal success—both on the road and on the track where it scored numerous victories. Some of the winning drivers included Stirling Moss, Peter Walker, Peter Whitehead, Leslie Johnson and Ian Appleyard. Indeed, in XK 120C/C-Type form it won Le Mans in both 1951 and 1953, while its engine was to power three more Sarthe winners and a whole host of Jaguars right up to the present day.

Finished in white with contrasting red hide interior, the roadster pictured here has been the subject of a meticulous "body-off" restoration by its former owner. The chassis was cleaned and painted, the body well was stripped to bare metal and prepared with particular attention being paid to the body fit and line. Where necessary, all parts were renovated; however replacement parts include leather trim, hood, side screens, wiring loom and all the chrome work.

The restoration was completed in 1981; since that time LAB 730 has been properly dry-stored. The quality

"Without doubt, the most beautiful car in the world."

"The XK 120 became a colossal success — both on the road and on the track where it scored numerous victories. . .winning drivers included Stirling Moss, Peter Walker, Peter Whitehead, Leslie Johnson and Ian Appleyard."

of workmanship and the sheer number of man hours spent on this car has given LAB 730 a character and patina rarely found in modern restorations. The condition of the car today is testimony to the quality of the aforementioned restoration.

At the December 3, 1996 Coys Auction in London, SN 661032 sold for $38,580, leading one to believe that the emphasis on the condition of the car was more on "patina" than on "quality of restoration." True, high-90-point 120 roadsters have been selling in the $50,000-$60,000 range for the past year. Great 120s continue to be a good investment, because even at $60,000 you are paying only for the restoration, and getting the car for free.

(Photo and description courtesy of the auction company.)

From the January 1997 issue of *SCM*. ◆

1952 XK 120 Roadster

The world's first high-volume twin-cam engine was nothing less than sensational—this sleek, beautiful, and strikingly modern automobile was the car of choice for Clark Gable and Frank Lloyd Wright

by Gary Anderson

Chassis number: 672051

Looks and sounds magnificent, with performance to match.

During the Second World War, Sir William Lyons and his colleagues envisioned a new car that would feature the world's first high-volume twin-cam engine. Called the XK series, it would be a short-wheelbase chassis mated to a two-seat sports roadster body. When combined with the new engine, the result would be nothing less than sensational—a sleek, beautiful, and strikingly modern automobile.

At the Earls Court Motor Show in October 1948, this XK made its first public appearance, and what an introduction it was. Spectators marveled at the new Jaguar. One journalist commented at the time that "all preconceived notions as to what was a series-production sports car disappeared overnight." It was a show stopper.

The XK Jaguar was given the body-type number 120 to represent its top speed. This proved to be an understatement of the car's capabilities when factory test driver Ron Sutton was clocked in a prototype at over 132 mph. Race versions of the XK 120 were potent in the hands of drivers like Stirling Moss and Phil Hill, both of whom scored important victories in 1949. With its 160-hp, inline-six engine with twin overhead cams in original tune, the production XK 120 not only looked and sounded magnificent, but had the performance to match.

Finished in red with tan Connolly leather, the example pictured here has benefited from a professional frame-off restoration to concours standards. It's fully equipped, including a factory tool set and side curtains.

The SCM analysis: This car sold for $44,000 including commission at the RM Auction in Phoenix, Arizona, January 20-21, 2000. RM Classic Cars has found a fitting architectural backdrop for its newest vintage car auction in the Frank Lloyd Wright-style Biltmore Resort and Spa in Phoenix. Unfortunately, invitations and announcements about the auction didn't circulate until less than a month before the sale. While the bidders in the audience clearly had money in their pockets, there weren't quite enough of them to make a quorum on many cars. The result was that relative bargains like this traditional Jaguar—similar to the ones driven by people like Clark Gable and, yes, Wright himself—could be found. XK 120s in this condition aren't difficult to find, but someone spent more on the restoration than this car fetched on that Friday afternoon.

This "open two-seater" (or OTS, Jaguar's term for a roadster) had been recently restored and appears to be as accurate as claimed. The chrome side lights and lack of footwell vents on the front fenders, and the body-colored vinyl piping on the rear fenders place it as pre-1953, while the bolts on the domed timing chain covers place it as post-1951, all matching a chassis number that indicated the car was produced in June of 1952.

With the standard body-colored steel wheels and hub caps, and the "spats" (fender skirts) on the rear (wire wheels were optional and

their knock-offs won't fit under the spats), it offered all the stunning good looks that first electrified the crowds when the XK 120 was introduced at the 1948 Earls Court Motor Show. The appropriate wide white sidewalls and bright crimson paint job against the carefully groomed green of the Biltmore's grass similarly drew the attention of the crowd at the RM reception the night before the auction.

Only a few small details detracted from its overall appeal. For example, a half-inch gap between the driver's door top pad and the matching pad on the scuttle suggested that final assembly may have been hurried to get the car to this sale. However, the panel fit was otherwise excellent and the paint was impeccable. For the medium-stature person who can fit under and behind the big black steering wheel, this should make a fine car for vintage tours as well as Jaguar meets. It will be able to keep up with the Ferraris on the road and probably outdraw them in the parking lots. At this price, the new owner will still have five grand left to make sure that all the details are properly sorted before this car faces a thousand miles of Copperstate highway or a thousand points on a JCNA judge's clipboard.

(Photo and description courtesy of the auction company.)

From the April 2004 issue of *SCM*.◆

> "While the bidders in the audience clearly had money in their pockets, there weren't quite enough of them to make a quorum on many cars, resulting in relative bargains."

Years produced: 1949-1954

Number produced: 7,631

Original list price: $3,345

SCM Price Guide: $38,500-$47,500

Tune-up/major service: $300

Distributor cap: $20

Chassis #: on VIN plate on firewall and on frame near foot pedal pivot

Engine #: on VIN plate and stamped on block above oil filter and on head just behind timing chain cover

Club: Jaguar Clubs of North America, 888.258.2524; 8am-6pm PST

Web site: www.jcna.com

Alternatives: Aston Martin DB2/4 Drophead, Austin-Healey 100 Le Mans, AC Bristol roadster

1954 XK 120 SE

A little pain and suffering (like driving around in summer with the heater on to cool the engine) helped make owning a sports car seem less of an indulgence and more of a statement of stoic endurance

by Keith Martin

Chassis number: S 676285
Engine number: F 4008 S

A t the 1948 London Motor Show, Jaguar virtually threw the sports car world into turmoil with its stunning XK 120. Here was a car with outstanding style and looks, a powerful six-cylinder engine installed in an outstanding chassis and a remarkably low price—a quarter that of a V12 Ferrari with similar performance. The combination was unbeatable, and without doubt the XK 120 was an absolute milestone for both Jaguar and the motor industry as a whole. XK 120 orders flooded in; ironically, Jaguar had only planned to produce 200 of the XK 120, a car designed merely as an interim model to publicize the XK engine for the new MK VII saloon.

At the heart of the William Lyons-styled roadster was an all-new 3,442cc twin overhead-camshaft XK engine, producing 160 bhp via twin SU carburetors—sufficient for 126 mph and 0-60 mph in 10.0 seconds. To further push the performance point home, in October, 1948, with an aeroscreen and aluminium undershield the only modifications, an XK 120 recorded 132.6 mph for the flying mile in Jabekke, Belgium, making it indisputably the fastest off-the-shelf production car in the world.

The massive success of the XK 120 became immediately apparent, on the road as well as the racetrack. It stacked up win after win, with a host legendary drivers from Ian Appleyard to Peter Whitehead at the wheel. It also scored victories in the hearts of many less famous drivers, who lined up all over Europe (as well as across the pond) for the thrill of wind tousled hair and rakish style at a possible, if not practical, 120+ miles per hour.

The left-hand drive XK 120 shown here was exported to the United States in August, 1954. Little is known of the car's history until 1967 when it underwent an engine overhaul and was then stored for almost 30 years. Once removed from storage the car continued to be restored, the work including a bare metal respray and a new interior. Attractively finished in Old English White with black leather upholstery, this useable, three-owner car comes with a Jaguar Daimler Heritage Trust certificate.

The car pictured was a post-block sale for $28,034 including buyer's commission at Coys' auction in London on November 20, 1997. Known as an SE (Special Equipment) model in Britain and an M in the States, this late car incorporates a package consisting of wire wheels, special cams and dual exhaust. Coys' estimate was modest enough (even for a left-hand drive car in England) at $30-37,000. Good

The XK 120 stole the thunder of the MK VII saloon.

> "Here was a car with outstanding style and looks, a powerful six-cylinder engine installed in an outstanding chassis and a remarkably low price to boot— a quarter that of a V12 Ferrari with similar performance."

XK 120 M roadsters in the U.S. are over $40,000; a superb XK 120 M freshly restored to showroom condition can bring $60,000. Ones without the SE/M package seem to sell for about $5,000 less.

This car seems suspiciously reasonably priced, perhaps reflecting its lumpy front valence, swoopy sill line, dangerously dropping driver's door and the uncertainty created by a restoration started with an engine overhaul in 1967 and finished with a final lick of paint in 1997. It might turn out to be a good value, but is just as likely a can of worms waiting to be opened.

Once in a while it's useful to take a fresh look at Jaguar's XK 120. Not particularly rare (7,391 steel-bodied XK 120 roadsters were built), the XK 120's combination of decent performance and handling with William Lyons' landmark styling helped create the sports car market. The XK 120's styling and panache seduced many (including the writer) into their first sports car, fortunately setting modest reliability expectations that subsequent Jags and Alfas could meet. A little pain and suffering (like freezing when the mercury drops below 60° F, after driving around all summer with the heater on to help cool the engine) helped make owning a sports car seem less of an indulgence and more of a statement of stoic endurance.

The XK 120 roadster's stature makes it a reliable investment (if not necessarily reliable transportation) that will mirror the market's performance. This price was fair enough if the mechanicals hold up.

(Photo and description courtesy of the auction company.)
From the June 1998 issue of *SCM*. ◆

1956 XK 140 Roadster

While the 140 models have superior horsepower and handling when compared to the 120s, they lack the visual simplicity that often makes first models of any successful serial production car attractive

by Keith Martin

Chassis No. S812714
Engine No. G865885

In October 1954, at the London Motor Show, the XK 140 was introduced as the successor to the XK 120. The XK 140 was easily distinguishable from its predecessor because of its Mk 7-type front and rear bumpers, the traditional radiator grill but with fewer slats and a chrome strip which ran along the center of the bonnet and the boot. Under the bonnet, the XK 140 had the traditional 6-cylinder unit of 3.4 liters with bore and stroke of 83 mm x 106 mm. This was basically the same as the Special Edition XK 120 engine, and thus capable of producing 190 bhp at 5,600 rpm, compared to the 160 bhp of the standard XK 120. Like the 120, however, it had independent front suspension with semi-elliptic leaf springs at the rear.

The XK 140 sold very well indeed, with orders flooding in. This was for two reasons: first, due to the excellence of the old 120 (which had won the hearts of so many), but also because of the enormous success Jaguar was having in international motor racing, winning Le Mans in 1951 and 1953 with the C-type and in 1955, 1956 and 1957 with the D-type.

The XK 140 roadster pictured here was originally delivered to America and therefore has left-hand drive. It was re-imported into the UK several years ago and soon after was purchased by the current owner at one of Coys Auctions. He spent further money to bring it to its present condition, describing the body, chassis, interior and paintwork as "good" and the engine and transmission as "excellent." Bills for the work carried out

Quicker but more visually complicated than the XK 120.

"The XK 140 sold very well indeed, with orders flooding in. This was for two reasons: first, due to the excellence of the old 120 (which had won the hearts of so many), but also because of the enormous success Jaguar was having in international motor racing, winning Le Mans in 1951 and 1953 with the C-type and in 1955, 1956 and 1957 with the D-type."

are available. The coachwork is finished in red while the upholstery is black.

Offered at No Reserve, S/N S812714 was sold at $31,185 on January 24, 1995 by Coys.

While the 140 models have superior horsepower and handling when compared to the 120s, they lack the visual simplicity that often makes first models of any successful serial production car attractive. XK 140s in true concours condition will cross the $50,000 mark, which is no great success story as it usually takes $100,000 to get them to the 99-point level.

In strong driving condition, as this car was represented to be, $30,000 is the right number. Driving condition 120/140/150s in this price range are a decent buy, but will only increase along with the market, never being at the forefront of appreciation.

(Photo and description courtesy of the auction company.)

From the April 1995 issue of *SCM*.◆

1956 XK 140 MC Drophead Coupe

For those of us approaching a certain age, the notion of driving vintage sports cars with roll-up windows, weathertight top and a posh leather interior is quite appealing

by Dave Bownell

Chassis number: S818074DN
Engine number: G5933-8

The XK 140 was introduced in October 1954, retaining the classic XK lines but with major changes in engineering and appearance. A chrome strip ran down the length of the hood and another on the trunk lid drew attention to the medallion in the middle proclaiming the marque's Le Mans wins. The car wore sturdier bumpers and a tougher grille and with the C-type head developed for the XKC Le Mans race cars, the motor made 210 hp at 5,750 rpm.

Inside, the front seat and dashboard remained the same, but with considerably more leg room than the XK 120 because the engine block was moved forward on the chassis. There was also space behind the front seat. The Special Equipment models were designated "MC" and, like the car represented here, were fitted with wire wheels and Lucas FT576 foglamps mounted above the front bumper. The dual exhaust system had two separate silencers and ran through holes in the chassis cross members, emerging below the rear overriders.

This fabulous XK 140 MC drophead special equipment model was originally supplied through Jaguar main agents Charles Hornburg Inc. of Los Angeles, having left the factory on December 7, 1955. It is a full matching-numbers car that was professionally restored to the highest of standards by marque experts in California. The body was removed and the chassis stripped, prepared and powder coated, with all suspension bushes and running gear refurbished or replaced. A completely new braking system was fitted, as well as a completely new electrical system. The engine was rebuilt and blueprinted with balanced crank and new pistons, before dyno testing. The driveshaft was reconditioned and the differential received new seals. The Jaguar

The new owner paid two times the price for one of the finest XK 140 dropheads extant.

"These Jags earned an undeserved reputation as troublesome and temperamental machines, mainly because of a lack of understanding among the service-station Goodwrenches and shade-tree mechanics who tried to keep them running in tune without proper tools."

is also fitted with a new stainless steel exhaust system. The car has been beautifully repainted in deep burgundy and retrimmed throughout in beige Connolly leather upholstery with new carpets and new beige Stayfast soft top.

On a test drive in August 2002, the car drove superbly, having an excellent gearbox with overdrive, a responsive engine and proper brakes. The coachwork is unmarked, and more recently this car won a JCNA Best of Class award at the Houston, Texas regional meeting.

This car sold for $128,500, including buyer's

Years produced: 1954-57
Number produced: 2,740
Original list price: $4,315 POE New York
SCM Price Guide: $42,500-$62,500
Tune-up/major service: $450
Distributor cap: $35
Chassis #: Data plate on firewall
Engine #: Right side of block
Club: Jaguar Clubs of North America 1000 Glenbrook Road, Anchorage, KY 40223
Web site: www.jcna.com
Alternatives: Aston Martin DB2/4 drophead coupe, Austin-Healey 3000 Mk III, Chrysler Dual Ghia
SCM Investment Grade: B

premium, at the Christie's Rockefeller Center auction held June 5, 2003.

For those of us approaching a certain age, the notion of owning and driving vintage sports cars with such amenities as roll-up windows, weather-tight top and a posh leather, walnut and Wilton wool interior is quite appealing. Add to that a car whose mechanical specifications and race-proven credentials give you all the performance and bragging rights you need, and the proposition becomes even more so. That is what this Jaguar offered in abundance, and to two bidders at Rockefeller Center, it was attractive enough to climb to double the top end of the SCM Price Guide before selling.

> "Whatever care (or lack thereof) this Jag was treated to, surely its second incarnation is a glorious one, reflected in its stunning appearance, lavish interior, excellent running condition and award-winning credentials."

In fact, there wasn't much this Jaguar didn't have, including a Laycock-DeNormanville factory-option overdrive and a complete and correct factory tool roll. I could have done without the chrome wire wheels and whitewalls, but at least the wide whites were the proper size and appearance for the year of the car. The C-type engine spec didn't harm things either.

The restoration was hard to fault inside or out, being on a level certainly equal to if not higher than when the car sat on Charles Hornburg's showroom floor. The engine and engine compartment were immaculate, the workmanship and materials on the interior correct and flawless, and the paint had a lovely depth and luster.

While we can reasonably presume the car was restored from a sound example, that isn't automatically the case. As XK 120s and 140s grew into used cars, with little value, back in the '60s and '70s, they were subjected to all the ravages of time, including road salt, careless owners and accidents. On top of that, these Jags earned an undeserved reputation as troublesome and temperamental machines, mainly because of a lack of understanding among the service-station Goodwrenches and shade-tree mechanics who tried to keep them running in tune without proper tools. But there is nothing fundamentally wrong with the design of an engine which won the Le Mans 24-hour grind and countless

other important races. As a talented mechanic friend said when he was rebuilding his first 120 engine: "It's really nothing but a Chevy stovebolt with an extra cam and carb."

That's where a careful inspection, on a lift, can come into play. A good body shop (you don't need a mechanic to check for previous rust and collision repairs, you need a specialist in sheetmetal) can tell you if the car has ever been abused, and if it has, just how well its revival has been completed.

> "This is a car whose mechanical specifications and race-proven credentials give you all the performance and bragging rights you need."

With this particular car, I am sure that Christie's had the documentation necessary to answer whatever questions potential bidders might have had. And truly, it would be very odd for a car that is restored to this extraordinary level to have undealt-with sins lurking underneath.

Whatever care or lack thereof this Jag was treated to, surely its second incarnation is a glorious one, reflected in its stunning appearance, lavish interior, excellent running condition and award-winning credentials. The new owner paid the price times two for the car but should derive an enormous amount of psychic satisfaction and pride in owning one of the finest XK 140 dropheads extant. And that's a pleasure beyond price.

(Photo and description courtesy of the auction company.)
From the November 2003 issue of SCM.◆

A 1956 XK 140 roadster

1959 XK 150 S 4.1 Liter

This new car with major American influence had lost some of the svelte looks of its predecessors, but it was more luxurious

by Keith Martin

Chassis number: T. 825 192 DN
Engine number: VAS 1149-8

Jaguar's new six-cylinder twin-overhead camshaft engine was ready by 1948, and, launched in the XK 120 sports car, took the motoring world by storm. Some 12,000 XK 120s were subsequently sold. This was succeeded in 1954 by the XK 140, and the final evolution example was the XK 150 in 1957.

This new car with major American influence had lost some of the svelte looks of its predecessors, but it was more luxurious, with a larger cockpit, wind-up windows and a one-piece curved windscreen. The first XK 150 models were 3.4-liter fixed-head coupe and drophead convertibles, and in 1958 the roadster was reintroduced at the same time as the "S" series option for all models. This Harry Weslake "straight port head" version with three large SU carburetors provided 250 bhp and then in 1959 a 3.8-liter "S" version giving 265 bhp was introduced providing the ultimate performance, coupled to superb braking.

The very special 1959 XK 150 3.8-liter "S" fixed-head coupe pictured here was delivered to Australia's premier dealership BRYLAWS of Melbourne owned by Jack Bryson in April 1960. The first owner was Darryl Matthews who wanted the equivalent of a competition D-type but in the guise of a 150. The engine was given to legendary tuning expert Bob Jane, who modified it with his 4.1-liter competition conversion, which included D-type speci-

"Stirling Moss" is the name engraved on one of the alloy spokes of the steering wheel.

fication exhaust valves, forged pistons and special profiled camshafts. The gearbox has close ratio internals and the suspension was suitably modified to cope with the greatly increased performance, and to add the final touch, original polished magnesium D-type wheels were fitted.

Jack Bryson was a personal friend of Jaguar chief Sir William Lyons and when he asked for the best Jaguar to be loaned to his niece for her honeymoon, this was the car they used, and his daughter Pat drove it when she visited Australia. Stirling Moss drove the car in the early 1970s and his signature is engraved on one of the alloy spokes of the steering wheel. In 1972 the car was retired from events and stored in a vacuum-sealed air conditioned container which accounts today for

its low mileage of just under 45,000. In 1989 it returned to the UK and its present owner has since pampered the car back to its previous excellent condition.

The leatherwork, paint and mechanics are completely original and Prowess Racing have completely checked the car over replacing incidentals where necessary to make this the most original and best S-type right-hand drive XK 150 fixed-head coupe in the world.

We watched as this stunning FHC failed to sell, despite a high bid of $61,120, on May 6, 1991 at the Christie's Monaco auction. Despite the collapse of the market since then, this particular car might still bring $60,000 if presented in the right venue. It was a handsome 150, with an assortment of exotic add-ons, all desirable, all attractive, and all done properly.

(Photo and description courtesy of the auction company.)

From the August 1996 issue of *SCM.*◆

> "We watched as this stunning FHC failed to sell, despite a high bid of $61,120...despite the collapse of the market, this particular car might still bring $60,000 if presented in the right venue."

1960 XK 150 Drophead Coupe

Perfect to tour, show, or simply covet: beauty and value had the celebrities lining up for the most sensuous body ever seen on a production automobile

by Gary Anderson

Chassis number: S838844DN

Jaguar turned the motoring world upside-down and inside-out when it introduced the XK 120 in 1948. It combined a powerful 160-bhp twin-cam straight-six with the most sensuous body ever seen on a production automobile. The combination of the 120-mph top speed, beauty and value had the celebrities lining up for their copies. Basic specifications called for mating the gorgeous 3.4-liter twin-cam engine to a four-speed Moss gearbox. Front suspension was independent by torsion bars, while the driven solid rear axle was suspended—and located—by longitudinal leaf springs.

A fixed-head coupe and a drophead coupe soon joined the original OTS (open two-seater). In 1954, the XK 120 was displaced by the more luxurious XK 140, which adopted the 190-bhp engine as its base power plant and offered much more comprehensive bumper protection. Using the cylinder head from the Le Mans-winning C-type, the Special Equipment XK 140—often referred to as the MC—was propelled by a 210-bhp version of the lusty 3.4-liter engine.

The final iteration of the classic Jaguar XK came along in 1957 with the XK 150. The 3.4-liter engine remained essentially unchanged, as did the 102-inch wheelbase. However, the extensive alterations to the body made this look almost like an entirely new car, although the Jaguar family resemblance was still striking. The big news, though, was that every XK 150 came standard with four-wheel disc brakes, the innovation that had helped the famed Coventry marque conquer Le Mans repeatedly. Like the XK 140 it replaced, the 150 was offered from the onset in open two-seater, fixed-head coupe, and drophead coupe forms. Arguably the most elegant of the XK 150 line, the drophead offered greater comfort and superior weather protection than the OTS model.

This spectacular XK 150 was delivered new to Vancouver, British Columbia, in 1960. Although it has always been a Canadian car, it is absolutely rust-free. In the mid-'90s, the car was stripped to the base metal and refinished in gleaming British Racing Green. The owner proudly states that the body was prepared by "an English panel beater" who used only lead solder in those instances where filler was required. Inside, the interior is trimmed in tan leather and the top is of black mohair cloth. To set off the gleaming rich green paint and contrasting tan upholstery, the car rolls on correct 16-inch chrome wire wheels.

Although this genuine, three-owner, 83,000-mile car has never required any major mechanical work or restoration, it has had a complete overhaul of the braking system, a new fuel tank and stainless steel exhaust. The original 3.4-liter engine runs beautifully and the overdrive Moss gearbox is in fine fettle.

In every respect, this is an excellent example of a most sought-after British classic, in a most appealing color scheme. This car is perfect to tour, show, or simply covet.

This car sold at no reserve for $29,900, including buyer's premium, at the Bonhams & Brooks Quail Lodge sale, held August 17, 2001.

The most striking feature of the XK 150 drophead coupe is that there really isn't any collectible car that is directly comparable. With more

When the bidding stalls at $29,000, it's time to get the paddle up.

than 200 horses on tap, an all-day cruising capability at speeds over 100 mph, four-wheel disc brakes (more than able to rein those horses in) and a spaciously elegant, leather-trimmed wood interior with a lined top, it was really the first true convertible touring car. It certainly wasn't a sporting automobile; leave that to its XK 120 and XK 140 predecessors. This was, in fact, the convertible version of the executive-express sports sedan, the Mark I, which Jaguar created during the same period.

The XK 150 was fatter, heavier and less responsive—one of the period road tests called it "podgy"—than other two-seat sports cars of the day. But it was also more reliable and more comfortable while giving up nothing in top speed. If you're thinking of taking a thousand-mile tour among New England's forests or the mountains of Colorado, this is the car for you. Just don't expect to make fastest time of day in the Jaguar Club autocross.

Buying an XK 150 should be done very carefully. Philip Porter, one of the world's experts on all things Jaguar, says, "Buying an XK is a high-risk sport…The cars are without doubt among the most difficult to restore."

If any rust is encountered, bodywork can be complicated and expensive, and it takes a Jaguar specialist to do a decent job of rebuilding mechanical systems. Even with everything intact, at 83,000 miles this car is going to need a full mechanical overhaul soon, though the buyer can probably expect two years or so of decent use. At least the paint and bodywork have already been refreshed.

On the other hand, when bidding stalls at $29,000, it's time to get the paddle up. For the price of an average Austin-Healey, this buyer got a marvelous car to drive and enjoy until he decides to restore it or sell it.

(Photo and description courtesy of the auction company.)

From the February 2003 issue of *SCM*.◆

Years produced: 1957-60

Number produced: Approx. 2,600

Original list price: $4,763

SCM Price Guide: $32,500-$47,500

Tune-up/major service: $500

Distributor cap: $45

Chassis #: plate riveted to engine compartment firewall on right side of car

Engine #: stamped on engine block above oil filter

Club: Jaguar Clubs of North America, 888.258.2524

Web Site: www.jcna.com

Alternatives: Jaguar XK 140 DHC, Austin-Healey 3000 BJ8, AC Ace Bristol, Porsche 356B Cabriolet, Aston Martin DB2/4 DHC

C, D, & XKSS Registry

This was just the beginning of a decade of domination at Le Mans for the Jaguar Factory, a domination of dimensions that no other marque has achieved, before or since

by Terry Larson

After seeing the racing success of the stock Jaguar XK 120 in 1950, Sir William Lyons gave Bill Heynes the go-ahead to design and build a lighter, more aerodynamic car using stock 120 mechanicals. This was to be a purpose-built car, constructed with one objective: to win the 24 Hours of Le Mans. The car was labeled the XK 120C, or C-type.

The three Le Mans C-types were built with only six weeks in hand. Not only did the C-type of Peter Whitehead and Peter Walker win the 1951 Le Mans, they also came in 77 miles ahead of the second place car. In addition, they were the new holders of the new 24 hour speed record, fastest lap and the greatest distance. Quite an impressive showing for the first time out.

This was just the beginning of a decade of domination at Le Mans for the Jaguar Factory, a domination of dimensions that no other marque has achieved before or since.

The C-type again won Le Mans in 1953. The next year, the more refined, more aerodynamic D-type arrived and won at Le Mans, a feat it repeated for the following three years. 1957 was the most famous Le Mans race, when the D-types took 1st, 2nd, 3rd, 4th and 6th. No other marque has ever matched this achievement (incidentally, my own D-type, XKD 153, placed third in this race).

Many consider the D-type to be the ultimate '50s sports racer. Uniquely, the D-type combined a tubular chassis with a monocoque center section. Besides being anchored to the bulkhead, it also penetrated the alloy center section to the rear bulkhead cross members, to which the rear subframe is attached.

This racing Jaguar was able to reach nearly 200 mph down the Mulsanne straight at Le Mans and then reduce speed very quickly with its fantastic new disc brakes.

In the '50s, the D-type was clearly the car to beat.

THE REGISTRY

I own a C-type (XKC 017) as well as a D, use them both on a regular basis for the track or road, and have occasionally jumped into one to go out for dinner in the evening. Great cars, and an important part of road racing history, they have always had a reputation for being one of the most reliable and drivable race cars of the '50s.

I have also been a member of the Classic Jaguar Association for 20 years, and have been gathering information on the C- and D-types for several years. Knowing this, CJA President Jack Hilton, who is also a friend, asked if I would take on the responsibility of doing a Register of the C, D, and XK-SS, which I agreed to do.

REQUIREMENTS

In order for a car to be listed in the Register, it must have an unbroken history and the original chassis, or a proper replacement chassis. If the chassis, or any other component, was damaged in a known accident and replaced (hopefully the original discarded chassis was destroyed and not built into another made-up car) and the car has an unbroken history, then the owner has claim to the chassis number and can be listed in the Registry. Obviously there

A replica can be a thing of beauty—but it's still just a replica.

are circumstances which can affect the degree of authenticity to the car. The most important component is that to which the factory has affixed the identification number, which is the chassis. This is the ruling of the CJA (Classic Jaguar Association) as well as many other clubs.

A Register will ensure that the unbroken history of proper cars is recorded. With so many replicas being built, it becomes extremely important to make sure that these replicas stay recognized for what they are, and are not confused with proper C- and D-types. While a replica may be an acceptable alternative for some people, it is hoped that those people do not lose sight of the fact that they are indeed replicas. It is probably reasonable to say that the time when a reproduction becomes counterfeit is when the serial number from a missing or destroyed genuine car is affixed to a replica (or is some cases, simply the number from another proper car which still exists). It also needs to be understood that you cannot take some components from a genuine car, build a replica and make it genuine.

A record is also being kept of anyone owning a replica who represents the car as genuine.

I was at a recent event where a replica was entered and the owner was very misleading, giving many people the impression that the car was genuine. This was not only disturbing to those aware of the truth, but also caused the people who knew the facts to lose respect for the owner.

If replicas are to be allowed in events with genuine cars, it is the responsibility of the owners to make it absolutely clear that their car is indeed a replica.

If you have an interest in acquiring a C or D (or any other high-dollar car), just make sure the history doesn't go "cold" in the mid '80s *(there are reputed to be more C- and D-types driving around than ever left the factory – ED).*

If you own a C,D, or XK-SS, or have any relevant information about one, or about a replica which is being represented as real, please contact me. In addition, I am always glad to be of assistance to those considering purchasing a C, D, or XJ-SS.

From the January 1995 issue of *SCM*.◆

1955 Ecurie Ecosse D-Type

Even the most rabid exponents of red or silver sports cars admit that the D was—and is—one of the very best looking cars ever to come thundering down the Mulsanne straight

by Dave Brownell

Chassis number: 18081
Engine number: 259843

Back in the '50s, high performance car makers—seeking to boost the reputation of their marque—pointed their most gifted engineers toward the Le Mans GP d'Endurance 24-hours races. Well-organized, deep-pocketed factory teams battled for supremacy in a series of epic battles. Jaguar's magnificent legend was built and established at Le Mans, where their initial C-type specialized roadsters first won in both 1951 and 1953. For 1954, a far more sophisticated sports racing car was developed and became known as the D-type.

At Le Mans that year, the leading Jaguar factory-team car of Rolt and Hamilton ran a gallant second behind the mighty 4.9-liter Ferrari V12 of Gonzales and Trintignant. The winning speed average at Le Mans was 105.1 mph, but Jaguar quickly had their revenge a few weeks later, when the D-types came in first and second at the 12 hours of Reims, averaging 104.55 mph. In the 1955 Le Mans, the Jaguar factory returned to claim first and third place, and returned to Le Mans in force in 1956, knowing this was to be the last year that the factory would run a team of long nose D-types. Two team cars crashed in damp conditions, and the third was hampered by a misfire; but the Ecurie Ecosse team from Scotland saved the day for Jaguar with their short-nose D-type. The car pictured, driven by Flockhart and Sanderson, emerged victorious in the 24-hours classic; a feat the private Scottish team was to repeat in 1957 with a remarkable clean sweep.

This D-type hat-trick of GP d'Endurance victories, against the strongest of opposition, sealed the Jaguar marque's charismatic image. D-types have been acknowledged ever since as one of the greatest classic sports racing cars. In addition to its outstanding and long competition record and capabilities, the D-type can also be used as a remarkably docile yet extremely exhilarating road car.

This car must be considered to be the most original, most authentic, most unaltered D-type in the world, and hence perhaps the most desirable. It will be the pinnacle of any collection, no matter how exceptional the other cars around it may be.

The SCM analysis: The car pictured was sold at Christie's London auction on November 1, 1999 for $2,815,725. The D-type Jaguar was the spiritual, stylistic and structural ancestor of the E-type with its monocoque center section and engine nestled in a tubular frame in front of it. More important than that is the enviable record of these cars, at Le Mans and elsewhere. These wins against relentless competition resulted in the D Jaguars becoming one of the most formidable and successful factory-built sports racers in the history of motor sport.

The selling price of over $2m surprised some of the punters and Christie's experts alike. It reflected what astute collectors in today's market seek in such cars: important competition victories, impeccable

Demand for documented D-types far exceeds the supply.

provenance, great originality and superb engineering. What is more remarkable is that this car's Le Mans victory was achieved by a private team rather than through a factory effort, albeit with quiet, sympathetic support from Jaguar.

The few sensible modifications added to the car for road use do not detract from its value in the least, and for some, may give it a further attraction as both a vintage racing car and eligible for international rallies such as the Colorado Grand and Mille Miglia revival. Not only that, even the most rabid exponents of red or silver sports cars would admit that the D was and is one of the very best looking sports racers ever to come thundering down the Mulsanne straight.

When this car was last sold in 1970, it brought a then-record-breaking £10,000 ($23,900 USD). In the intervening years, interest in historic race cars and sports racing cars and participation in historic racing events, has grown exponentially. Demand for "real" cars like this D-type far exceed the supply. Did the new owner pay too much? The selling price with premium rose nearly $716k above the high estimate in the catalog, but that has to be balanced by the car's credentials and the good chance that it won't be on the market again for a very long time. For the successful bidder it was decision time and we think he made the right decision.

(Photo and description courtesy of the auction company.)
From the January 2000 issue of *SCM*.◆

> "This car must be considered to be the most original, most authentic, most unaltered D-type in the world. It will be the pinnacle of any collection, no matter how exceptional the other cars around it may be."

Years produced: 1954-56
Number produced: 77
SCM Price Guide: $900k-$1.2m
Price new: £3,663 including purchase tax, $10,256 USD
Tune-up: $250-$450
Distributor cap: approx. $75
Chassis #: hand stamped into right front shock absorber mount
Engine #: stamped in right side of block above oil filter housing
Club: Jaguar Clubs of N. America, 9685 McLeod Rd, RR.2, Chilliwack, BC, Canada V2P 6114
Web site: www.jcna.com
Alternatives to consider: Aston Martin DB3S, Ferrari 375MM, Maserati 450S

1956 D-Type Roadster

We're reminded of the ax that a museum curator claimed was the original ax with which George Washington chopped down the cherry tree. "Of course," he noted, "the handle has been replaced five times and the head replaced twice"

by Gary Anderson

Chassis number: XKD530

Early years were spent racing in Finland.

In the 1950s, the magnificent Jaguar legend was enhanced at Le Mans, where their initial C-type specialized roadsters first won the 24 Hour race in both 1951 and 1953. For the 1954 race, a far more sophisticated sports racing car was developed, which became known as the "D-type." Entered at Le Mans as factory team cars in 1954, the first D-types were only narrowly beaten by a much larger-engined Ferrari V12. Jaguar quickly got their revenge a few weeks later when the D-types came in first and second at the 12 hours of Reims with an average speed of 104.55 mph. The works team won the 1955 Le Mans, and this was repeated twice more by the private Ecurie Ecosse team in 1956 and 1957.

This D-type hat trick of Le Mans victories against the strongest opposition sealed the Jaguar marque's charismatic image, and these handsome machines have been acknowledged ever since as one of the greatest classic sports racing cars. In addition to its outstanding competition capabilities, the D-type can also be used as a remarkably docile yet extremely exhilarating road car.

XKD530 was tested in October 1955 at the Motor Industry Research Association track. Finished in the traditional colors of British Racing Green and Suede Green upholstery, it was dispatched on February 13, 1956, via the Finnish agents Suomen Maanviljeligain Kauppa to the well-known sportsman Kurt Lincoln of Helsinki. Correspondence throughout Lincoln's ownership is held on file, and makes fascinating reading.

Throughout the next four years the car was actively campaigned as part of Lincoln's Scuderia Askolin. Files with the car include race programs and even videos of the significant events.

In May 1959, apparently disappointed with his results, Lincoln returned the car to Jaguar, later remembering he sent the car with a tag on the engine asking for 100 more horsepower. The engine was bored out to 3.8 liters, a Thornton Powerlok differential was fitted, and the car was repainted to a white Finnish livery.

During the following two years, the car was raced successfully, on a number of occasions by a young Finnish driver Timo Makinen, who later became a world-famous rally driver in Austin-Healeys.

Between 1961 and 1965, the car was raced in Finland by a succession of three owners, with full race and ownership records on file.

In 1966 the Jaguar was sold to Nigel Moores in the UK. Paul Kelly, the mechanic and curator for Moores, later described the external body-work on its arrival in the UK as "deplorable and hardly recognizable as a D-type." The body had suffered extensive damage and modifications, including cutting out the cockpit and cutting off the back like a bobtail Cooper.

Consequently, the bodywork, including monocoque, hood and tail, was sent to Williams & Pritchard, who were

> "Some might argue that precedence in claiming identity should be given to the car with the greatest amount of original content. However, in the world of classic and valuable collector cars, the rule is different."

Years produced: 1954-57
Number produced: 77
Original list price: approx. $6,000
SCM Price Guide: $800,000-$1,000,000
Tune-up/major service: $750-$1,000
Distributor cap: $30
Chassis #: stamped on right front shock tower
Engine #: stamped on block between carburetors
Club: Classic Jaguar Association, Jaguar Clubs of North America, www.jcna.com
Web site: www.classicjaguar.org
Alternatives: Aston Martin DB3S, Ferrari 500 TR, Lister Jaguar

XKD530, in red, on the ice

commissioned to rebuild the car in the form of a long-nose D-type. Usable metal and the original body tag were attached to a new monocoque. In addition, a new 3.8-liter D-type engine was fitted, dating from 1957 and built for use in XKD530 for the Sebring race but not used.

The original engine and remains of the damaged bodywork were retained in the back of the stores by the Moores collection. In 1982, the remaining parts of the damaged monocoque and tail were sold to John Harper, who used them with a new subframe from Lynx Engineering to build another D-type (which ultimately made claim to the same serial number, XKD530).

After Nigel Moores' death in 1988, his collection was sold to Evert Louwman. Six months later, XKD530 was sold to its present owners and in 1990 they commissioned Nash Morgan & Co. Ltd. to remake the nose and tail in its original short-nose configuration.

The engine and part of the gearbox originally fitted to XKD530 were also sold and were fitted to the D-type build by Harper. Making claim to the XKD530 chassis number, a subsequent owner sold the Harper car at the Brooks Monaco sale in 1990 to a long-time Jaguar enthusiast in the U.S. who still owns it.

After some dispute, FIA papers were issued to both cars claiming the XKD530 chassis number, one set from the British FIA to the car on sale today, and one set from the American arm of the FIA to the U.S.-owned car.

Owing to the fact that D-types can essentially be split into two halves, on more than one occasion two cars have evolved claiming the same identity. However, the car on sale today is offered with the benefit of a continuous and documented chain of ownership.

This car sold for $518,013, including buyer's premium, at Christie's Nine Elms sale, June 11, 2002.

Confused? I suppose that's understandable. Two D-types exist, both claiming the same chassis number. One has an unbroken existence and documented ownership, though during its lifetime much of the body as well as the engine and gearbox have been replaced by new parts or original parts intended for other cars.

> **"Owing to the fact that D-types can essentially be split into two halves, on more than one occasion two cars have evolved claiming the same identity. However, the car on sale today is offered with the benefit of a continuous and documented chain of ownership.**

The other has the engine, most of the gearbox, and much of the bodywork from the original car, though during some of the intervening period, those parts were simply a pile of metal in a storeroom behind an auto collection.

Someone might argue that precedence in claiming identity should be given to the car with the greatest amount of original content. However, in the world of classic and valuable collector cars, the rule is different. It is the unbroken sequence of ownership with documented transfers of title that gives a car claim to the identity of an originally produced car, rather then its content.

We're reminded of the ax that a museum curator claimed was the original ax with which George Washington chopped down the cherry tree. "Of course," he noted, "the handle has been replaced five times and the head replaced twice."

In fact, though this car was in good racing condition when sold, it fetched just over half what a D-type with unquestioned provenance might have obtained at the same sale. Clearly, the cloud of challenged identity cost the car a significant amount of its value.

Not to worry, however, since everyone is now living happily ever after. The American enthusiast and long-time SCM subscriber who bought the other XKD530 in 1997 for just over half of its then-current market value was the happy buyer of this car at the Christie's sale. If we've done our arithmetic correctly, he did quite well. He has been able to buy both halves of the identity at approximately half-price each. Now, once he's swapped all the original pieces from the American car with the Christie's car, he will own one car with unquestioned provenance and a good amount of original content. As a bonus, he will also have a very nice D-type replica, valued at perhaps $150,000, that he can use as an everyday driver.

Editor's note: In Monterey 2001, I had the chance to speak with the subscriber who owns "both halves" of XKD530. Our advice to him was to create one good, complete car, then send all the other non-authentic pieces to the crusher. The last thing the vintage car world needs is another faux D-type running around. There are just too many unscrupulous types who would take the "parts-left-over" D-type and begin to make claims of originality.

(Photo and description courtesy of the auction company)

From the November 2001 issue of *SCM*.◆

1954-56 Lynx D-Type Replica

The D-type dominated the international racing scene from the outset—today, the surviving examples are highly sought-after. For some, this re-creation of the immortal D-Type represents about the most motoring fun that can be had for the price

by Keith Martin

The Jaguar D-type was one of the most beautiful and charismatic sports racing cars ever made, not to mention one of the most successful. First appearing in 1954, the D-type featured bodywork of a highly aerodynamic nature, complete with tail-mounted fin for top speed stability, penned by ex-aircraft designer Malcolm Sayer. The center section of the car was of mono-coque construction, similar to that of an aircraft fuselage, while power came from the now legendary twin-cam, dry-sump, 3,442 cc six (later 3,781 cc), which produced some 250 bhp at a relatively unstressed 5,750 rpm. Top speed was in excess of 170 mph, while 60 mph from standstill could be achieved in a breathtaking 4.7 seconds. Not surprisingly, the D-type dominated the international racing scene from the outset until its demise, by which time just over 70 examples had been built. Today the surviving examples are highly sought-after and still make their presence strongly felt in historic racing.

This beautifully constructed recreation of the immortal D-type represents for some about the most motoring fun that can be had for the price. It uses a Lynx chassis, probably the most faithful to the original, but the rest is all hand-drafted. The exceptional specification includes: dry sump, 280 bhp, 3.8-liter engine; correct 1954 style wraparound dashboard with correct switches and instruments; Moss gearbox with D style lever; authentic type seats covered in old, worn dark brown leather, original D-type aluminum bonnet, bearing numerous blemishes and nicely patinated; all-aluminum bodywork to short nose, small-fin 1954 works specification; oversized D-type brakes; rubber safety fuel cell; 16" D-type wheels; Le Mans supplementary driving light; and Appendix C-style full-width screen. The only real deviation from an original car is the rear suspension, which is by trailing arms rather than by torsion bar. This gives improved roadholding, but could be altered if one so desired.

The SCM analysis: This car looks the part, sounds the part and feels like D-type to drive. One would be hard pressed to tell it from an original without checking the chassis number. It has taken more than money to build: it has taken time, hunting everywhere to find the "right" bits, expertise and patience.

These hand built Lynxes, of all the replicas, have the best reputation.

"These replicars, to me, represent a waste of time and money. I would personally question the sanity of a Lynx owner who would not take that kind of money and run, not walk to the nearest bank."

This ersatz winged flivver made a high bid of $85,800 at the May 11, 1995 Coys Auction, but remained unsold. I would personally question the sanity of a Lynx owner who would not take that kind of money and run, not walk to the nearest bank.

Popularized during the late '80s and as "affordable" alternative to million-dollar-plus authentic D-types, Lynxes changed hands in the $150,000+ range. They are hand built, and of all the replicas, have the best reputation.

However, just as with the Tupperware Autokraft Cobras so popular on our side of the pond, these replicars to me represent a waste of time and money.

It is the purpose of a high-performance car to address the questions being asked at the time of its creation. Any number of firms could today create a "more-than-perfect" D-Jag or Ferrari 250 LM or 300SL that would outperform the originals.

So what?

I remain unconvinced as to the purpose, utility, value or philosophy behind these recreations, and recommend you purchase one only if you need something to make into stylish sandbox for the children.

(Photo and description courtesy of the auction company)

From the June 1995 issue of *SCM*. ◆

What's in a Name, True Colors and More

Perhaps we needn't warn you about the ergonomic shortcomings of the Jaguar XK 120, and the particularly British attitude that steering wheels should be at least 17 inches in diameter and positioned within inches of the driver's thighs and chest

by Gary Anderson

Dear Mr. Anderson: *I recently read that the source of the "SS" of Sir William Lyons's first cars is a mystery. I always thought the initials were taken from Lyons's original company, "Swallow Sidecars." I didn't realize that information was in dispute.—***Jay Laifman, via e-mail**

Quoting from Andrew Whyte's marvelous book *Jaguar: The History of a Great British Car* (Patrick Stephens, Cambridge 1980), featuring a foreword by Sir William, "What 'SS' actually meant was something between [Sir John] Black and Lyons," meaning that the world may never know exactly what they were thinking when they created the name.

Probably the most reasonable assumption is that the marque was an abbreviation of Standard and Swallow. Standard was Black's company that supplied the chassis for the SS I. Swallow was Lyons's company, which by then was known as Swallow Coachbuilding, having dropped the "sidecar" from its name a few years earlier.

Alternatively, it might have been a shortened form of "Swallow Sports" since the term "sports" was quite fashionable for small-production cars of the time with sporting bodies. The first public use of the new name appeared in *Autocar*, July 31, 1931. "'SS' is the symbol adopted for a new car which will be put on the market in due course by the Swallow Coachbuilding Co., though at the moment it is still in the 'unrevealed secret' stage." The headline of that article was "The SS and the Swallow—Specially Adapted Sports Type Standard."

The Swallow Company went public as "SS Cars Ltd." in 1935. The first "SS Jaguar" models were introduced in 1935, with the most famous being the SS 100. During World War II, SS Cars did go back to making sidecars as well as other wartime conveyances. When civilian production resumed at the end of the war, the entire company was renamed "Jaguar" because of the unpleasant, Nazi-related connotations of "SS."

From the May 2001 issue of *SCM*.

> "The Swallow Company went public as 'SS Cars Ltd.' in 1935. The first 'SS Jaguar' models were introduced in 1935... at the end of the war, the entire company was renamed 'Jaguar' because of the unpleasant, Nazi-related connotations of 'SS.' "

This 1939 SS 100, from the days before Jaguar was Jaguar.

British Racing Green, or Suede Green?

Dear Mr. Anderson: *Some months back, a reader asked how to determine the correct shade of Jaguar British Racing Green for an XK 120. While it is true that BRG varies from marque to marque and year to year, it is usually possible for a good paint supplier or restoration shop to match the old formulas with mixes of modern paints. If an unfaded sample of the original color can be found on the car, this is even better since new paint can be computer-matched to the exact original shade of that car. However, what bothers me is that people aren't replicating the original colors when they restore Jaguars (and other cars). I have never understood why having the correct hose clamps and getting the nuts lined up on the manifold receives more judging attention than the fundamental question of correct period colors.—***Jack Triplett, via e-mail**

I couldn't agree with you more. If cars are going to be judged in concours, then they should be limited to colors available for that model and year. Your comment led me to do some more research. I found that the Jaguar XK 120 wasn't ever produced in British Racing Green, much less the almost-clichéd combination of BRG with biscuit interior.

As noted in Philip Porter's *Original XK*, the only shade of green used to paint the XK 120s was Suede Green, with a matching Suede Green interior. Don Pikovnik, who is working now to produce a paint color sample book for Jaguars, describes Suede Green (ICI code 2397) as a "deep blue-green with a lot of grey in it."

The biscuit interior was available with several other exterior colors, but not the Suede Green cars. British Racing Green (ICI code 2539) only became available on the XK 140s and is described as a "clean dark green, almost black." This would have been about the same time the works C-types were raced at Le Mans in dark green livery so it seems likely that dark green was used on the production cars to emulate the race cars. On the XK 140s, BRG paint could be ordered with either a Suede Green interior or a "tan" (rust-brown) interior, but still not biscuit.

I can only imagine what Sir William Lyons would say if he were suddenly transported to a modern day Jaguar concours or auction. "I don't recall ordering any 120s to be painted in the works C-type colors, and besides, how did so many of them get fitted with that strange tan hide interior?"

From the April 2001 issue of *SCM*.

> "What bothers me is that people aren't replicating the original colors when they restore Jaguars (and other cars). I have never understood why having the correct hose clamps and getting the nuts lined up on the manifold receives more judging attention than the fundamental question of correct period colors."

Dear Mr. Anderson: *I have wire wheels on my Jaguar XK 120 and they are in pretty sorry shape. The paint is chipped, and many spokes are broken. Should I have them rebuilt, or should I just buy new ones?*—**Jan Griffin, Sunnyvale, CA**

We discussed this issue with Mike Edgerton, manager of customer service at Dayton Wheels in Ohio, the primary manufacturer of wire wheels in this country, as well as specialists at Hendrix Wire Wheel and British Wire Wheel. They all agree that it is still possible to rebuild wire wheels as long as the splines are in good shape. However, they point out that for most wire wheels, it just isn't cost effective any longer.

To rebuild a wheel so that a company is willing to certify it as safe to drive, all spokes have to be removed—not just the broken ones—and the hub and rim have to be stripped of their paint or chrome. Then the spokes have to be replaced and the wheel trued, a process that must be done by hand. After that, the wheel can be repainted or rechromed.

Rebuilding wire wheels is a costly proposition.

For wheels in sizes that are still being produced, it's much less expensive, and probably safer, just to buy a new one. Dayton produces wire wheels in nearly every standard size used on postwar British cars, including 14-, 15-, and 16-inch diameters and 4-, 4.5-, 5- and 6-inch widths. There are also some overseas companies that produce the 18-inch wheels fitted to prewar Jaguars and MG-TCs for sale by U.S. parts sources, again at prices that are considerably less than the cost to rebuild a wheel.

However, for the concours-focused enthusiast who cares about the subtle differences between these new wheels and the original wheels, or for the individual with a car that can't be fitted with one of these standard sizes—like the Duesenberg or Packard owner—Dayton Wheel (www.daytonwirewheels.com) does offer a rebuilding service. There are also various local specialists who can do this demanding job. Just expect to pay a significant premium over what a manufactured wheel would cost.

From the July 2002 issue of *SCM*.

Dear Mr. Anderson: *I read with interest SCM's description and comments on the Christie's Pebble Beach sale of Lot #55 (October 2001, page 36), the very early (S/N S-810589) Jaguar XK 140MC OTS. This was apparently an exquisitely restored example about which the reporter commented "…and one of the earliest XK 140MCs extant." I actually have an earlier 140MC roadster and have always wondered if very early cars command a premium over later production, assuming the conditions are comparable.*

According to the Jaguar archivists, my car, carrying chassis number S-810440 was built by Sir William and his associates on December 10, 1954. There are only a few small cosmetic differences between the early and late XK 140s, such as the width of the bootlid handle, and the contours of the armrest between the seats.

Would you have 140 Registry or other reliable information to support that S-810440 might be the earliest surviving left-hand drive XK 140MC OTS? Additionally, in general, are the earliest cars more desirable and, by extension, of potentially higher value on an equivalent condition comparison basis?—**Fred Hammerle, via e-mail**

Earlier models and variations are often considered more valuable than later ones if there were significant changes during production. For example, your XK 140 is considered to be worth less in the marketplace than a comparable XK 120, and an early "flat-floor" Series I E-type has greater value than a later Series I in spite of the fact that in both cases, the later car is more practical.

However, I don't believe that lower serial numbers will be

XK 140 roadster—the earlier, the better?

worth more than later numbers in the same production run if there isn't anything significant to distinguish them from each other. Looking at Philip Porter's book Original XKs, there actually were few running changes during production of the 140s, and none that look significant enough to influence valuation.

Moving on to your first question, your best source of Jaguar production data will be the Jaguar North American Archives (800.452.4827). However, even they might not be able to tell you whether there are XK 140s with lower serial numbers than yours still in existence. According to Porter's book, the first left-hand drive XK 140 OTS was serial number 810001, so yours would have been the 440th produced. It certainly could be the oldest now surviving. Whether or not that will make the car worth more, it certainly makes an interesting comment when describing your car.

From the February 2002 issue of *SCM*.

Dear Mr. Anderson: *I have a 1952 Morgan +4 Special that I plan to sell in part to fund the purchase of an early Jaguar XK-series fixed-head coupe. I like the design of the fixed-head coupe but am a little concerned about how drivable it might be. Can you give me any directives on what to look for in a fixed-head coupe? I like the 120 best but am wondering if the 140 or 150 might be a better choice?—**Paul Davidson, Potomac, Maryland***

First off, you will be selling an open roadster and replacing it with a tin-top, which means no more wind in your hair and sun in your face but, of course, you knew that.

On the other hand, since you're already used to squirming into the Moggie, perhaps we don't need to warn you about the similar ergonomic shortcomings of the Jaguar XK 120. Both share the particularly British attitude that steering wheels should be at least 17 inches in diameter and positioned within inches of the driver's thighs and chest.

If you are prepared to seal yourself into a coupe and are interested in drivability, I would lean towards the 140. Think of the 120 as the show prototype that it really was, and the 140 as the practical version. On the exterior, functional bumpers, a sturdier grille and a few trim pieces were about the only changes. On the inside, however, the changes were more fundamental. The pedal box was expanded and the steering was repositioned so that the wheel is closer to the dashboard and a little higher, giving the

driver more clearance. Other than that, the 140 has the same lovely wood fascia of the 120 and, of course, the lovely sweeping fender lines that were drawn in so many schoolboys' notebooks in the early '50s. In my mind the 150 is simply not in the same category as the 120/140, being more of a luxury cruising convertible than a sports car.

The 120 and 140 dropheads generally have similar prices, though, being the original, the 120 might have a little more appreciation potential. If you do decide to buy, you should be most concerned about the quality of the wood interior. Finding a good craftsman to restore a poor interior will be challenging, and the work will be expensive. Second in order of concern, check the panels and frame carefully for any signs of rust or badly done body repairs. While bodymen with Jaguar experience can be found, repairs can eat up money in a hurry. Mechanical problems are not of as much concern, though you should want to make sure all the parts are there and the car has the right engine, transmission and accessories. Don't shy away from paying more than the *Price Guide* numbers for a good car. You'll still come out far ahead when compared to dragging home a project.

From the March 2003 issue of *SCM*.

Note: We received several letters in response to our answer in the February 2002 issue to Fred Hammerle's question about early Jaguar XK 140s, and whether there might be any surviving with an earlier serial number than his S-810440. Clark Wilson, a rocket scientist from Austin, Texas, informed us that he owns S810229. Ken Beck told us that he owns S810123 and knows of the existence of S810027. Tom Miller can beat that with his XK 140—S810017—which he believes was the 14th built.

If you're interested in getting more data on your XK, John Elmgreen wrote to say that he keeps records of all XKs worldwide. He recommends the Jag-Lovers Web site (www.jag-lovers. org), which includes his XK-Lovers group (www.jag-lovers. org/xk-lovers/). He is aware of several XK 140s with serial numbers that place them in the first 20 built. However, John notes that since Fred's car is an "MC" model—a designation that means it was a Special Equipment car built with a C-type head—it would be more valuable than a standard XK 140. John would be happy to receive information from all owners of XK 120s, 140s and 150s, and is pleased to provide any information he can from the database he has created. He can be reached at elmgreen@compuserve.com.

From the April 2002 issue of *SCM*.

The XK 140 is more practical than the 120, but with less financial upside.

Dear Mr. Anderson:
I enjoy SCM, *but why the constant harping about replicas not being good investments and unable to hold their value? Do you really think of buying a Jaguar D-type for $2.8 million or more as an investment? Do you realize what tying up nearly $3 million in a car represents in lost income or lost opportunity, compared to what you could realize in an average index fund? Most of us collect cars because they are beautiful, mechanically interesting and fun to drive and show. Who cares if an excellent D-type replica won't hold its value—it has all the benefits aforementioned at one-twentieth the cost.—**Paul Emple, via e-mail***

Replicas may be fun, but they won't garner any invitations to Goodwood.

Photo by RM Auctions

Paul, you've just taken the first step down a slippery slope when you start to compute the value of a vintage car relative to the potential return from some bits and bytes on your broker's computer system. (I would have said "a piece of paper in your lockbox" but most investments don't even have that level of tangibility any more.)

When a car is discussed in terms of its "investment potential," I hope most buyers realize we are discussing values relative to other cars, not non-automotive opportunities to use your money. It is the rare automobile (or artwork or sculpture) that will outperform a paper investment. There was a brief moment, in the late 1980s, when money put into a mediocre Van Gogh or a second-rate Vanwall would bring a higher rate of return than an index fund, but those days are gone. Of course, just a few months ago, an investor who didn't have half his money in an Internet fund was derided by some as not being "with it."

The financial point being made in our discussions of replicas is that they will depreciate. For an investor who only has $50,000 or $100,000 to spend on his car hobby, and who wants to get as much of his money back as possible when he sells his car, he would be better off monetarily buying a very good XK 120 or E-type rather than a replica of a C-type, even one made of alloy with a Jaguar engine. He should also

> "Even if his replica isn't likely to appreciate over time at the rate of a genuine car, in one sense, it may be a significant bargain."

keep in mind that the replica won't gain him an invitation to Goodwood or the Monterey Historics, or even bragging rights at the next Jaguar Club field meet unless he parks next to someone with a plastic-bodied replica.

On the other hand, even if his replica isn't likely to appreciate over time at the rate of a genuine car, in one sense, it may be a significant bargain. Many of the high-quality replicas with $60-75,000 asking prices may have originally cost well into the six-digit range to build. The original owner has already absorbed most of the depreciation and they aren't likely to go down much further.

And for that price, the new owner can obtain many of the same psychic satisfactions only otherwise available to the high-rollers. A well-executed replica that is built as much as possible with authentic components and techniques should provide a similar driving experience to the real thing, and it will be accepted at many of the second-echelon rallies and vintage races. In effect, high-quality replicas, when bought at current aftermarket prices rather than at MSRP from their creators, may actually be a pretty decent "investment" both financially and emotionally. The real question for the buyer to ask himself is: Given a specific amount of money to spend, should I buy an affordable re-creation of a much more expensive car for what it offers, or should I instead buy the real version of a less-expensive collectible automobile that won't require lengthy explanations of economic theory to justify?

From the December 2000 issue of *SCM*. ◆

SSs, XK 120s, 140s and 150s Cross the Block

"On-site auction reporting is the trademark of SCM. When an *SCM* expert attends an auction, his job is to personally evaluate the cars crossing the block, taking note of everything from the chassis number to the originality of the seat stitching. They analyze each car as if they were going to buy it for themselves. As you'll see in the Jaguar reports below, *SCM* experts **don't hesitate to call a prince a prince and a toad a toad.** Their reports are always honest, sometimes witty, and always make you feel as if you were there looking at the car with them."

— *Keith Martin*

SSs

#47-1937 SS JAGUAR 1 1/2 Litre sports sedan. S/N 22089. Eng. #60475. Black/beige. LHD. Odo: 31,815 miles. Genuine total mileage. Fully restored in mid-1990s, repaint and rechrome still quite shiny, interior good apart from shabby trunk area. Unusually, all tools lining trunk lid are present. Cond: 2+. **SOLD AT $15,260.** *Although $1,440 less than guide price was accepted here, other SS 1-1/2 sedans have made $16,700 or more on this side of pond. I would call this one very well bought.* **H&H Auctions, Buxton, UK, 10/03.**

XK 120s

#1025-1951 JAGUAR XK 120 rally coupe. S/N 679132. Pale green/green. LHD. 220-hp engine, C-type head.

Limited slip. Restored and much modified for rallies in the mid-1990s by fussy specialist Nigel Dawes. Has all requisite Heuer and Halda equipment. Still very nearly mint with great detailing, louvered bonnet, leather strap, Monza filler. Cond: 1. **SOLD AT $97,180.** *Quality restoration to super spec in great condition, hence result. Their UK auction results shows Dawes XKs are much sought after. A lot of money, but a lot of car for the money, and from a reputable builder.* **Bonhams, London, UK, 12/03.**

#213-1952 JAGUAR XK 120 roadster. Body by factory/Chatham. S/N 672306. Birch Gray/burgundy. RHD. Odo: 5,985 miles. Ex-US car restored 1999 with current 3.8 motor on triple Webers and very sexy exhaust manifolds. Cosmetics still sharp. Minimalist, bumperless, no brightwork, mesh in place of grille, two aeroscreens. Left- to right-hand drive conversion. Cond: 2+. **SOLD AT $54,280.** *Following several unsuccessful attempts to sell at auction in UK, vendor welcomed $3,000 under-estimate result here. For someone who wants a mock bad-boy racer or rally car, a good buy. For an originality fanatic, hopeless.* **Bonhams, Monte Carlo, Monaco, 5/03.**

#773-1952 JAGUAR XK 120 roadster. S/N 677552. White/blue leather. LHD. Odo: 53,165 miles. Very good paint and good chrome, some window chrome fair to poor. Wood is just good, will need refinishing. Some poor bodywork under paint, gaps in rear decklid show out of round areas. A good driver, possible local show contender. Needed (and very expensive) chrome work brings overall appearance way down. Cond: 3. **SOLD AT $28,890.** *Cost new in 1952 (U.S. delivery): $4,039. Total production from 1949 to 1954 was 12,078, 7,631 of which were roadsters. I'll count this one as a good buy, perhaps a little bargain. If no rust is found, this is a car to drive and enjoy for a long time before "investing" in a restoration.* **Kruse International, Scottsdale, AZ, 01/04.**

#111-1953 JAGUAR XK 120 roadster. S/N 674450. Eng. #G6735-8S. Gray/maroon. RHD. Odo: 9,280 miles. Older restoration, paint thick, rechrome good, leather retrim slightly marked, two Lucas flamethrowers, correct hubcaps on front wheels and rear spats in place. LHD to RHD. Cond: 2. **SOLD AT $37,028.** *Mid-estimate valuation about right.* **Bonhams, Goodwood, UK, 9/03.**

#126-1954 JAGUAR XK 120 road-ster race car. S/N W587085. Red/black. LHD. Odo: 29,432 miles. Vintage racer. La Carrera Pan-Americana campaigned 1992-96. Old repaint flat and battle-scarred, shabby presentation, trim-less, peaked roll-over bar braced to dash. Hurst shifter, Tilton brakes, fiberglass body. Cond: 4+. **Not Sold At $32,680.** *Too rough, specialized and, with $48,160 lower estimate, far too pricey for audience here. Ideal for "anything-goes" UK XK Series Open Class racing, nearly worthless for anything else.* **Christie's, London, UK, 12/03.**

#721-1954 JAGUAR XK 120 competi-tion coupe. S/N 5669125. BRG/green. RHD. Odo: 8,267 miles. Very well documented racing history. Always been a race car. Carries distinctive registration DVV 200. Paint to front of the car has bubbles, engine compartment appears dingy and untouched. Very good leather, dash wood very good, as are carpets. A racer meant to be hammered, and it has been. Cond: 3-. **SOLD AT $61,059.** *Race history is the big element in pricing here. Catalog presentation has list of this*

car's victories in 1954, photos of car on the track. A well-known car to British race fans, ex Jack Sears and Peter Sargent. Three times the price of a 120 FHC without provenance, but fair enough everything considered. **Coys, London, UK, 12/03.**

#U89-1954 JAGUAR XK 120 roadster. S/N S674845. Silver/red leather. LHD. Odo: 7,840 miles. Car card described as a "complete frame-up restoration." My recollection is that that should include the interior and chrome also. Fresh paint, new top, some sections of leather seats possibly replaced. Steering column and plastic cap left untouched. Cond: 3. **NOT SOLD AT $38,000.** *Better described as "restored like they used to be," which is not a good thing. No harm done in restoring a car and replacing only the "needed" bits. Problem is, you are competing with those cars where every bit was replaced or made new again.* **Kruse, Las Vegas, NV, 5/03.**

#SP117-1954 JAGUAR XK 120 Drophead coupe. S/N S678201. Dark blue. Odo: 26,571 miles. Paint good, some fisheye at driver's door sill, dime-size pop on rear fender. Chrome to front and rear bumpers, mirror bases peeling. Interior shows little wear but needs com-plete cleaning. Top dirty, wood is very good. Quickly deteriorated restoration due to salty seaside air. Cond: 4+. **SOLD AT $41,998.** *Lots of pre-sale interest here. I heard plenty of speculation as to what this car would bring on the block, from a low*

of $15,000 to a high of $30,000. The even-tual winning bid was pricey for condition, however, this car will clean and buff up to be a much better one in short order. With $2,500 in parts and a little less than that for labor, this will be a #2-condition car. **RM Auctions, Boca Raton, FL, 2/04.**

140s

#520-1956 JAGUAR XK 140 MC Drophead coupe. S/N S817703. Eng. #G4593-8S. Red/tan leather. LHD. Older restoration showing age, still some shine to paint but multiple bubbling, chips, cracks. Interior leather worn through color in spots, left door panel frayed badly on corner. Chrome okay. Wires weary. Chassis and engine not detailed. Cond: 4+. **SOLD AT $30,475.** *US spec. Aftermarket air conditioning installed in rear deck, original manual trans was switched to automatic. Sale price in line with condition. For someone who needs an automatic, this was a fair price. But that's a rare buyer.* **Bonhams & Butterfields, Carmel, CA, 8/03.**

#7-1956 JAGUAR XK 140 roadster. S/N 812766. Eng. #68665-8. Pearl Gray/red leather. LHD. Odo: 72,398 miles. A few chips to paint on front end. Chrome, while good, is not perfect in brightness and does not line up piece to piece. Older vinyl tonneau cover. Very slight bubbling to paint in license-plate area. Scratches on edges of doors, hood and spats. Cond: 3-. **SOLD AT $52,875.** *Sale price achieved was a bit of a shocker, as this was a driver and not a particularly nice one, at that. Restored cars with just a few miles of use are available for just $10k more, and similar ones on the market for $10k less; no bargain here.* **Christie's, NY, NY, 9/03.**

#33-1956 JAGUAR XK 140 MC Drophead coupe. S/N S818074DN. Eng. #G5933-8. Burgundy/tan leather. LHD. Odo: 72,398 miles. 210-hp six-cylinder, four-speed synchromesh with overdrive. Splendidly and correctly restored throughout, complete with new braking and electrical systems, rebuilt engine. New Stayfast top. Lovely example ready to collect a lot of awards. Cond: 1. **SOLD AT $128,500.** *Big money for an XK but this was an XK to die for. Superb automobile made all the more desirable with MC engine option. Almost too nice to drive. Perfect Jag XK prices have returned to the heights of 1989.* **Christie's, NY, NY, 9/03.**

#786-1956 JAGUAR XK 140 MC roadster. S/N S810190. Light blue/tan leather. Odo: 2,616 miles. 4-sp. Highly modified Jag that has languished in a garage for years. '53 Buick headlights and frenched tailights. Dents in body,

paint shot. Fender mirrors. Strange windwings. Leather interior gone. Top stained and ripped. Wire wheels. Cond: 4. **NOT SOLD AT $15,000.** *"MC" signals the optional performance package. Once owned and modified by Seattle hydroplane driver and Gold Cup winner Bill Muncey. Question is, what do you do with this? It asks for a needs-everything restoration and is just a weird oddity left as-is.* **Kruse International, Seattle, WA, 3/04.**

#181-1956 JAGUAR XK 140 roadster. S/N S81-1589. Eng. #G45958S. Old English White/tan leather. Odo: 87,085 miles. Striking presentation. Paint and bodywork excellent. Six-year frame-off restoration with photos to document the process. Leather interior excellent. Cooling system modified for high-altitude driving. Jack and tools correctly dispayed in trunk. Claimed show driven only, little to fault. Cond: 1-. **NOT SOLD AT $55,000.** *The 140 gives a few more inches of legroom than the 120 and still maintains styling that many prefer compared to the 150. Bid was light by about ten grand, but there was plenty of interest as people were around the car all weekend talking to the owner. Good 140s, like this one, will always have a market. Just not at this auction on this day.* **McCormick, Palm Springs, CA, 2/04.**

> "Big money for an XK but this was an XK to die for...almost too nice to drive."

#352.1-1957 JAGUAR XK 140 FHC. S/N S815710BW. Red/grey vinyl. Odo: 87,956 miles. Automatic. Nothing special, but an honest-appearing car with lots to like. Decent older paint, shows signs of aging, no need to repaint yet. Good quality chrome, no pitting found. Chrome wires appear to be new. No help found with vinyl interior. Cond: 3. **SOLD AT $21,330.** *Also ran as lot #41 and was declared sold at $35,100. I don't know the reason behind the rerun; let's just assume that it was a non-registered bidder. Automatic transmission is unusual, no longer the big minus it once was because of changing tastes. Pricey at $35k, a great deal at $21k.* **Barrett-Jackson, West Palm Beach, FL, 3/04.**

#130-1957 JAGUAR XK 140 MC roadster. S/N S813096. Eng. #G9790 85. British Racing Green/green and biscuit leather. LHD. Odo: 11,519 miles. Tonneau cover, Lucas fog lamps, left and right exterior mirrors. Restoration not quite as fresh as new but very recent appearing. Unfortunate divot to driver's door and front fender, paint otherwise unmarked. Excellent chrome, good quality throughout. Cond: 2. **NOT SOLD AT $75,000.** *Sorry—this one should have changed garages at this price. Perhaps the seller counted his car's condition as being nicer than it is, or perhaps he figures after repairing the dings it will bring more. I don't agree.* **RM Auctions, Monterey, CA, 8/03.**

150s

#176-1958 JAGUAR XK 150 coupe. S/N S8345640N. Green/black. LHD. Odo: 70,868 miles. One-owner car, original except some paintwork to top and hood. Body straight and solid. Extra set of painted wires. Original leather very presentable. No abnormal fluid leaks in clean engine compartment—just normal Jaguar leaks and streaks. Cond: 2. **SOLD AT $39,900.** *The delightful owner was selling his car due to advancing age and was with his car to answer any questions for most of the day. It did not meet reserve but he came down a bit and a deal was made after the fact, so it worked out well for everyone.* **McCormick, Palm Springs, CA, 11/03.**

#41-1958 JAGUAR XK 150 3.4 FHC. S/N SB35664DN. Eng. #V4678-8. Green/red. LHD. Odo: 19,024 km. An older restoration—paint now has many marks, the front quarter light surrounds are corroded, retrim is still good but the trunk is dirty. Successfully completed the 1992 Liège-Rome-Liège retro rally. Cond: 3. **SOLD AT $27,291.** *In view of a necessary repaint, the near mid-estimate result is slightly generous. Its 1992 rallying was really a very long time ago, and no guarantee that it is still in fine fettle.* **Christie's, Apeldoorn, Holland, 8/03.**

#145-1958 JAGUAR XK 150S 3.4 roadster. S/N S830600DN. Blue/red. LHD. Odo: 69,713 miles. Acquired 1983 in Oklahoma, 1993 UK restoration, repaint and rechrome good, leather retrim marked and crazed, floor-mounted speakers in front of seats. Cond: 2. **SOLD AT $60,977.** *Mid estimate result was retail valuation for most desirable of open 150s with 250 bhp motor and optional overdrive.* **Bonhams, Goodwood, UK, 9/03.**

#29-1958 JAGUAR XK 150 drophead coupe. S/N S824443DN. Eng. #V2639-B. Red/cream leather. RHD. Odo: 18,634 miles. 4-sp. Great finish on poorly prepared repaint, door fit poor, paint crack atop right wing, very good chrome. Cream seats no longer pristine, wires hanging from modern radio. Non-original engine well detailed. Cond: 2. **SOLD**

AT $38,760. *A fast, classic '50s British motorcar that had a $135k conversion/resto from a fixed-head coupe around 1991. Well bought, despite the blemishes.* **Shannons, Melbourne, Australia, 3/04.**

#31-1958 JAGUAR XK 150 convertible. S/N S837545. Red/red leather. Odo: 73,300 kilometers. Orange peel in paint, incorrect wood veneer added to dashboard, trunk and door fit off, excellent interior. Cond: 2-. **SOLD AT $60,041.** *Records indicate a total of 2,004 XK150 convertibles were produced with LHD. This one got a full and generous selling bid for a car in driver, rather than show, condition.* **Artcurial, Paris, France, 3/04.**

#348-1958 JAGUAR XK 150 coupe. S/N NA. Black. LHD. Odo: 5,668 miles.

The Twenty Year Picture

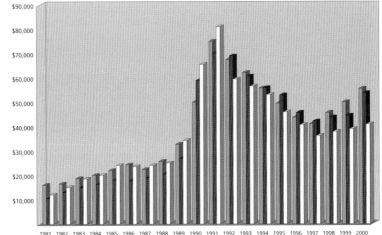

Legend:
- XK 120
- XKE S1
- XKE S3

Values courtesy of the Black Book and CPI, www.blackbookusa.com

Nice interior including wood dash. Turn signal stalk not chromed. Gaps good, paint good except chip on right side of hood. Rear passenger glass cracked and some scratches to rear window. Chrome excellent, including wire wheels. Cond: 2. **SOLD AT $24,413.** *Comes with generator in the trunk, wisely replaced by alternator. A very solid #2 car with a recent, thorough restoration. I'd give it a 2+ with a new passenger window. Best buy of sale, if you want a closed XK 150—a thin market.* **Mecum, St. Charles, IL, 10/03.**

#6-1959 JAGUAR XK 150 convertible. S/N S838636DN. White/red leather. Odo: 42,227 miles. Good and straight but door seams off, interior showing slight wear. Jaguar leaping cat mascot added at some point. Cond: 2. **SOLD AT $70,548.** *Optional 3.8-liter engine, first year it was offered. One of 2,489 built during the production run. Strongly bid, well sold.* **Artcurial, Paris, France, 3/04.**

#081-1959 JAGUAR XK 150S roadster. S/N T-831621DN. Red/biscuit leather. LHD. Odo: 99,916 miles. Very good doors, panels and paint. Beautiful new interior and excellent new top. Fresh mechanicals, according to catalog. On second engine. Cond: 2. **SOLD AT $66,000.** *36 of the S-Types offered the extra oomph of the larger 3.8-liter, triple-carb Jag engine as fitted to the E-Type. This car now carries such a unit. Selling price was on the money.* **RM Auctions, Phoenix, AZ, 1/04.**

#71-1959 JAGUAR XK 150S roadster. S/N S830981DN. Black/red leather. LHD. Odo: 40,674 miles. 3.4 liter. Very nice paint and bodywork, excellent leather and chrome. Looks like a no-longer-fresh restoration: Cloth top needs full cleaning, lots of detailing work would help. Carpets excellent, very good glass and dash. Cond: 3+. **SOLD AT $77,000.** *I have seen lots of upward movement in XK 120s, 140s and 150s, and this car continues the trend. It will make it all the way to a 2+ with a heavy detail, but the buyer already paid 2+ money to own it. Sold by an SCM'er.* **RM, Meadow Brook, MI, 8/03.**

#262-1960 JAGUAR XK 150 DHC. S/N S838408. White/maroon leather. LHD. Odo: 66,996 miles. Very nice paint and panel fit, almost all chrome replated. Lucas fog lights, chromed exhaust tips. Very light motor grime from limited use. Somewhat high idle speed (1600 rpm). A very thorough professional restoration done in the early 1990s, but holding up exceptionally well. Cond: 2+. **SOLD AT $55,650.** *Reserve lifted when the bidding surpassed $51,000. If the owner had the restoration performed for him, and even lightly enjoyed driving and showing the car for a decade, then he did all right.* **Silver Auctions, Fountain Hills, AZ, 01/04.**

#63-1960 JAGUAR XK 150 3.8-Litre drophead coupe. S/N S838695BW. Eng. #C4953. Light green. LHD. Odo: 71,738 miles. Chrome flaking off and scratched, doors don't fit properly, marked whitewalls. Some carpets missing. Gearbox clunky. Engine bay not detailed. Cond: 4. **SOLD AT $46,000.** *Only appreciation by the market at large will save this buyer. Dropheads are more expensive to restore than roadsters, due to their complex interiors, and generally bring less when offered for sale. Fully priced.* **Bonhams, Nurburgring, Germany, 08/03.**

D-type

#56-1955 JAGUAR D-TYPE replica. S/N E2090-9. Eng. #CAD001. Green/green leather. RHD. Odo: 1,227 miles. Good panel fit, paint settling over countersunk rivet heads, minor orange peel, odd bubbling. Typical XK engine rear oil seal leak. Constructed very accurately about 20 years ago using many genuine D-Type components. Cond: 1-. **NOT SOLD AT $319,960.** *A replica is a replica, even an excellent one. The estimated low of $335,160 was very hopeful—shocking, actually. The market tends to value real Ds at well over a million, and fake ones at under $100,000. It's not much fun to brag about your genuine cylinder head, after all.* **Shannons, Melbourne, Australia, 3/04.**

Section II
E-Types

With the E-type, Jaguar once again rewrote the rules about how sexy-looking, fast and and affordable a GT car could be. Think about it: a monocoque frame, triple-SU engine, and independent rear suspension for around $6,000.

I've owned all three variants of the E-type in both coupe and convertible versions, the lithe Series I, the more refined Series II, and the rather strange but powerful V-12 Series III. Each was different, and in their own way, special.

My memory of the first Series I coupe (a 4.2 liter) I owned is a little skewed, as the bronze with black leather interior car arrived with a long-dead mouse somewhere deep in the air ducts, which meant that the perfume of rodentus-mortuus was overpowering throughout the interior. At first, not quite knowing the origin of the smell, I decided that it might be mold, so I rolled up all the windows and let the car bake in the hot summer Oregon sun for a few days.

Whew. At that point, I had two options, either wear scuba diving apparatus to breathe when behind the wheel, or let the car become someone else's adventure in de-smelling. I advertised the car as "coming with free dead mouse decaying in the airvents" and sent it on to someone more talented than I at deodorization.

My favorite Series II roadster was baby blue, and had just been fully restored. Light blue with a dark blue interior, it had a subdued, elegant air about it, very different from the rough-and-tough

Series I. I recall thinking how extraordinarily attractive it looked in blue, and also how extraordinarily frustrating it was to fix all the little things the restorer either hadn't gotten around to or had just forgotten. Things like water temperature senders that didn't send, and winkers that didn't wink. All of which lead me to develop, as part of *SCM*'s creed on how to buy a car, to always look for cars that have been driven a couple of thousands of miles after a restoration is completed. Let someone else do all the sorting out, or "fettling" as the English like to call it.

I confess to never quite getting the Series II V12s. They seemed so tiny inside, with their narrow footwells, and so huge in front of the windshield, with a hood and engine that seemed to go on forever. Saddled with a Rube Goldberg approach to smog regulations, they never seemed to run very well for very long. But when they did, they cruised effortlessly at high speeds, and were comfortable so long as you stayed on only moderately challenging roads.

With today's technology, the SIIIs can be made to run quite reliably, and I note that at auction they are finally starting to creep up in value once again.

A well-done E-type, of any flavor, is an enthusiast's delight. If you've owned one before, I invite you to buy another one. You'll be surprised at just how good they've become. And if you're a newbie to the world of E-types, be prepared to wonder how you let so much of your life go by without experiencing one of motorcars great creations.—*Keith Martin* ◆

1961 3.8 "Flat Floor"

Always the most sensual of cars, it's no coincidence that this was Austin Powers' chariot of choice in that quintessential send-up of Sixties attitudes

by Gary Anderson

Serial number: 875898
Engine: 3.8 Liter

Introduced in 1961, the Jaguar E-type caused a sensation when it appeared, with instantly classic lines and a 140 mph-plus top speed. The newcomer's design owed much to that of the racing D-type: a monocoque tub forming the main structure, while a tubular spaceframe extended forward to support the engine. The latter was the same 3.8-liter unit first offered as an option on the preceding XK 150, and the E-type's performance did not disappoint. Weighing around 500 pounds (227 kg) less than the XK 150, aerodynamicist Malcolm Sayer used experience gained with the D-type to create one of the most elegant and efficient shapes ever to grace a motor car. Tall drivers, though, could find the interior somewhat lacking in space, a criticism addressed by the introduction of footwells (and other, more minor modifications) early in 1962. But of all the versions of Jaguar's long-lived and much-loved sports car, it is the very early "flat floor" 3.8-liter cars built prior to February 1962 which, for many enthusiasts, remain the most desirable of all.

Acquired in Canada by the French vendor in 1995, this restored 3.8-liter "flat floor" is, we feel, fully deserving of its owner's description of "concours." Finished in Old English White with black interior, the car has French papers and is accompanied by sundry invoices and Controle Technique.

The SCM analysis: The Series I E-type (referred to as the "XKE" in U.S. marketing literature) is an ideal benchmark for overall prices at classic car auctions because there is at least one in excellent condition for sale at every auction. These cars' specifications are well-known and parts are generally available, so if the example has been restored, the work has generally been done to a high standard. In the U.S. this year, comparable condition Series I E-types were selling for around $45,000, so the sale of this E-type at $40,183 by Brooks in Monaco in May of 1998 suggests that prices are fairly comparable in the U.S. and Europe, allowing for shipping, and that general market conditions haven't changed much in the past year.

A solid E-type that has been carefully restored is an excellent automobile. Even with the less-than-ergonomic seats in the early Series I, the cars are comfortable, and the nearly bulletproof 3.8-liter engine makes it practical for long-distance cruising, though the awkward four-speed transmission could have been better. E-types have always been the most sensual of cars—no coincidence that one was Austin Powers' chariot of choice in that quintessential send-up of Sixties attitudes. The Series I is the most stylish of them all, with its smooth, elegant fender lines terminating in clear glass covers over recessed headlamps and cloth soft-top easily dismounted for top-down touring.

The later Series I with the bigger 4.2-liter engine is a good driv-

For many enthusiasts, the most desirable of all sports cars.

ing option but has less investment potential. Many people prefer the added power and more comfortable seats, even with the lack of headlight covers.

The Series II, introduced in 1968, was mechanically a better car, though additional safety changes to headlamps, a different soft-top mounting and an awkward radiator opening were steps backward in styling.

By 1971 the high-revving six no longer could meet U.S. emission standards, so the Series III was introduced, powered by the torquey V12 from the big sedan. It had the visual styling cues of the earlier E-types, but huge rubber bumper overiders and a larger grille detracted from the classic curves.

If you decide to satisfy your nostalgia for Sixties sensuality, the Jaguar E-type proves the rule of paying a reasonable price for a good car rather than looking for a cheap restoration project. A good E-type is very good, but a bad example can be horrid. If much body-work needs to be done to get that enormous multi-curved bonnet to look and fit properly and if there's any rust in the monocoque tub, your bill just for paint and bodywork alone could exceed the sale price of this Brooks car.

(Photo and description courtesy of the auction company.)
From the July 1999 issue of *SCM*.◆

> "If you decide to satisfy your nostalgia for Sixties sensuality, the Jaguar E-type proves the rule of paying a reasonable price for a good car rather than looking for a cheap restoration project...a good E-type is very good, but a bad example can be horrid."

Years produced: 1961-68
Number produced: Series I 3.8, 7,820; Series I 4.2, 9,550
SCM Price Guide: $32,500 - $45,000
Original list price: $5,595
Chassis #: ID plate on center of firewall
Engine #: Stamped on engine block above oil filter
Tune-up: $300
Distributor cap: $22.50
Club: Jaguar Clubs of North America info: 888.258.2524
Web site: www.jcna.com
Alternatives: AC Bristol roadster, Austin-Healey 3000 convertible, Porsche 356 Cabriolet

1964-67 XKE Series I 4.2 Coupe

The coupe is really a better car in every way than the roadster. But to give yourself that vintage look, you'll have to muss your hair with a blow dryer, and go to a tanning booth to singe your skin

by Gary Anderson

A t the Monterey auctions this year, roadster-bodied Series I Jaguar E-types that were brilliantly restored were selling for $75,000 to $100,000. Yet at the same auction, a Series I E-type coupe in similar condition sold for less than $30,000. For the motoring enthusiast, as opposed to the investor, this anomaly is one of the great bargains in the marketplace.

In 1961, when Sir William Lyons introduced the replacement for the long-in-the-tooth XK 150, the E-type coupe was the car on the display stand. It was an instant sensation, recognized by the automotive press as an exceptionally pure form of automotive design.

In addition to the graceful body style, the E-type coupe offered a comfortable, leather-trimmed interior, adequate luggage space accessible through a convenient rear hatch, and the ability to cruise all day on the new divided highways at speeds above 100 mph. The roadster was introduced later, with its drop-top coming at the expense of all-weather comfort and luggage space.

The coupes, like the roadsters, offered four-wheel independent suspension under the monocoque body. The engine was easy to work on because the entire nose of the car tilted forward. The rear suspension was assembled in a single unit that could be removed to service the inboard disc brakes and other components.

Most Jaguar aficionados believe that the Series I E-types are the quintessential version of this sleek sports car. Between 1961 and 1967, a number of improvements were made to the car without changing the elegant styling. In 1964 the original 3.8-liter engine was upgraded to 4.2 liters and the engine was modified to improve cooling. The flat floor and minimalist seats were changed to provide better interior comfort. The dash trim, originally pebbled aluminum that rapidly lost its new look, was replaced with vinyl. Sadly, in 1968 the covered headlamps and triple SU carbs were lost to zealous U.S. regulators when the Series II E-type was introduced.

So why today does the coupe sell at such a discount to the convertible? The answer is that most of us buy our hobby cars for sunny weekends, show fields, and short cruises. Our collector cars are rarely driven in bad weather, and seldom on long trips. Because of this, the driving enthusiast who really wants to use his car can come out on top. The coupe is really a better car in every way than the roadster, except that you'll have to use a blow dryer to muss your hair, and go to a tanning booth to singe your skin. The coupe's chassis is more taut, resulting in better handling, and no roadster soft top, no matter how well fit, will ever equal the weathertightness of a closed car.

Because of the low market value relative to the roadster, the E-type buyer should be especially careful to buy the very best example that can be found, with particular attention paid to body condition. The hood is especially vulnerable to damage, and expensive to get right if it needs repair. Mechanical problems are less critical, but if the clutch has to be replaced, the entire drivetrain has to be dropped to get to it. Overall, if you don't need a top that goes down, this coupe may be the best bargain in the sports car market.

From the November 2001 issue of *SCM*. ◆

Possibly the best bargain in the sports car market.

> "Open Jaguar E-types that were brilliantly restored were selling for $75,000 to $100,000. Yet at the same auction, a Series I E-type coupe in similar condition sold for less than $30,000. For the motoring enthusiast, as opposed to the investor, this anomaly is one of the great bargains in the marketplace."

Years produced: 1964-67
Number produced: 7,770
SCM Price Guide: $23,000-$30,000
Tune-up: $300
Distributor cap: $45
Price new: $5,625
Chassis #: ID plate on center of firewall
Engine #: stamped on engine block above oil filter
Club: Jaguar Clubs of North America, c/o Nelson Rath, 1000 Glenbrook, Anchorage, KY 40223; 888.258.2524
Web site: www.JCNA.com
Alternative: Porsche 356 SC coupe

1966 E-Type Series I 4.2 Roadster

Arguably the best recognized sports car of its era, the E-type had a perfect combination of curvaceous lines and high performance, and was priced economically to boot

by Gary Anderson

Chassis number: 1E11389

Upon its introduction in 1961, the E-type roadster proved an immediate success. With its timeless design, it was immediately proclaimed one of the prettiest sports cars ever built. Designed under the guidance of Sir William Lyons, the car was a longer and lower version of Jaguar's D-type, a car that is widely regarded as the best-looking race car of its time.

Arguably the most widely recognized sports car of its era, the E-type had a perfect combination of curvaceous lines and high performance, and was priced economically at $5,595 to boot. These factors helped establish it as an instant hit; its popularity has only grown stronger as a collector car.

The evolution of the E-type is well documented. The original 3.8-liter model had a lack of footwell space, uncomfortable seats, massive brake fade and an engine prone to overheating. Later 4.2-liter Series I and Series II versions solved many of these problems, with bigger brakes, better cooling and an improved interior. One of the most important updates from a driveability point of view was the vastly-improved full-synchromesh transmission, replacing the antiquated Moss "crash box" of the earlier cars.

The example pictured here is the most desirable of all E-type configurations—a covered-headlight Series I car with the 4.2-liter engine. It has benefited from a comprehensive professional body-off restoration with exceptional underbody and engine bay detailing. The caliber of the restoration is attested to by a recent score of 99.9 in rigorous JCNA judging.

The mechanical restoration was performed to factory specifications, with all major components replaced or rebuilt. Cosmetically, a full bare-metal strip and repaint was carried out to concours standards. All brightwork, rubbers, top and interior trim were replaced during the restoration.

The SCM analysis: This car sold at the RM Monterey auction on August 18, 2001, for $115,500, including buyer's premium.

When one British journalist first reviewed the new E-type roadster, he christened it "the best crumpet-catcher ever devised." Certainly, the glorious and sexy lines of this Jaguar have attracted men and women alike ever since the first version was shown to the press in Geneva in 1961. Like the XK 120 that earlier had put an end to sports cars with square radiators and cycle fenders, the E-type revolutionized the way enthusiasts would think about the way a sports car should look.

Incidentally, these models are most often referred to by aficionados as "E-types," following the usage of the European brochures that hearkened back to the racing C-types and D-types. The term "XKE" was used primarily in American marketing literature to remind we colonists of the XK 120s, 140s, and 150s that were better known here.

As noted in the RM catalog information above, many changes were made during the first five years of production, including a larger engine, better transmission and more comfortable seats. The catalog is accurate in referring to the "covered-headlight Series Is" as the most desirable of the line. The DOT-complying, rocker-switch, open-headlight and EPA-satisfying detuned Series II cars that followed may have been slightly more practical, but vastly less powerful, and not nearly so romantic.

As to why this particular car sold for more than twice the Sports Car Market Price Guide range, we can only respond: How much

Proclaimed one British journalist, "The finest crumpet-catcher ever devised."

is perfection worth? Even Jaguar Club judges could find only the most minor of flaws. Every single bolt, nut and screw is original or matched to original appearance and specifications. The restoration work was such that every seam and panel match is as nearly perfect as the best body and paint man could achieve.

In one striking departure from originality, the exterior color of opalescent maroon has been matched to a black interior, when as original the interior would have been beige or dark maroon. Nevertheless, the maroon is a welcome change from the cliché red of many E-type restorations, and is quite pleasing combined with black trim.

The bidders either didn't know or didn't care about this issue. All it took was two or three bidders who wanted the best Jaguar on the lot to blow the top off the RM estimate of $80,000-$90,000. The fact that two Series Is sold later in the evening for $75,000 and $93,000 suggests that the underbidders eventually found cars that were nearly as good to take home, and saved enough to pay for several New England 1000 entry fees as well.

Further, it is the curse of every near-100-point car that to drive it is to sully its restoration, and hence its value. The owner of this $115,500 E-type has more of a trophy than a car that can be used.

This RM trio of E-type sales may be watershed prices for some time to come. As an aside, these prices provide enough room for most good restorers to make a little money off a project car, so we may see a few more project cars being restored to their former glory in the next couple of years—something that simply wouldn't happen when $50,000 was all you could expect for a perfect car.

(Photo and description courtesy of the auction company.)

From the November 2001 issue of *SCM*.◆

Years produced: 1961-68
Number produced: Series I 3.8: 7,820; Series: I 4.2: 9,550
SCM Price Guide: $35,000-$50,000
Tune-up: $300
Distributor cap: $45
Price new: $5,595
Chassis #: plate on center of firewall
Engine #: stamped on engine block above oil filter
Club: Jaguar Clubs of North America, c/o Nelson Rath, 1000 Glenbrook, Anchorage, KY 40223; 888.258.2524
Web site: www.jcna.com
Alternatives: AC Bristol roadster, Austin-Healey 3000 Mk III convertible

1970 Series II E-Type Roadster

This superb roadster underwent a meticulous, Pebble Beach level restoration documented at $75,000; yet the owner stresses that this Jaguar was built to be driven

by Keith Martin

Chassis number: 4R7581
Engine number: 7R11451-9

To some, the Series II E-type represents the best of all worlds. The styling and design is unmistakably classic; recognized as one of the finest roadsters ever built, this car has several design advantages over its Series I predecessor.

These include the newer cross-flow radiator with twin electric fans for better engine cooling, bigger Girling-made brakes, collapsible steering column, stronger chrome-plated wire wheels, better clutch with higher-rated diaphragm spring and new camshafts with redesigned profiles to give quieter operation. The 1970 Series II offers all of the refinements of the E-type historic line with the low-maintenance operation inherent in Jaguar's powerful straight-six twin-overhead-cam engine—a definite advantage over the more complicated Series III twelve-cylinder, which arrived in 1971.

The roadster pictured here was purchased new in 1970 by Mr. Douglas of South Carolina. He bought the car from a Ft. Lauderdale/West Palm Beach area dealer as a birthday gift for his wife, who had requested a model with factory air conditioning. It remained in the same careful ownership for the following 23 years, until they sold the vehicle to a good friend who lived about 30 miles away. The second owner kept the vehicle for two years and put the mileage up from 45,000 to 47,800 before selling the car in February 1995 to the current owner.

While the intention was to simply enjoy driving the vehicle, after a couple of months there were some items that needed fixing or correcting. Meeting Jaguar historian and contributor to Jaguar's U.S. Archives, George Camp (who has a passion for congeniality and making sure a car is "correct") helped convince the new owner that a proper restoration was in order. This superb roadster then underwent a meticulous, ground-up restoration documented at $75,000. No expense was spared. The restoration, documented by photographs, was carried out to Pebble Beach standards.

The automobile was trailered to four JCNA shows, Boca Raton, Boone Hall (Charleston), Hilton Head and Atlanta with a score that averaged 99.950, good enough to achieve top national honors. The car also did well in non-JCNA shows, winning a special award from the Atlanta Jaguar Society.

One man's quest for the perfect Jaguar.

While the car was restored to concours condition, the owner stresses that the Jaguar was built to be driven. When not touring, the car is kept in a special climate controlled display room. Attention to detail included brand new correct Dunlop SP sport 185VR15 tires specially ordered from England. The vehicle also has custom-installed rear stereo speakers and a specially-designed stereo unit and console which can be installed by simply sliding out the center console and inserting the stereo unit.

With just three owners from new, limited use and being subject to a concours-winning restoration, this vehicle may be considered by some to be one of the finest Series II roadsters in the world. The present owner, who originally purchased this car to drive, says of the subsequent restoration work: "I went overboard in every minute detail in my quest for the perfect Jaguar, and this is the result."

On April 26, 1997, at the Christie's Tarrytown auction, SN4R7581 sold for $57,500. This is a price not seen since the late '80s for an SII roadster.

Hampered stylistically by open headlights and clumsy U.S.-legal tail lights, and forced to endure the indignity of power-sapping Stromberg carburetors, SIIs will always lag behind SIs in price. However, given the quality of the automobile, this car was well bought.

(Photo and description courtesy of the auction company.)
From the May 1997 issue of *SCM*.◆

> "With just three owners from new, limited use and being subject to a detailed, concours-winning restoration some may consider this vehicle one of the finest Series II roadsters in the world."

1971-74 E-Type V12 Roadster

Something of an enigma, the new E-type looked at first glance just like the car it replaced; on the other hand, its character was completely different

by Keith Martin

Perhaps no other manufacturer but Jaguar could be expected to pull off the same trick twice and get away with it.

Certainly the brilliant E-type was going to be a very hard act to follow when, a decade on, some aspects of its design were beginning to show their age. The increasing demands of US emission and safety regulations had caused the six-cylinder E-type Series II to be noticeably less powerful and, to many eyes, a less handsome vehicle than the initial "clean slate" S1s. Notably the E-type had been putting on weight as it approached middle-age—a phenomenon sadly known to cars as well as human beings—and its legendary performance was not what it once was.

Jaguar's solution was, effectively, to give the car a heart transplant. Thus the upcoming V12—an engine of some magnificence—was brought into early service to create the Jaguar E-type Series III. This 5.3-liter engine was originally developed for racing, and was tested in the then super-secret XJ13. Jaguar's original plans were to offer this new engine, first in a four-door saloon, and then in a sporting two-seater. However, the new XJ6 was ready before the V12 engine was, so the saloon was launched with the XK six-cylinder engine, the twelve following at a later date.

Thus, the new engine made its debut in the revamped XKE. There were historical echoes here too, because the legendary XK-Series engine, (now being superseded) was also originally proposed to power a saloon but found itself diverted into an equally successful sports car.

Yet this course of action created something of an enigma. The new E-type looked at first glance just like the car it replaced—on the other hand, its character was completely different. Closer inspection showed that the styling had been considerably enhanced with a larger hood bulge, re-radiused wheel arches with prominent flares, the steeper 2+2 windshield for the roadster, dual wipers to clear it and, on US models, big black-rubber bumper guards reminiscent of the visual excesses of early '50s American Cadillacs. Set in the famous race-bred nose apertures was a chromed chip-slicer grille. A detachable factory hardtop arrived as an option, and as an indicator of the more refined nature of this Jaguar, many were delivered outfitted with automatic transmissions and air conditioning, certainly a far cry from the shrieking exhaust note of the original C-types as they flew down the Mulsanne straightaway.

The massive engine featured a 60-degree angle between cylinder blocks, which were made of aluminum, as were the heads and crankcase. Each bank had a single overhead camshaft. Combustion chambers were formed in the top of the pistons rather than in the head casting, which was machined fully flat. Aspiration was via a quartet of constant-vacuum Zenith-Stromberg carburetors.

The new engine, which turned out 272 bhp—a figure no

Before purchasing an SIII, take it out for a bit of an exercise.

standard XK unit ever approached—finally restored the E-type's critical 140-mph-plus top speed and was able to improve considerably on its acceleration figures. The 0-60 times of 7.5 seconds were of Ferrari/Lamborghini proportions, but for far less money. The US POE price was round $8,000 basic in 1972, making this the cheapest 12-cylinder sports car in the world.

The SCM analysis: It's no secret that we at SCM have always been slightly confused by the SIII E-types. With their nose-heavy handling and prodigious horsepower, they resembled their American muscle car brethren like the Road Runner and the Chevelle 396 SS more than their lithe, nimble S1 3.8 and 4.2 E-type predecessors.

Sales were never strong for the SIII, and up to the year 1984 decent-enough roadsters could be purchased for under $10,000. With the surge, prices of concours examples crossed the $100,000 mark with regularity.

Prices now have stabilized. 95+ point SIII roadsters, with manual gearchange, wire wheels, factory air conditioning and hardtop will bring $60,000 at auction and in private sales. While SIIIs will appreciate with the market, they will lag behind the earlier S1 covered headlight cars.

The most desirable models are those from 1971, as they have higher-compression engines and fewer emissions controls.

Before purchasing an SIII, you would be well advised to take one for a bit of an exercise. As magnificent as the V12 engine is, the problems of a tight cockpit, vulnerable bodywork and suspect electricals were carried over from the early 6-cylinder E-types.

The SIII handling and performance characteristics are extremely appealing to some, and less so to others. You should decide for yourself.

From the March 1994 issue of *SCM*.◆

1972 XKE V12 Coupe

There is a mystique surrounding twelve-cylinder cars....and to think that less than $20,000 will buy the budget-minded enthusiast entrance into this exclusive club

by Gary Anderson

Chassis number: 1872914

Since its introduction in 1961, the E-type has been critically acclaimed as having some of the finest lines ever penned for an automobile. Even today, the long, cigar-like nose and short rear deck lid remain the standard by which other sports cars are judged.

Much of the design inspiration came from its racing predecessor, the D-type. With the E-type's monocoque chassis construction, it was both longer and lower than its predecessor, but the racing heritage was undeniable.

Ten years and numerous tweaks later, Jaguar launched a V12 engine in its E-type, transforming it with an infusion of turbine-like torque and horsepower. Along with the engine, other more plush modifications were made, including power steering and power brakes.

The result was a very fine, if somewhat sophisticated, grand touring car. The primrose yellow Jaguar E-type 2+2 coupe shown here has fresh exterior paint. Its black leather interior is in excellent condition. Overall, the car has been very well maintained, and has all the correct trim, including original chrome wheels and hub caps. It is perfectly suited for Jaguar club events and cruises.

The SCM analysis: The car pictured sold for $17,600 at the RM Auction in Amelia Island, Florida, on March 11, 2000. There is a mystique surrounding twelve-cylinder cars. Ferraris, Lamborghinis and other super cars of that ilk have these sophisticated, silky-smooth engines. There's even an historic rally each year that can only be entered by twelve-cylinder cars. And to think that less than $20,000 will buy the budget-minded enthusiast entrance into this exclusive club. The Jaguar Series III E-type fixed-head coupe is a great car for that money.

So what's the catch? For one, the "tweaks" carried out between the classic Series I E-type roadster and this cat built at the end of E-type production resulted in a car that, to be generous, has few graceful angles. The wheelbase, stretched to accommodate the longer engine and extra seats, is too long. The roof line, raised for rear headroom, has a hunchbacked appearance. And the car is heavier than earlier E-types, which didn't help either mileage or handling. Gas mileage was probably the worst complaint. Drive the car at all aggressively and the twelve cylinders can have trouble delivering the same mileage as a sport-ute. Produced under the new EPA restrictions, the engine is strangled by four Zenith-Stromberg carbs that had replaced the three two-inch SUs of the previous model. At least a 1972 model-year car no longer has to be smog-certified in California and several other states.

But at the price of a barely average Austin-Healey, how can you go wrong? Actually, there are a lot of ways. Like any other bargain-priced but complicated car, if the Series III E-type requires any work at all, it is cheaper to back off and wait to buy something better later. Just the body work to correct a bent and misaligned bonnet and rusty outriggers could cost as much as the price of this Amelia Island car. While the V12 engine is actually very sturdy, it can be expensive to fix if it has been allowed to severely overheat, a typical problem on these cars.

On the other hand, all mechanical parts and most trim parts are easy to find. In addition, there are a variety of proven steering, suspension and drivetrain upgrades that can turn this car into

A great car for the money.

a practical daily driver that can make the words "grand tourer" a true compliment instead of faint-praise criticism. The V12 coupe was just as fast as the first-series E-types and could actually get to 100 mph sooner. At that speed, the aerodynamics make the car very stable and quiet. The large rear hatch opens to a generous luggage area and the coupe is totally weatherproof. This combination means that miles can be consumed at a great rate in pleasant comfort, which is what grand touring was all about. Just don't try to win any slaloms. With the increased weight and wheelbase, the SIII understeers badly in tight corners and the slim, leather-covered steering wheel doesn't increase one's confidence. Bob Tullius and his Group 44 did manage to win the SCCA B production championship with an SIII in 1975, but he said later the car "didn't want to be a race car."

At the low end of the SCM Price Guide, this car was probably well bought. It does have a manual transmission, more fun than the just-adequate automatic, but has the original standard chrome disc wheels, not as desirable as the optional chrome wires. The decent repaint and a nicely worn but still serviceable original interior are consistent with the price. It's notable that the convertible version in the same condition would have sold for at least 50 percent more. Most people who buy a vintage Jaguar today want the wind in their hair. But as entry-level transport into the Jaguar world and the incomparable experience of the V12 engine, a good Series III E-type coupe provides great value for the money.

(Photo and description courtesy of the auction company.)

From the July 2000 issue of *SCM*.◆

Years produced: 1971-1974

Number produced: 7,300 FHCs; 7,990 roadsters

Original list price: $7,325

SCM **Price Guide:** $17,500-$24,000

Tune-up/major service: $500

Distributor cap: $75

Chassis #: Main plate pop-riveted to top center of firewall in engine compartment; shown on sticker on rear face of door aperture and stamped under the heater in engine compartment

Engine #: Stamped on head on rear in V between cylinder banks

Club: Jaguar Clubs of North America, 888.258.2524

Web sites: www.jcna.com; www.Jag-lovers.com

Alternatives: Jensen Interceptor, Porsche 911

1973 XKE SIII V12 Convertible

The initial model lacked footwell space, had uncomfortable seats, massive brake fade and an engine prone to overheating—yet it was loved

by Gary Anderson

I f ever there was an auto manufacturer to take lessons learned from racing and apply them to their street cars, it was Jaguar. The legendary D-type was a formidable competitor on the track, and Jaguar included all the D's best traits when it debuted the E-type in 1961.

Arguably the most well recognized sports car of its era, the E-type had a perfect combination of curvaceous lines, high performance and affordable price. This winning combination helped establish it as an instant hit and its popularity has only grown stronger.

The evolution of the E-type is well documented. The initial 3.8-liter model lacked footwell space, had uncomfortable seats, massive brake fade and an engine prone to overheating—yet it was loved. Ten years and numerous improvements later, Jaguar launched a V12 engine in its E-type that provided lots of torque and horsepower. The V12 was not the only improvement for the third and final series of E-types—it was now well appointed with features, while drivability benefited from power steering and brakes. The result was a sophisticated grand tourer.

The V12 model pictured here is fresh from a complete nut-and-bolt restoration to JCNA standards. The no-expense-spared restoration was completed four years ago; since then, the car has remained in a bubble, virtually untouched. It is beautifully finished in red with biscuit interior and is complete with optional wire wheels. The four-speed gearbox makes best use of the powerful 12-cylinder engine and the air conditioning will keep you cool in warm weather.

These late-model E-types mark the end of an era, and their user-friendly operation makes them highly suitable for all enthusiasts to enjoy on a regular basis.

The SCM *analysis: This car sold for $50,600, including buyer's premium, at RM's Meadow Brook sale, August 3, 2002.*

Denis Jenkinson, legendary English motoring journalist and co-driver for Stirling Moss when they won the Mille Miglia in the Mercedes 300 SLR, tested the brand-new Jaguar Series III V12 in comparison to his SII daily driver. His conclusion was that it could do everything the earlier six-cylinder E-types could do, just at 20 mph faster and at seven fewer miles per gallon. Concluding that he no longer had the reflexes or will to outwit the constabulary by cruising at 120 mph, nor would his expense account handle the double hit of rising petrol prices and decreased gas mileage, he decided to stick with his Series II.

In today's market, enthusiasts seem to make much the same decision. In spite of the fact that the 5.3-liter V12 engine with its four Zenith Stromberg carburetors, two on each cylinder bank, offers much the same verve and performance as a V12 Ferrari, collectors aren't willing to spend a premium over the six-cylinder cars.

In many ways, the Series III really was the best of the E-types. With a lengthened wheelbase, the model offered more space and comfort on the interior. Stylists would argue that in many ways, the design sorts out some of the awkward details of the SII, while preserving the voluptuous lines that characterize the entire E-type

Series III: in many ways, the best of the E-types.

line. Of course, there was the problem of the punching-bag rubber bumper overriders that were Jaguar's answer to the US bumper regulations instituted in 1974, the last year of the model.

At first glance, the V12 engine looks very complex. Pollution-control equipment, as well as standard power steering and air conditioning, with which most SIIIs were equipped, add a plethora of pipes, compressors, condensors and hoses to the engine compartment. Nevertheless, experienced Jaguar mechanics say the engine is one of the best features of the car. If it has been well maintained, it is quite reliable, and the one-piece bonnet makes all parts of it quite accessible. As an added bonus, in states with a rolling 30-year exemption for smog testing, modifications can now be made. Jason Len of XKs Unlimited says a replacement SU carb kit and removal of extraneous smog equipment can add 30 horsepower while improving gas mileage.

On the interior of the Series IIIs, safety regulations undermined the charm of traditional Jaguar design. Wood and metal trim had been replaced by padded vinyl. Metal toggle switches had been replaced by plain plastic rockers. And the lovely wood-rimmed steering wheels with polished plastic horn buttons had been replaced by a leather-wrapped rim and molded rubber hub. However, a large tachometer and large speedometer still bracketed the steering column, supplemented by a clock and four no-nonsense gauges above the console, all with black faces and white lettering.

This particular car was in excellent restored condition and the buyer was willing to pay at the upper end of the normal trading range for the quality of the restoration. There's no indication that the car has been entered in any Jaguar Clubs of North America concours events, so the true test of the point-quality of the restoration is yet to come. And since the car has not been driven in the four years since it has been restored, it will surely need to be fettled.

Nonetheless, given the apparent thoroughness and quality of this restoration, this car should be considered well bought. If properly maintained and driven sparingly, it should do nothing but appreciate in the future.

(Photo and description courtesy of the auction company.)
From the February 2003 issue of *SCM*.◆

The Appraiser's Corner

1973 XKE V12 Roadster

Excerpts from Actual Appraisals

by Steve Cram

Odometer:	17,427 miles (documented)
Exterior color:	British Racing Green
Top color:	Black
Equipment:	5.3-liter V12 engine, four-speed manual transmission.
Condition:	Using the traditional rating system of 1 to 5 for vintage and/or collector cars (1, mint/show/perfect/as-new; 2, very good; 3, good; 4, fair; 5, poor/rough), this vehicle is in low #1 condition.
Exterior:	Excellent specimen with no rust or accidents. Body is in low #1 condition. Paint is in fine original condition, #1. Chrome hardware, including bumpers and grille, all #1. Glass and lenses #1-. Grommets and seals #1, same for wire wheels and tires.
Soft top:	Original and in #1 shape. Rear light #1, all latches and receivers #1, same for bows and struts.
Hard top:	#1 shape.
Interior:	Excellent condition and totally original. Leather is in low #1 condition, same for carpet and dash top. Wood is #1. All instruments and systems controlled from within operate as they should and are in #1 shape.
Trunk:	Immaculate and detailed, with all items accounted for and in #1 condition.
Engine compartment:	Also immaculate and detailed. Body wiring and cooling system #1.
Undercarriage:	Immaculate and detailed. Suspension system redone to top standards by cognizant owner. Steering, exhaust system, and rear end same.
Mechanics:	Car started quickly and then performed to #1 standards in all tests.
History:	Continuation of Jaguar's lithe roadster, with a V12 powertrain. Values of these cars are rebounding very well. This unit was built in January 1973 and delivered to first owner. Purchased in 1984 with 9,000 miles by current owner, who has kept the car in spotless original condition. Fine original cars such as this one are almost never seen.

Base value for this vehicle: $37,000

Add for documented original condition: $10,000

Appraised value: $47,000

Cat Q & A:
Investments, Copycats, and Why You Should Never Teach a Kid to Drive in Your Series I E-Type

Dear Mr. Kerb: *I am married, with two children, ages two and five. I've always dreamed of having a sports car, but now need one that can carry the kids as well. I'd like to spend under $25,000, and have narrowed my choices to a Lamborghini Espada, a Series III Jaguar V12 coupe and a Maserati Indy. I don't do much work on cars myself, so I would like something fairly reliable. Do any of the cars above have fatal flaws that would keep me from enjoying them? What should I watch out for? How much should I pay? And which would you choose for yourself?—***J.M., Hollywood, CA**

Early '70s Jaguar will require a fair amount of fiddling to keep them right.

Dear Mr. M: The conquest for a sporty and affordable 2+2 has challenged parents for generations.

You have put together a list of candidates that fit your criteria and are common enough that it will be possible to find a good example in your general area. No matter which car you consider, the trouble areas will be rust, accident history and the quantity (and quality) of the service history. The "fatal flaws" that you mention are actually present in all three cars and it is the same flaw: age.

A car can have excellent compression readings, a good gearbox and functioning cooling system but still fail weekly due to the dozens of small parts that have simply gotten old. To a hands-on enthusiast, this is usually not much of a problem. Most of us can change a starter, wiper motor, heater core, water pump or door handle when they fail. If you have to set aside the time and money to have these failures repaired by a professional, your enjoyment of the car might fade.

Over time, the list of things that you haven't repaired will shrink and you might learn to live with intermittent failures, but an older, exotic "driver" will always be full of surprises.

Now that I've said all that, my personal choice would be the Indy. The Maserati V8 is a great engine and not fussy or unreliable, something that you might not expect in a four-cam V8. They have a very nice gearbox and brakes and overall the feel is that of a substantial GT car. I also find their stretched Ghibli styling more pleasant than other 2+2 models (like the Series 2 XKE coupe 2+2). Expect to pay high teens to low twenties for a good driver.

The Lamborghini, if you find a good one, is a very roomy, great driving car, but has limited appeal to many people due to its "Bertone on LSD" styling. Mechanically, the Espada is an evolution of the 350 and 400 models, so they are fairly well sorted out and don't have any huge shortcomings (if you don't count the styling). Prices begin in the teens but can go well into the twenties or even low thirties for a really good one.

For you, however, I recommend the Jaguar. All XKEs have excellent parts availability, which is a good thing because the quality control and assembly quality of the early '70s Jaguar will require a fair amount of fiddling and parts changing to get things right. That might make it sound as though the Jag should be taken off your short list but look at it this way: whoever owned and serviced the car before you has been improving and changing pieces for decades. There is a chance that you can find an XKE coupe that is fairly well sorted out but still reasonably priced, simply because it is not the more desirable roadster. Given that you are not mechanically inclined, it might be wise to start shopping for a good mechanic before you buy. If a mechanic performs a pre-purchase inspection with the knowledge that he will be looking after the car in the future, it is likely that his inspection will be more thorough and you will get a better car.

From the April 2000 issue of *SCM*.

Dear Mr. Anderson: *I would like to get your words of wisdom on purchasing an E-type Jaguar. I have found a nice (condition #2) 1970 Series II, no rust, with an engine rebuild, for around $21,000. I've also found a 1973 Series III V12 (condition #2+) in red for about $25,000.*

*I plan on keeping the car for at least five years and likely more. My question to you is: Do you feel the V12 is a better investment in the long run than the Series II automobile?—***N. P., via e-mail**

As a former economist, I feel obligated to tell you that serial production cars are generally not good investments, at least not in relative terms. I can't think of any car that would have beaten an equivalent investment in a diversified index fund over almost any five-year period, even taking into account the recent stock market corrections. (The only exception to this might be limited-production cars with extraordinary provenance, such as Maserati 200/300/450Ss and a variety of 250 Ferrari competition cars.—*ED.)*

I don't think there is any way of saying whether a Series II or III E-type in equivalent condition is going to appreciate significantly over the next five years. For one thing, you need to factor in the uncertainty involved in buying any car. When you buy a share of stock, the final price is that day's market quote plus a broker's commission. Period. But with a car, chances are that a problem is going to appear that neither you nor the seller would have anticipated, one which could cost 20 to 25 percent of the purchase price. And that's just the beginning. Let's not think about insurance, title and registration fees, tune-ups and other maintenance.

Today, we can say that the purer Series II cars have appreciated faster than the more refined, but more complicated, Series III cars over the past five years. However, in the next five years, who knows? Having reached their peak relative to the more desirable, and hence more expensive, Series I E-types, prices for Series II cars might stabilize while demand shifts to Series IIIs, pushing their prices up. Or not.

The main thing for you to realize is that these are dramatically different cars that happen to share common styling themes. The Series II is a true sports car, the ultimate development of the original E-type. While it may not have the raw performance of the early Series I, it has vastly improved creature comforts, better brakes and engine cooling that actually works, even on hot days. The Series III, by contrast, is longer, heavier and more powerful, with an even more comfortable interior, but isn't nearly as agile on the twisty bits. You'll also find that its 12-cylinder engine, which is burdened with an extraordinarily complicated emissions system, may be very expensive to maintain properly. But there is no other car whose engine makes quite the same sound as the marvelous Jaguar twelve.

So, my bottom-line suggestion is to take both of the cars out and drive them. Think about how you're going to use them—long-distance tours, short backroad spins, cruising down the boulevard on Sunday ice-cream runs? Then make your decision based on the one that you think will be the most fun for you. On the plus side, if you buy a good car and take care of it properly, neither an SII nor an SIII is likely to go down in value over the next five years. In the end, though, the expectation of significant financial gain is simply not the reason to buy either one of these cars.

Dear Mr. Anderson: *The clutch on my Series I E-type is fried. (Maybe this wasn't the best car with which to teach my 15-year-old daughter how to drive a stick shift.) My classic Jaguar mechanic tells me the whole drivetrain has to come out of the car to fix it. That's ridiculous; who would design a car that way? Anyway, do you think I could cut the transmission tunnel inside the car and lift the gearbox out that way?*—**C.F., Boulder, CO**

Will a V12 Jaguar be worth more in the future than a Series II?

Unfortunately, your mechanic is right; he's not just trying to set you up to make a few of his boat payments. One aspect of the Jaguar's drop-dead styling is that the car is built with a monocoque chassis from the firewall back, with a tubular frame and front cross-structure (sometimes called the picture frame) forward of the engine. This structure had originally been developed for the Jaguar D-types that won at Le Mans.

There is no way of simply lifting off a tranny tunnel and pulling out the clutch and transmission (the way you might do, say, on an Austin-Healey). Instead, the mechanic will have to remove that huge front bonnet/fender structure, then drop the engine and transmission out of the main chassis before changing the clutch. The last thing you want to do is to start cutting on the monocoque to avoid this task. Anything you saved in mechanic's time would be lost two or three times over in resale value. It's just one of the realities facing the owners of these gorgeous cars.

From the June 2001 issue of *SCM*.

Dear Mr. Anderson: *I am in the process of restoring my 1963 Jaguar E-type roadster, which I have owned for 18 years. Can you tell me definitively what would be the proper finish for the undercarriage and wheel wells? Was undercoating used? My E seems to have had some original undercoating. Most restored E-types I've seen have wheel wells in plain metal painted body color, but this seems inappropriate for a car that is driven, as every stone chip would penetrate and lead to rust.*—**Peter Bowman, via e-mail**

Experts we spoke with agreed that E-types were not undercoated from the factory, at least not with the tar-like substance that dealers applied to make a little extra money on new-car sales. On the bottom of the monocoque and back to the rear subframe on some original E-types, there may be a discernible texture to the paint, but the paint will still be body color. This texture came from a factory coating called "Flintkote," which can be found on several different English marques. It was a sort of sealer that looks

> "Before buying consider: How are you going to use your car? Long-distance tours, short backroad spins, cruising down the boulevard on Sunday ice-cream runs?"

as if it was applied with a trowel over the primer before the final color coat was applied. Most restorers don't try to imitate this feature since it didn't appear on all cars and wasn't very attractive.

You will have to take care of the underside of your car with the same attention you would take with the front end, but modern paints are pretty durable. You'll need to clean out the wheel wells and the underside of the chassis at least once a year and touch up stone chips that penetrate the paint, but this

Plentiful parts and talented mechanics keep these cars in better running condition today than when new.

isn't difficult and will keep the car worthy of the admiring glances it receives. Should you or your heirs want to sell the car, it will be an easier sale without the undercoating, even with a few stone chips, since the new buyer won't be wondering whether there's any metal under that tar, or just nicely-shaped Bondo.

From the March 2001 issue of *SCM*.

Dear Mr. Kerb: *I just got back from the Kruse Auction in Auburn, Indiana and I was surprised how few English sports cars were there. Can you suggest an auction that has better English car representation? Can you give me any information on why the XKE market has taken such a nosedive? Do you think it will come back?*—**DS via e-mail**

Dear Mr. S: I see a fair number of English cars at auction, but they are usually higher-end, more expensive models. Jaguar, Rolls, Bentley, Aston, Alvis, Lagonda etc. are your typical auction faire.

The less expensive models of English sports cars (MGB, TR-4 etc.) are usually pretty easy to sell; as a result, their owners don't often use or need auctions. The normally affordable British sportscars that do turn up often will be cars that for reasons real or imagined, priced well above the average car. Which auction to choose? Odds are that a huge auction will have more sports cars, on a percentage basis, than a small auction. Barrett-Jackson in January is a good start or even better, a trip to Monterey in August will put you in the middle of at least three auctions—although you may have a hard time finding a bargain MGB at Christie's at Pebble Beach.

Now, E-types. The history of restored E-types in the marketplace has only taken one sharp turn. Back in the summer of 1989 the best S1 roadsters were fetching north of $100,000. This activity inspired more than a few investors and a few restoration shops to get started on their own let's-make-some-money restorations. At the time, this didn't seem like a stupid idea. If you could

get $100k for a done car, there was (for a few minutes) money to be made. The high point of the E-type price curve was regretfully short-lived and this left quite a pile of not-quite-finished cars that would soon become hastily finished ones; all wallowing in the shallow end of the buyer's pool. So, you had a situation where the price was dropping, the guys with the best cars were not quite ready to take less money (but would be convinced later) and the alleged "restored cars" foisted onto the market were at best, uneven restorations and at worst, a project car with a quickie paint job and a Bartlett interior kit. (I think the term "Auction Queen" was invented for just that kind of E-type.)

It took a long time to sell off this stock of cars; a few fell as low as $25,000. The average price has hovered for a long time in the $35-40,000 bracket with exceptional cars capable of fetching $50-60,000. Really, the nose dive that you mention was that original 1989 correction and since that time, the prices have held at the current, less than restoration cost figures. Will they come back? I think that the prices for good cars will continue to firm up, however, I don't have much hope for the XKE to consistently reach 1989 levels for a long, long time.

From the November 1999 issue of *SCM*.

Dear Mr. Kerb: *I am interested in buying a Jaguar XK 120 roadster, a 1966 XKE (or earlier covered-headlight roadster) or a Ferrari 308 series car. I know a little bit about Jaguars, but not too much about Ferraris. Which of the above do you feel will have the best appreciation and/or best value? Can I rely on my* Sports Car Market Pocket Price Guide? *If not, can you recommend a reliable price guide?*—**R.C., via e-mail**

Dear Mr. C: I don't see much upside for the Ferrari 308 in the near future. The V8 cars that began with the Bertone-bodied 308 GT4 and evolved into the Pininfarina-bodied two-seat 308 GTB,

308 GTS, Si and QV were in production for many years. As a result, there are quite a few out there. We can't consider their investment value based on rarity. The real problem is that the cars had more low points than high points during their production history. The looks, fit and finish and horsepower really didn't come together until after the V8 had grown to 3.2 liters.

So, as we look back on the panorama of three-liter Ferraris, we don't see anything resembling a milestone car or a stylistic tour de force. As a transition between the slow and lovely 246 GT and GTS Dino and the later V8-powered cars, the 308 did a good job of keeping the marque alive during the years of ever-strengthening emission and safety regulations. If it weren't for the teething pains of those early models, the current batch probably wouldn't be as good as they are.

Old Jaguars are a different story. They have a dedicated following and despite the marque's reputation for rust, overheating and electrical gremlins, the legion of fans continues to grow. The likely reason for this interesting phenomenon is the fantastic availability of spare parts and the ample mechanical talent to keep the cars alive and actually in better running condition than when they were new. The oldest XK 120s are now over fifty years old. In that half century, most of the Jaguar's gremlins and mysteries have been solved—or, since these cars are no longer daily drivers, the idiosyncrasies that used to drive us crazy are now accepted as part of their charm.

Compared to the Ferrari 308, the Jaguar XK 120 and XKE are both stylistic standouts and are probably burned into more memories than any 308 will ever be. All these factors make a well-chosen Jaguar a good investment. You also mention "value." Sometimes the value in a car isn't the purchase price subtracted from the selling price. Value can also be found in the usability of your car. Here, for drivers of certain statures, the XK 120 has limited value and both the E-type and 308 just a bit more value.

There is also the issue of driving pleasure. The XK 120, though acceptable when new, embodies the "vintage" experience out on the road. The steering is vague, the brakes even more vague and the weather protection vaguer still. The XKE is more of a long-

Garage Queen or Auction Queen?

"The oldest XK 120s are now over fifty years old. In that half century, most of the Jaguar's gremlins and mysteries have been solved—or, since these cars are no longer daily drivers, the idiosyncrasies that used to drive us crazy are now accepted as part of their charm."

legged GT car than a sports car and as a result, seems to prefer smooth, fast roads to the really twisty bits. The 308, the newest design in the group you mentioned, feels laser-guided through the twisties. It has firm damping combined with very direct steering that makes the Ferrari respond in a way far different from the Jaguar.

A price guide is time sensitive; the fresher the data, the more useful it will be. It also takes more than a listing of the high, low and average price to really get the marketplace in your cross hairs. Auction data is useful, but can also be a source of skewed information. A high price doesn't necessarily set a new high point any more than a low-ball sale price can set a new bottom of the market. It takes a fair amount of experience to compile and filter all of the data that can slide across your desk or computer screen.

The guys at *SCM* are very experienced in the car arena and can help the average shopper sort through the often confusing data. But even though I read everything that I can get my hands on, nothing is a substitute for a chat with a good dealer. Those folks are in the trenches seven days a week. The cars they are selling and how much they are selling for is information as up-to-the-minute as you can get. Combined with a good price guide, this information will be as close as you can get to informed shopping without going into the market on a full-time basis.

From the October 2000 issue of *SCM*. ◆

XKEs Cross the Block

XKEs

#113-1962 JAGUAR XKE roadster. S/N 875821. Carman Red/black leather. Odo: 1,632 miles. Reported full restoration by marque specialist, 2003 JCNA National Champion, numerous concours awards and Heritage Certificate. Paint finish of high quality, yet not flawless. Right door hinge a bit sloppy. Chrome good, right rear bumper guard loose. Interior well done, some switch chrome slightly pitting. Engine and chassis well detailed and finished better than new. Cond: 1-. **SOLD AT $90,200.** *It's not that unusual for high-quality full restorations on Series I roadsters, especially when backed up with appropriate awards and documents, to bring $90k-plus, as this one did.* **RM Auctions, Amelia Island, FL, 3/04.**

#207-1962 JAGUAR XKE roadster. S/N 875994. Opalescent Burgundy/tan leather. Odo: 54,308 miles. Reported total restoration by famous specialist. Paint finish good quality, shows well. Chips touched up on bonnet and nose area, left rocker panel dented. Both door fits off and stiff opera-

tion, chrome good. Interior well done. Engine bay and chassis detailed. Cond: 2. **SOLD AT $52,800.** *Claimed matching numbers and Jaguar Heritage Certificate on hand. Nicely done and shows well but not a #1, sold in correct range for condition. What a difference condition makes—almost 50% compared to the other E-type in the sale.* **RM Auctions, Amelia Island, FL, 3/04.**

#474-1962 JAGUAR XKE SERIES I convertible. S/N 876754. Light blue metallic/blue leather. LHD. Odo: 9,699 miles. Quite nice exterior. Very good paintwork, cloth top, wire wheels and chrome. Driver's seat side shows quite a bit of wear, some dings in console. Very clean underhood, shows some light wear. Cond: 3+. **SOLD AT $50,051.** *Anywhere else, this Jag would have struggled to get into the high $40,000s. Monterey, however, is where XKE prices tend to trend high if not soar. This one, adjusted to Monterey prices, was a fair buy.* **RM Auctions, Monterey, CA, 8/03.**

> ## "Monterey is where XKE prices tend to trend high, if not soar."

#9005-1963 JAGUAR XKE convertible. S/N 876843. Old English white/red leather. Odo: 48,609 miles. One-family owned from new. Claimed one repaint 10 years ago. Redline Michelin tires. The quality of the repaint ranges from good to fair, chrome is no better with plenty of scratches, outside mirror de-silvering. Wood steering wheel, leather seats well patinaed. Aluminum insert in console is well worn. Nothing close to exciting here. Cond: 4+. **SOLD AT $48,600.** *Very surprising result. I would have pegged this no more than in the mid-$30s. With a still-ample supply of restored early E-types for not much more money, I hope the new owner either enjoys the patina of an honest used car, or decides he didn't mind paying a premium for a solid base for a complete restoration.* **Barrett-Jackson, West Palm Beach, FL, 3/04.**

#821-1963 JAGUAR XKE Series I roadster. S/N 877947. Red/beige leather. LHD. Sharp car all around with excellent paint and interior; in fine show-or-go condition. Cond: 1-. **NOT SOLD**

AT $38,000. *The right car, the right color, is simply worth more. Even the low estimate ($40k) would have been a bargain. We'll see this car again, and it will bring more.* **Bonhams and Butterfields, Hummelstown, PA, 10/03.**

"As close to factory new as you're ever likely to see. Trouble is, it looks too nice to drive. And at this price, a rock chip could lead to a nervous breakdown."

#513-1963 JAGUAR XKE SERIES I coupe. S/N J64889695. Silver blue metallic/blue leather. LHD. Odo: 63,223 miles. Older restoration showing some age, paint still presentable. Panel fit fine. Lots of sealer around the front and rear windows. Interior clean and tidy, worn-through spot on console leather. Engine compartment clean, chassis appears sound but not detailed. Cond: 3. **SOLD AT $26,450.** *Reported ownership history with past concours Jaguar Club wins. Seems honest enough car. With a major detail, could look like a $35,000 car.* **Bonhams & Butterfields, Carmel, CA, 8/03.**

#200-1963 JAGUAR XKE convertible. S/N 878299. Steel blue/gray leather. LHD. Odo: 312 miles. Customized and nice. Venolia pistons, aluminum radiator, stainless steel exhaust and headers. Lightweight flywheel. 4.2 series brakes, Wildwood calipers. T5 Borg-Warner 5-speed, Aldan shocks, Suffolk & Turley interior. Hardtop included. Cond: 1. **SOLD AT $79,380.** *A crowd favorite and a difficult car to value. Basically a new car that has been engineered for a modern lifestyle with performance, dependability and safety upgrades. The best of the old and new. However, all the money for a modified E-type.* **Barrett-Jackson, LA, CA, 6/03.**

#75-1964 Jaguar XKE 3.8 racer roadster. S//N 890554. Eng. #RA6770-9. Primrose/black. RHD. Odo: 34,611 miles. Built in 2001, well painted, interior stripped out for serious comp work. Full cage with sidebars, fancy pedals, safety gas tank, Aeroquip hoses, modern looking engine bay excellent. Getrag 5-speed, 300-hp Rob Beere 3.8 engine on Webers. Surprisingly, only low-back buckets. Some competition successes. Cond: 2+. **SOLD AT $53,310.** *Although raising $11,500 more than forecast, this non-period racer was said to have cost $113,000 to build. Fully street legal, someone's going to have fun on Saturday nights cruising the village.* **H & H Auctions, Buxton, UK, 12/03.**

#216-1964 JAGUAR XKE, SERIES I convertible. S/N 881063. Eng. #RA5488-9. Red/black leather. LHD. Odo: 52,496 miles. Claimed all-original car. Paint getting a semi-gloss sheen to it, trunk lid doesn't match remainder of car. Fresh engine work. Missing one wiper arm. Taillamp gaskets shot. Leather heavily worn, but no tears. Top heavily worn but not badly torn. Cond: 3-. **NOT SOLD AT $33,500.** *Most likely the consignor was looking more for an "auction appraisal" than to seriously sell the car. Originality is wonderful, patina is all right, but then there's plain old-fashioned wear, tear and age. Not an outlandish bid if new driveline is sorted out.* **Mecum, Elhart Lake, WI, 7/03.**

#105-1964 JAGUAR E-TYPE S I 3.8 LIGHTWEIGHT REPLICA race roadster hardtop. Body by Bryan Wingfield DRL Engineer. S/N 861439. Eng. #RA 4577-9. Silver/black. RHD. Acquired 1987 as crashed project, rebuilt as lightweight aluminum-paneled racer by Bryan Wingfield, hardtop roof and trunk vents, more recent $40,000 race-prep bills, Stirling Moss retro-driven, stone chips, knock-on alloys hammer marked. Cond: 1-. **NOT SOLD AT $103,350.** *Authentic looking, this rep failed to raise ambitious £126,000 ($210,000) being sought.* **Bonhams, Goodwood, UK, 9/03.**

#51-**1964 JAGUAR XKE SERIES I 3.8 roadster.** S/N 881185. Eng. #RA5667-9. Silver/red leather. LHD. Odo: 16 miles. Stunning restoration; car absolutely glows. As close to a factory-new car as you're likely to ever see. Engine rebuilt with new pistons, bearings, valves, guides, seals and timing chain. Rebuilt head, carbs, clutch. Cond: 1+. **SOLD AT $111,625.** *Meticulous refurbishment in every respect and worth the money. Trouble is, the car looks too nice to drive. And at this price, a rock chip could lead to a nervous breakdown.* **Christie's, Pebble Beach, CA, 8/03.**

#991-**1965 JAGUAR XKE roadster.** S/N 1E11149. Brown metallic/brown leather. LHD. Odo: 76,648 miles. Older, poor-quality respray. Uneven finish; dirt, fisheye and small rust bubbles in paint. Panel fit poor especially the all-important bonnet. Brightwork off, large dent in rear bumper. Front bumper fits poorly. Interior intact but looks tired. Hose clamp patch on rear exhaust pipes. Chassis dirty. If the mechanicals are anything like the cosmetic appearance, restoration might be the only answer at this point. Cond: 5+. **SOLD AT $34,560.** *Reported numbers matching and owned by the current owner for past 25 years. Even with the upward price movement in the XKE market,*

this is a big number for a substandard example in most situations. However, bought by an SCMer who was looking for a good car to restore. Viewed in that light, the perfect prospect, as it appears complete and unmolested. So long as the new owner doesn't charge himself more than $5 an hour for his own time, he'll come out just fine. **Barrett-Jackson, Scottsdale, AZ, 1/04.**

#537-**1965 JAGUAR XKE 4.2 coupe.** S/N 1E 21051. Eng. #7E 8504-9. Black/tan. RHD. Odo: 63,383 miles. Only 383 miles since full resto, with authenticating bills and photos on file. Webasto sunroof. Hood section renewed, along with many other items, though not by any well-known specialists. Cosmetically sharp. Cond: 1. **SOLD AT $52,164.** *Top-estimate valuation correct for retail-ready example. We all know the coupes drive better than the roadsters, but they lag in the market. While a top price, the buyer got good value due to the quality of the restoration.* **Bonhams, Sussex, UK, 7/03.**

> "Originality is wonderful, patina is all right, but then there's plain old-fashioned wear, tear and age."

#68-**1965 JAGUAR XKE 4.2 Special FHC.** Body by Frua. S/N 7E 6388-9. Eng. #7E 6388-9. Silver/black. RHD. Odo: 34,404 miles. A Frua redesign, commissioned by John Coombs. Originally red. Paint is now totally flat with some ravine-sized shrinkage. Leather is crazed. Despite air scoop in hood, a shortened rear end, and a larger rear window, it's still ugly, although unique. Cond: 3-. **NOT SOLD AT $37,604.** *Nobody wanted it at Christie's London sale either. This is the kind of car where the seller parades around proclaiming, "It's a custom one-off by a famous designer," and the audience replies, "Who cares? Nasty looking thing."* **Christie's Apeldoorn, Holland, 8/03.**

#182-**1966 JAGUAR XKE roadster.** S/N 1E11733. Silver-blue/black. LHD. Odo: 1,551 miles. Recent restoration completed to high standards. Respray well applied, body straight and solid. Interior flawless. Engine compartment highly detailed. Cond: 2+. **NOT SOLD AT $55,000.** *Some minor pitting in the chrome was all that held this car back. The Series Is have been moving up the value chart of late so the buyer made a wise decision in not letting his go at this price. Could be worth $10,000 more to the right buyer.* **McCormick, Palm Springs, CA, 11/03.**

#421-1966 JAGUAR XKE SERIES I roadster. S/N 1E13101. Dark blue/biscuit. LHD. Odo: 322 miles. Your basic as-new, freshly restored XKE. Glass-like paintwork. Excellent chrome. Interior as new, wood original-style, AM/FM/SW a nice touch. Darn close to visually perfect. Cond: 1-. **SOLD AT $101,201.** *As pretty as a shiny new penny. Think pretty doesn't sell? Look again, as this Jag brought home twice what a decent example in #2 condition could bring. Fully priced today, even by Monterey standards. But next year it might look a bit low.* **RM Auctions, Monterey, CA, 8/03.**

> "Fully priced today, but next year it might look a bit low."

#084-1966 JAGUAR XKE SERIES I 4.2 roadster. S/N 1E12689. Red/biscuit leather. LHD. Odo: 1,047 miles. Very correct in all areas and restored to better than new by Jag specialist. On the button right down to Lucas battery. Cond: 1. **SOLD AT $85,700.** *100-point JCNA winner driven minimal miles since full and accurate resto. Desirable covered headlight, all-synchro tranny. Strong but fair price paid.* **RM Auctions, Phoenix, AZ, 1/04.**

#5405-S126-1967 JAGUAR XKE convertible. S/N 1E15398. Blue Steel/black. LHD. Odo: 14,353 miles. Trunk and gas door gaps uneven. Hood is wide at the bottom left. Dent in the left chrome headlight trim and the weather-stripping loose around right headlight. Paint chips on driver's door and trunk lid edges. Windshield scratched on driver's side. Engine clean but driven. Undercoated. Driver's seat bolster showing patina. Cond: 2. **NOT SOLD AT $43,500.** *Looks like a decent driver to me, and it looks like the present owner thinks so too. He will continue to drive it a while longer. Bid was very fair for condition. Perfection can bring double, but that's not this car.* **Russo and Steele, Scottsdale, AZ, 1/04.**

#29-1967 JAGUAR XKE SERIES I coupe. S/N 1E33307. Opalescent Silver blue/navy blue leather. LHD. Odo: 987 miles. Interior has original headliner, radio console. Claimed matching numbers. Good-looking, well restored, needed nothing except a new owner. Cond: 1-. **SOLD AT $44,650.** *Reported $45,000 in restoration receipts. Unusual to see a coupe restored to this level, obviously an emotional decision, not a financial one. Excellent E-type coupes and convertibles continue to edge up.* **Christie's, NY, NY, 9/03.**

> "As pretty as a shiny new penny. Think pretty doesn't sell? Look again."

#825-1967 JAGUAR XKE 4.2 roadster. S/N 1E13293. Green/biscuit leather. LHD. Odo: 32,487 miles. Sharp car all around. Slight top fit problem, fine interior, good doors and panels, clean engine room. Cond: 1-. **NOT SOLD AT $34,000.** *Worth at least low estimate ($34k) and maybe more, considering it's a covered headlight car with the big engine and all-synchro gearbox. 1967 was really the last and best year of the pure E-types, due to impending US smog and safety regs.* **Bonhams and Butterfields, Hummelstown, PA, 10/03.**

#160-1969 JAGUAR XKE roadster. S/N 1R8613. Ivory/black leather. LHD. Odo: 50,196 miles. Older mediocre repaint showing age, cracks on driver's door, overspray on interior door panels. Door gaskets deteriorated. Dash nice and looks original, seat leather worn to nice patina. Fuel leak at left front? Cond: 3. **SOLD AT $38,340.** *Claimed to be authentic, mostly original and true 50k miles. Might be, but how about some documentation to back up those claims and some recent service records! Strong price, considering overall condition and lack of documentation of anything.* **Barrett-Jackson, Scottsdale, AZ, 1/04.**

#460-1970 JAGUAR XKE roadster. S/N 1R12332. Black/red leather. LHD. Odo: 84,204 miles. 4-speed, wires. By no means perfect, but a quite nice example. One or two dings to otherwise good paint, chrome is good but not show quality. Fresh tires are classic radials —not a smart place to save money when you're trying to get top dollar for a car. A very good, high-quality driver. Cond: 2-. **NOT SOLD AT $31,000.** *Bad Series II Jag convertibles bring in the middle to high teens; over-the-top restorations can bring $45,000 and above. This very nice driver was appropriately bid.* **Kruse International, Ft. Lauderdale, FL, 1/04.**

#L30-1972 JAGUAR XKE SIII convertible. S/N 1520155. Red/saddle leather. LHD. Odo: 51,414 miles. A refreshing change from Pebble Beach. Medium quality respray and fresh tires, the remainder is old and worn instead of fresh and new. Original seats are flat, dry, have wear and some tears. Carpets clean but worn, soft top rear window is brown with age. Cond: 4+. **SOLD AT $28,355.** *Scratched and pitted chrome, turn signal lens cracked right front. Quite pricey for condition. I don't know where the next owner can escape before he is totally underwater—unless the market tightens and prices shoot skyward.* **Kruse International, Auburn, IN, 8/03.**

#741-1973 JAGUAR XKE roadster. S/N UD1522668. Medium blue/beige leather. Odo: 54,256 miles. 4-speed, wires. Claimed stored for 22 years and recently restored to great driver standard. Paint quality overall is decent, sanding marks evident, a few chips. Right door fit off a bit. Chrome nice but has multiple small scratches. Interior appears original, shows well, tidy. Chassis clean and appears honest. Car was locked—a stupid way to show a car at an auction. Cond: 2-. **SOLD AT $72,900.** *Another huge price for a good but not exceptional E-type roadster, almost twice SCM Price Guide. I'd like to say that V12 E-types are roaring back in value, but I think I'd best say only this V12 is roaring. The rest are still mewing in the $35,000-$50,000 corner they've been stuck in since 1991.* **Barrett-Jackson, Scottsdale, AZ, 1/04.**

#9-1971 JAGUAR XKE V12 SERIES III coupe. S/N 1S71943. White/black leather. Odo: 44,680 miles. Wires. Originally a U.S.-delivery car with factory air. Fair chrome plating, excellent paint; okay door and panel fit. Appeared to be well maintained and road-ready. Cond: 2-. **SOLD AT $29,845.** *Price was about right. Might have brought a better bid if the color was other than white, but it had pluses like the manual gearbox and chrome wires to compensate.* **Christie's, Paris, France, 2/04.**

#14-1972 JAGUAR XKE SERIES III convertible. S/N 1S2051BW. Silver/gray cloth. LHD. Odo: 39,674 miles. V12, auto, wires. Nardi wood steering wheel. Stock XKE with older, medium-quality respray. Very nice top, wire wheels show pitting, road grunge. Red painted front brake calipers. Pirelli P400 tires. Chrome trim on top of driver's door pulling up. Cond: 3-. **SOLD AT $31,900.** *Middle-market price for a middle-condition car, seems like a fair trade. The automatic and condition-related issues combined will keep the price here at mid-pack. Some easy repairs will make this a decent driver. SIIIs continue to creep up in value.* **Kensington, Bridgehampton, NY, 7/03.**

"Bought by an SCMer who was looking for a good car to restore. Viewed in that light, the perfect prospect, as it appears complete and unmolested. So long as the new owner doesn't charge himself more than $5/hr for his own time, he'll come out just fine."

#107-1973 JAGUAR XKE SIII roadster. S/N UD1S21824. Red. LHD. Odo: 44,391 km. Stick, disc wheels, extra wires included. Paint good, chrome faded in places, rubbers average. Luggage rack. Ugly steering wheel cover and wrong gear knob. Leather creased on headrests. Serviced regularly, runs well. Cond: 2-. **SOLD AT $29,900.** *These will never be the sporty cars that the six-cylinder E-types are, but they're terrific for long days of cruising at 100-mph plus on the autobahn. Prices have been all over the map, but this still seems cheap for what appears to be a sound car.* **Bonhams, Nurburgring, Germany, 8/03.**

#33-1973 JAGUAR XKE SIII V12 roadster. S/N ES3V/2UD/52239. Eng. #7S10248. Red/beige. LHD. Odo: 7,020 miles. Air conditioning, a rare manual transmission and still original apart from some repainting to bonnet. Delivered new to Illinois, acquired later by vendor via Jimmy Wanko of Miami for $100,000! Cond: 1-. **SOLD AT $67,577.** *Low mileage and originality responsible for $10,700 over low estimate paid. One of the strongest prices we've seen in years for the rather ponderous SIIIs. I'm sure the red color and manual gearchange helped.* **Christie's, Apeldoorn, Holland, 8/03.**

#S38-1973 JAGUAR XKE SERIES III convertible. S/N 1521908. Olde English White/tan leather. LHD. Odo: 98,561 miles. Modified with T-5 transmission, "special high-performance engine," Momo wood steering wheel, stainless steel brake hoses, suspension mods. Trunk rack, paint, interior and top all recently redone. Some light scratching to chrome. A/C, Sony AM/FM CD. Cond: 3. **SOLD AT $49,025.** *With the "improvements" included, this Jag brought an unexpectedly high price, in my view. While the "high-po" motor and 5-speed may make the car drive better, they decrease its value to collectors. If you just want a super driver, buy a new car.* **Kruse, Las Vegas, NV, 5/03.**

"Buying some other guy's hard won restoration is almost always a great way to find cars, and save you a lot of time and money; and doing so after a market drop is an even better idea."

#283-1974 JAGUAR XKE SIII convertible. S/N VE1S25811. White/black leather. LHD. Odo: 8,981 miles. 4-speed. Trunk fit off and dent to right side of bonnet. Panel fit good including hood. Some overspray. Interior dirty with a broken choke knob and poorly repaired console. Driver's seat worn and headrest collapsed. Engine bay clean, undercarriage coated. Cond: 3. **SOLD AT $32,550.** *If the low mileage is correct and the undercoating is not hiding anything, then it should be a nice buy. The price was low enough to spend a few thousand fixing things and still be okay.* **Mecum, St. Charles, IL, 10/03.**

#5407-S178-1974 JAGUAR XKE SIII convertible. S/N L1E1S24085BW. Red/tan. LHD. Odo: 77,322 miles. Driver's door and trunk gaps uneven. Chrome wearing thin on front bumper and headlights. Rear bumper shows scratches. Paint prep flaw at rear of trunk with numerous door edge chips. Some windshield scratches and stone chips. Engine is dirty with oil leaks evident; rust on intakes. Snags on top fabric. Undercoated. Air conditioning. Cond: 3. **SOLD AT $26,568.** *I found a receipt in the glove box for a new oil pan, transmission gaskets and a new rear seal. The trunk had numerous dents from something bouncing around and banging against the lid from the inside. The car has some issues but it appears to have been purchased with that in mind. Fairly bought.* **Russo and Steele, Scottsdale, AZ, 1/04.**

#226-1974 JAGUAR XKE SERIES III convertible. S/N UE1S25540. Silver/ burnt orange leather. RHD. Odo: 56,529 miles. Excepting a very nice older repaint, an original car. Minimal motor prep, but what little grime there is, it's congruent with the miles indicated. Newer stereo, LoJack. Atypical of Series IIIs, the headrest foam has collapsed. Seat leather good. Cond: 3. **SOLD AT $27,563.** *As a very honest lower mileage Series III, this was a good buy. Should prove to be a decent car if enjoyed in limited amounts.* **Mecum, Elhart Lake, WI, 7/03.**

#501-1974 JAGUAR XKE SERIES III roaster. S/N UE1S23476. Dark green/ tan leather. LHD. Odo: 84,227 miles. Auto. Older repaint of mediocre quality, dulling, chips, scratches, some bubbling. Interior looks tired, driver's seat loose and rattles, headrests imploded. Chassis not detailed. Chrome fair. Cond: 4+. **SOLD AT $18,975.** *U.S. model, originally had manual transmission that's been converted to automatic, no details given. Not an awe-inspiring example; price was more than enough, considering. Will always be a car with a story.* **Bonhams & Butterfields, Carmel, CA, 8/03.**

#9-1974 JAGUAR XKE SERIES III convertible. S/N VE1S2351. Burgundy/ tan leather. LHD. Odo: 23,243 miles. 4-speed, wires. Subjected to restoration said to cost in excess of $100,000 during the "silly season" a few years back. Very, very nice throughout, some scarring at top edge of driver's seat. Very correct, excellent paint and chrome. Top needs some cleaning. Cond: 2+. **SOLD AT $55,000.** *1974 was the final year of XKE production. Sale price appears to be market correct. Buying someone else's restoration is almost always a great way to find cars, doing so after a market drop (1991-1998) even more so.* **Kensington, Bridgehampton, NY, 7/03.**

#139-1975 JAGUAR E-TYPE S III 5.3 V12 COMMEMORATIVE EDITION roadster. S/N 1S2853BW. Eng. #7S16477. Black/black. RHD. Odo: 21,773 miles. Claimed to be genuine mileage. Repainted thickly, engine bay surfaces not included and poor, original leather dirty. Cond: 2-. **NOT SOLD AT $79,500.** *Even though one of the final 50 Commemorative edition (49 in black), unexceptional cosmetic condition resulted in $95,000 minimum being well out of reach.* **Bonhams, Goodwood, UK, 9/03.** ◆

The Twenty Year Picture

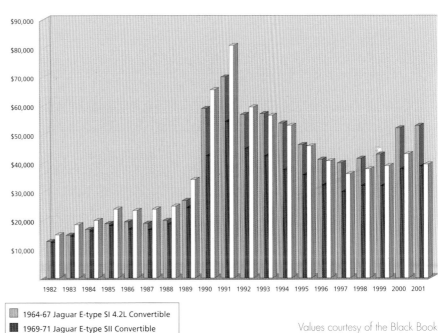

Legend:
- 1964-67 Jaguar E-type SI 4.2L Convertible
- 1969-71 Jaguar E-type SII Convertible
- 1971-73 Jaguar E-type SIII Convertible

Section III
Coupes & Sedans

Getting into an XJ6 has always reminded me of sitting in an English drawing room. Somehow, the folks at Jaguar do the best job in the industry of combining the rich smell of leather and the distinctive look of burled wood into an enticing interior.

Jaguar sedans have always been the automotive pinnacle one aspires to, the kind of car that announces you've got more taste and sophistication than someone who buys some sort of upscale Japanese car. Of course, in the pre-Ford ownership days, before 1989, owning a XJ6 generally meant you had a mechanic on retainer as well.

It's no secret that the Jaguar sedans from the '70s and

'80s had suspect electrics, constantly finding new ways to leave an owner stranded in the dark, and usually in a rainstorm as well. The farm-boy habit of installing Chevrolet V8s into Jag sedans always seemed a bit odd to me, as it was rarely the engines that failed. So these tinkers merely end up creating an Anglo-American hybrid with no residual value, and whose electrics would fail anyway.

Restored Jaguar coupes and sedans are hard to find, and impossibly expensive to restore. So if you come across a good one, don't be afraid to pay a premium for it, and prepare yourself to be transported in elegance and style—the Jaguar way.—*Keith Martin*◆

1948 Mk IV 3.5-Liter Drophead Coupe

Sometimes being first is more important than being better—in the world of collectible Jaguars, for instance, the first postwar Jag offering known as the Mk IV

by Brian Rabold

Chassis number: 637068
Engine number: SL2791

Like the majority of Britain's motor manufacturers, Jaguar Cars (as William Lyons' SS concern had been renamed in 1945) commenced postwar production with a range of pre-war designs. These comprised the compact 1.5-liter as well as the 2.5-liter/3.5-liter model, retrospectively known as the Mk IV.

Built on a 120-inch wheelbase, the Mk IV retained a separate chassis featuring beam/live axle suspension on semi-elliptic springs and Girling mechanical brakes. The stylish all-steel coachwork was available in saloon or drophead coupe form and featured the kind of luxuriously well-appointed interior that would become a Jaguar hallmark. The engine was Standard's seven-bearing six fitted with a Weslake overhead-valve cylinder head. In 3.5-liter form, the engine was capable of propelling the sturdily built Mk IV to over 90 mph.

In the immediate postwar years, the bulk of Jaguar's production was directed overseas, the majority of drophead coupes (like this left-hand-drive example) were sent to the United States. This car was built in April 1948 and sold directly to International Motors. The car returned to the UK around 1975 and was professionally rebuilt between 1988 and 1990. The vendor acquired the car on completion and informs us that it has been kept garaged and used sparingly, covering approximately 500 miles in the past ten years."

This superb example of the most desirable Jaguar of its day has been refinished in its original white livery with beige leather upholstery and matching carpets and is accompanied by a photographic record of the restoration.

The SCM analysis: This car sold for $33,120, including buyer's premium, at the Bonhams & Brooks Hendon sale, held April 23, 2001.

Sometimes being first is more important than being better. Take, for example, the Beatles or the good people who invented Kleenex. In the world of collectible Jaguars, this axiom is illustrated by Series I E-types, XK 120s, and the first postwar Jag offering, now commonly known as the Mk IV.

Following the end of combat in the European Theater, Jaguar turned its efforts to manufacturing automobiles instead of fighter plane parts, and quickly brought a saloon to market. Using the old six-cylinder pushrod engine of prewar days as well as an unchanged body design, the Coventry company returned to producing the SS Jaguar saloons last seen in 1940. These "new" cars were called 2.5s and 3.5s, and they became the first true Jaguars, as all SS references were now rightly considered gauche.

Minor variations distinguished the postwar models from the prewar ones: modestly updated axles and brakes, a retooled heating system, an altered dashboard, new badging. Mostly, though, the car was simply a quick way to satisfy motorists' cravings and pique interest until a brand-new model could be designed.

On the road, Mk IVs suffered from a soft chassis, poor brakes, and a prosaic suspension. Mk Vs, on the other hand, which were introduced in 1949, had independent front suspension, a stiffer chassis and smaller wheels. These adjustments made the Mk V more practical, and they are generally considered to be better vehicles.

A milestone in a long line of excellent Jaguar saloons.

Nonetheless, the Mk Vs don't have the same cachet. The Mk V's styling and engine were already long in the tooth at the time of its debut. The car was replaced in 1951 by Jaguar's flagship, the Mk VII. A stale design can be excused when you talk about the first postwar Jaguar, but not the second.

Mk IVs can go for as much as $20,000 more than the older prewar SS Jaguar DHCs, and $15,000 more than Mk Vs. The reasons are simple. Not only were the Mk IVs the first true Jaguars in name, but, thanks to the booming American economy, they were the first postwar Jaguars to be offered in left-hand drive and drophead coupe guise. Coupled with the fact that convertibles represented less than 6% of Mk IV production, and lefty DHCs with the desirable 3.5-liter engine accounted for only half of that number, the example shown here is a rare and appealing package.

Then why did this car sell for nearly $10,000 under the low estimate? There are two likely causes. First, some expense can be expected to arise in trying to fettle this car back to driving standards. Although once expertly restored, the car has almost assuredly begun to unravel in places. Second, on English roads, left-hand-drive is an impractical configuration for a not-so-practical car. Still, $33,000 doesn't come close to restoring another example. The new owner has shrewdly given himself a cushion for freshening up his new Mk IV, increasing the odds that he will at least break even when he goes to sell.

So, while the 3.5 isn't a paragon of engineering, it is the initial milestone in a long line of excellent Jaguar saloons. And, while less could be spent on "better" models, those examples wouldn't be firsts. Consider this car well bought, indeed.

(Photo and description courtesy of the auction company.) ◆

Years produced: 1945-49
Number produced: 11,952; 560 3.5L drophead coupes
Original list price: $4,745
SCM Price Guide: $45,000-$65,000
Tune-up/major service: $300
Distributor cap: $45
Chassis #: plate on firewall
Engine #: plate on engine
Club: Jaguar Club of North America, c/o Nelson Rath, 1000 Glenbrook, Anchorage, KY 40223
Web site: www.jcna.com
Alternatives: Bentley Mk VI DHC, Lagonda 2.6L DHC, Talbot-Lago Record cabriolet
SCM Investment Grade: B

1950 MkV Drophead Coupe

Though rare and distinctive, this beautiful drophead begins to look more and more like a money pit with steep sides

by Bill Neill

Chassis number: 647333
Engine number: Z3127

It was described in the April, 1950 issue of *The Motor* as offering "a standard of riding comfort which is outstandingly high, a standard which has not been bettered in any car of any nationality which it has been our good fortune to test." The Mark V introduced in September 1948 would be the principal model with which Jaguar established its name following the war years.

The Mark V was somewhat a transitional model, meant to bridge the gap between the existing cars of the pre-war concept and the new overhead camshaft model then under development. The well-proven six-cylinder pushrod overhead valve engine, which was little different from the SS 100 which epitomized pre war British sports cars, was retained, in both 2.5-liter and 3.5-liter forms, but a new box-section cruciform-braced chassis was used. The front suspension was independent by wishbones and torsion bars, with Girling telescopic hydraulic dampers, while Girling two leading shoe hydraulic brakes working in twelve-inch drums were used. Top speed was about 90 mph and the model proved to have extraordinary longevity; it was used extensively by British Police forces and some examples covered more than 200,000 miles in service. The Irish driver Cecil Ward achieved third place in the 1951 Monte Carlo Rally in a 3.5-liter Mk V saloon. The model was discontinued in 1952. Only around five hundred drophead coupes were made in left hand drive form; survivors are relatively few.

This example was imported to the UK in the late 1980s, following a period of restoration in America. It was offered for sale at Christie's Summer Vintage auction in 1989 where it was acquired by the present owner.

Today the car has a somewhat aged appearance and it is clear that any work carried out in America was largely cosmetic, rather than a thorough rebuild. As a result, the car is worthy of careful inspection and in Christie's opinion notable areas that need attention are the base of both doors and the wings.

Accordingly, the car is offered at a modest price level for its model, and so represents a usable project, which can be progressively improved on.

The SCM analysis: This car sold for $38,916 at Christie's London auction June 7, 2004. The price doesn't seem like much of a discount considering its condition.

Let's read between the lines for some words of caution. This car has a "somewhat aged appearance." Its restoration was "largely cosmetic" and not necessarily complete. Furthermore, Christie's believes that both doors and fenders "need attention." The dreaded word "project" is also mentioned.

Whoops. This beautiful drophead begins to look more and more like a money pit with steep sides. Christie's should be commended for raising such red warning flags since not all auction companies are so forthcoming. However, Mark V sheetmetal is not something you can pick up with a few phone calls to local wrecking yards, as you could a front clip for a mid '80s Ford Mustang. And since you can't find replacements, you need to fix the panels that came with the car.

Not much of a discount, considering its condition.

Repairing rusty fenders and doors could swallow up much of your Jaguar repair fund.

It's hard to understand how this car could be "progressively improved on," as the auction company suggests. It's not as though you could do bits and pieces on weekends in your spare time. It sounds more like a car that needs to be taken apart and its restoration begun again. Early Jaguars such as this one are prone to rust in the body and a skilled craftsman is needed to make proper repairs.

In any case, this is no car for the novice buyer. Its condition must have satisfied the successful bidder, who paid $40,000.

This Mark V makes an XK 120, available the same year, seem modern by comparison. With its upright grille, Mark V styling has more in common with prewar years than the 1950s.

About 60 percent of the 10,466 Mark Vs built were exported, and many went to America. Only about one in ten were convertibles, making this car rare and distinctive.

It is powered by a 3.5-liter six rated at 125 horsepower. Unlike an XK, which you could consider taking on public roads for special occasions, you might have a hard time finding a time and place to exercise this ancient car. But if your goal is to own a drophead that practically nobody else has in your JCNA chapter, then the Mark V could be a compelling choice. At least it has left-hand drive, making it more usable in the States. Just make sure that a body man you trust has delivered his opinion on all the suspect parts before you hand over the check.

(Photo and description courtesy of the auction company.) ◆

Years produced: 1949-1951
Number produced: 977 worldwide
Original list price: $3,850
SCM Price Guide: $40,000-$55,000
Tune-up/major service: $300
Distributor cap: $45 (not original style)
Chassis #: plate on firewall
Engine #: boss at rear of block, plate on firewall
Club: Clubs of North America, 1000 Glenbrook Rd., Anchorage, KY 40223
Web site: www.jcna.com
Alternative: Rolls-Royce Silver Wraith DHC, Mercedes-Benz 300S cabriolet
SCM Investment Grade: C

1963 Mk II 2.4

Under no circumstance should one view this fright kitty as a restoration candidate. To do so would be a Sisyphean chore, and the result will only be worth a fraction of the cost

by Brian Rabold

Chassis number: 115555 DN
Engine number: BH 9834-8

The Mk II Jaguar was a brilliant facelift of the original 2.4 and 3.4 Mk I saloon and became the mainstay of Jaguar production during the 1960s. With classic, uncluttered styling and compact dimensions, the short-block 2.4-liter engine endowed the car with a respectable 120 bhp. Other models became available, namely the 3.4-liter and, at the top of the range, the 3.8-liter. The model was Jaguar's first unitary construction car and by the time the Mark II was announced in 1959, any earlier shortcoming had been smoothed out. With this small-displacement engine, the cars were cheap to run and insure, and offered excellent value for the money.

A Mr. Colin Clarke purchased this example new in June 1963. On file are his original confirmation of order letter from K.J. Motors Ltd., and the agreement of partial exchange for his Triumph Herald. Even the envelope for the original invoice was retained by Mr. Clarke; such is the comprehensive nature of the history of this single-owner car.

The Jaguar was serviced locally in Bromley throughout its life, its service book being stamped up to date until 1970. Each invoice up to and from then onwards has seemingly been kept on file, the most recent being some attention to the bodywork in 1993. It is offered with the history file noted, which also includes an immaculate "Sales & Service Facilities in the United Kingdom" brochure and original handbook.

Today, having been left to stand in the open in recent years, the condition is a little tired, and in need of sympathetic restoration, surface corrosion is evident in the fenders, but on a cursory inspection the car appears solid underneath. There cannot be many examples of the model that were so cherished, so this is deserving of attention, to be returned to the road, by its next owner.

The SCM analysis: This car sold with no reserve for $1,845, including buyer's premium, at the Christie's London sale, held March 24, 2003.

Building on the success of its full-sized Mk VII saloon, Jaguar launched a new model in 1956. Sporting a 2.4-liter version of the XK engine and unibody construction, company executives hoped this new model would appeal to buyers who didn't want a car as large in size or price as a Mk VII, but still wanted a family-sized Jaguar. A 3.4-liter version was unveiled in 1957.

Both versions of the Mk I, as it was later unofficially called, were in production until 1959, and both met with mixed reviews. The styling, though penned by Sir William Lyons, was called stodgy in its day, and the cars' handling was a little skittish. The 2.4- and 3.4-liter engines were capable high-speed tourers, but neither was available with disc brakes. Nonetheless, more than 36,000 units were sold from 1956-59.

Encouraged by these figures, the car was redesigned and reissued in late 1959, receiving a new exterior, disc brakes, a wider rear track, and a new name: the Mk II. A 3.8-liter option became available along with the 3.4, and the 2.4 was relegated to European markets only. The 3.4s and 3.8s were successful in saloon racing through 1966, which helped make the Mk II the most popular Jaguar model of the '60s.

This rusty kitty has been left unserviced for more than ten years.

Sadly, for the car pictured here, the Mk II 2.4 was decidedly the least popular iteration of the three. Aside from its absence in the immense American market, the price differential between a 2.4 and a 3.4 when new was only $700, but the performance gap was quite noticeable. The 3.4 could reach 120 mph thanks to 210 hp. In comparison, the 2.4 only had 120 hp, causing it to max out just shy of triple digits. The 3.8 was the belle of the three, and boasted a top speed of 125 mph courtesy of 220 hp. Even though the 2.4 was able when compared to its competition, its own stable mates could put it to shame with ease. Sadder yet, the same still holds true.

Saddest of all, though, is the fact that this car has been left unserviced for more than ten years. With rust on the fenders and a decaying interior, one can only guess the amount of work this fright-kitty calls for. While it would be a lovely tribute to Mr. Clarke to restore his beloved Mk II and turn it loose on the road once again, to do so would be a Sisyphean chore. Best bet is to drive it when it allows, and perhaps tinker with the engine on occasion, and for amusement only.

Under no circumstance should one view such a Jag as a restoration candidate. It will cost the same to refurbish as the more desirable 3.8 and 3.4, and it will always be worth a fraction of the cost. Whereas you can hope to recoup at least some of the restoration expense of a 3.8 by selling it for upwards of $30,000, a perfect 2.4 will only fetch $12,000. And those numbers just don't add up.

(Photo and description courtesy of the auction company.) ◆

Years produced: 1960-67
Number produced: 25,070
Original list price: $3,843
SCM Price Guide: $7,000-$9,000 (Mk I 2.4)
Tune-up/major service: $300
Distributor cap: $15
Chassis #: plate on firewall
Engine #: plate on engine
Club: Jaguar Club of North America, c/o Nelson Rath, 1000 Glenbrook, Anchorage, KY 40223
Web site: www.jcna.com
Alternatives: Alvis 3-Litre, Gordon-Keeble GK1, Maserati Quattroporte, Mercedes-Benz 300d
SCM Investment Grade: D

1965 3.4S Saloon

The generous amount of glass made the interior seem spacious then... today, its tall side windows make it look like an aquarium on wheels—the world's fastest fish tank

by Keith Martin

Chassis number: PLB 3997 BW
Engine number: 7B 4623/8

Following a long line of sporting saloon production (from the earliest beginnings through the pre-war SS Cars and subsequent post-war developments), the Jaguar S type was almost the last in the line of what may be considered a true sports-saloon by this long-established manufacturer. It still used the well-proven trusted 3.4-liter power unit that had revolutionized the sports car market in the XK 120 back in 1949 and continuously developed over two decades installed in all the model range.

Jaguar had managed to produce a performance car with looks to match, with a quality of finish that offered excellent value for money. This particular car was delivered through the main London Agents Henley to a Commissioner of the Police based at Scotland Yard. Two years later it was purchased by the second owner who seldom used it; it was then put into storage, where it remained unused for the next 30 years.

It was then inherited by a family member in 1997, who commissioned Classic Coachbuilders of Sittingbourne, Kent to commence the painstaking restoration of the car to return it to its former glory. During this operation expenditure has exceeded £35,000 in which every aspect and detail has been renovated or renewed. During this refurbishment, some modifications have been incorporated in order to facilitate driving in today's crowded conditions. These include cylinder head and timing changes to run on lead-free petrol, gearbox to column-change operation, alternator replacing dynamo, electronic ignition and fuel pumps, oil-cooler fitted, modern Jaguar power-steering, graded anti-roll bar, road springs and dampers, modern serve-brake unit and wider rim chromed wire wheels.

The interior, too, has been the subject of further specialist restoration with complete re-upholstery in leather, matching carpets and trim, and all woodwork veneered in figured walnut to the utmost discerning standards. The bodywork has undergone a full bare-bones restoration, all rusted panels replaced, whilst paintwork has been resprayed in Jaguar opalescent blue, as a personal option from the original Warwick grey and a full-length Webasto sunroof has been fitted.

The SCM *analysis: This car sold for $26,583 at Christie's London auction on March 29, 2004. The price was smack in the middle of the* SCM *Price Guide.*

Most Americans are not aware of it, but in the early '60s Jaguar saloons earned a racing reputation in England, Australia and New Zealand. The car won the European Touring Car championship and performed well in the Tour de France Automobile.

When new, the generous amount of glass made the interior seem very spacious. Today, however, its tall side windows telegraph the car's age, and make it look like an aquarium on wheels.

So what's the difference between the S model and a regular Mk II sedan? S models cost an extra $514, measured seven inches longer and weighed about 300 pounds more. Changes were both cosmetic and mechanical. Coil spring rear suspension was adopted and the body enclosed the tops of the rear wheels more closely. The independent rear suspension and inboard disc brakes on the S model are the same

Tall side windows telegraph this car's age.

as fitted to the XKE, which gives S owners some bragging rights. In front, the headlights were recessed, the bumper was slimmer, and the turn signals wrapped around the front fenders. The visual effect was of increased streamlining. Inside, the S model included more walnut on the dashboard than the standard Mark II.

The S model was sold both with the 3.4-liter and 3.8-liter engine. (The U.S. got only 3.8-liter cars after 1961.) It borrowed the boxy trunk of Jaguar's larger Mark X sedan so it can hold more luggage. All the added length of the S model was at the rear; the wheelbase was the same as the normal Mark II.

The straight six engine was rated at 210 horsepower and is said to be capable of taking this conveyance to 125 mph. The "8" at the end of the engine number gives the compression ratio. (Some engines had a 9.)

Four-door sedans, no matter how capable, are not valued as much as the more stylish coupes and convertibles. Even so, this car made a very respectable $26,583.

This right-hand drive car sold at auction in England, and in the States its value would be slightly less. With only 40,000 miles and many years in storage, this particular car appeared to have been a good candidate for restoration. The seller may have undertaken to put it back on the road for sentimental reasons since the car had been in the family for so long. Certainly the money spent to refurbish it was not recovered at auction, but this is almost always the case.

The minor changes made during restoration to improve drivability should not detract from value and ought to make ownership more trouble-free.

Second-hand police sedans are not usually considered desirable automobiles. But in this case the price paid seems appropriate considering its thorough restoration and long ownership in one family.

(Photo and description courtesy of the auction company.) ◆

Years produced: 1964-1968
Number produced: 9,830
Original list price: $5,933
SCM Price Guide: $20,000-$30,000
Tune-up/major service: $300
Distributor cap: $15.59
Chassis #: right side of body under hood
Engine #: right side of block, above oil filter
Club: Jaguar Clubs of North America, 1000 Glenbrook Rd., Anchorage, KY 40223
Web site: www.jcna.com
Alternative: Mercedes-Benz 450 SEL 6.9, Maserati Quattroporte
SCM Investment Grade: C

1971 XJ6 SI

To achieve maximum value, this car is best left in its original condition. The conservative sort of umbrella-toting buyer is not the type to look kindly on modifications; gilding the lily, indeed

by Keith Martin

The marvelous XJ6 Saloon introduced in 1968 was a replacement for the outdated Mark X and Mark II's and was to survive for 18 years, carrying Jaguar through the most traumatic period in its history. Low and sleek in a thoroughly modern manner, it represented the acme of Sir William Lyon's *(sic)* stylistic talents, which were complemented by the outstanding engineering package created by William Heynes and his team. Little wonder then that the XJ6 was Lyon's all time favorite Jaguar, even though the name itself did not appear anywhere on the car.

The majority of XJ6s were fitted with an automatic transmission, and power steering was standard. A mere description of the XJ6's technical aspects does not, however, do justice to this Jaguar's extraordinary levels of refinement, quietness and general good manners which many motoring reviewers judged to be superior to those of Rolls Royce. Given these superlatives, an examination of our XJ6 may be called a case of "gilding the lily."

Built as a showpiece for his wife by the consignor who is the chairman of a well known Jaguar restoration and racing shop, this XJ6 sports many improvements from standard. The body restoration began with a strip to bare metal after which the perfect polyurethane silver metallic paint was applied. The interior has new dark blue Connolly hides, a quality wool headliner and a perfect refinishing of the original walnut wood veneers. The bumpers and other brightwork were rechromed as required. The original Philips multi-band radio was restored and an upgraded air conditioning system fitted. Being a shop that also prepares winning historic racing cars, the XJ6's improvements were not limited to cosmetics. The engine was totally gone over; Isky street cams installed, as well as ported and polished cylinder heads and intake system. A mild shift-kit accompanied the transmission overhaul and improved road springs, anti-sway bars and Koni shocks firmed up already excellent handling. Proving its pedigree, our Show Cat was driven hundreds of miles to several concours where it was judged second in JCNA National 2003 points.

The SCM analysis: This car sold for $15,400 at the RM Amelia Island auction held March 13, 2004. It barely reached the low end of the presale estimate, which was still a very good result for the seller.

Consider how many buyers there are for a hot-rod Jaguar sedan, few. This seller added aftermarket camshafts and cylinder head embellishments for his own reasons and it's singularly small group that is likely to appreciate them. This is no '32 Ford.

At least he was wise enough to leave the appearance of the car original, as enthusiasts don't look kindly on XJ6s that have been lowered, flared, spoilered, and fitted with custom wheels.

Stock is what XJ6 collectors prefer. After all, this conservative sort of umbrella-toting buyer is not the type to look kindly on modifications. At least the engine mods are invisible and not likely to attract attention. Better leave the Isky decal off the side window as well. "Gilding the lily," indeed. To achieve maximum value, this car is best left in its original condition.

To restore an XJ6 is not a cheap undertaking.

XJ6 production is divided into three series: Series I from 1969-73; Series II from 1974-79; and Series III from 1979-87. Jaguar sold almost 80,000 Series I XJ6s, and some survive today in running condition. Today only a few brave collectors seek out these admittedly attractive four-door sedans, so prices remain modest.

Most owners are reluctant to sink the money to restore an XJ6, which not a cheap undertaking. As a business proposition it makes as much sense as starting your own restaurant. The seller of this car is not likely to have recovered much of the cash lavished on new paint, upholstery and wood interior trim. On the other hand, since he owned a restoration shop, he probably got his parts at a significant discount.

It would be nice to know how many miles this car accumulated before it was restored, and also the condition of its six-cylinder engine. There is no mention of anything below the cylinder heads having been touched.

Let's face it; do you really want to own a car made during the "most traumatic period" in a company's history? It doesn't inspire a lot of confidence in its build quality.

The name of Jaguar founder Sir William Lyons (not Lyon, as the catalog called him) is invariably invoked by auction companies to add a sense of class and tradition to the marque. Born in 1901, he retired in 1972, so if you want to own a Jaguar built during his reign, here it is. But be prepared to set aside a good chunk of money in a maintenance fund. Just because this car has been restored is no guarantee it will not keep nibbling at its owner's wallet.

(Photo and description courtesy of the auction company.) ◆

> "How many buyers are there for a hot-rod Jaguar sedan?"

Years produced: 1968-1973
Number produced: 23,546 in 1971
Original list price: $7,620 in 1971
SCM Price Guide: $7,000-$9,000
Tune-up/major service: $500
Distributor cap: $23.53
Chassis #: fender panel under hood, brass plate on firewall
Engine #: right side of block, above oil filter
Club: Jaguar Clubs of North America, 1000 Glenbrook Rd., Anchorage, KY 40223
Web site: www.jcna.com
Alternative: Aston Martin Lagonda
SCM Investment Grade: D

1978 XJ12C Coupe

These coupes have little upside and trade in a thin market, meaning expensive repairs are ignored; but this car is a bit of an oddity in the Jaguar canon, guaranteed to draw attention at the club meet

By Brian Rabold

Chassis number: 2G1522BW
Engine number: 7P-346285A

Launched to much acclaim in 1968, the XJ6 refined concepts embodied by previous Jaguar saloons to create a car rivaling the best offered by Mercedes-Benz. Although introduced with XK six-cylinder power under the hood, it had always been Jaguar's intention that its flagship saloon would accommodate the new all-alloy V12 engine that had debuted in the E-type sports car, and the resulting XJ12 duly appeared in July 1972. With a top speed of 145 mph (courtesy of the 5.3-liter V12's 272 bhp), the newcomer combined high performance with a level of luxury unmatched by many a less accommodating Grand Tourer costing several times as much.

The authoritative magazine *Road & Track* tested a prototype XJ12C to US specification in 1976, enjoying the experience immensely: "All XJs are a fine cross between a Mercedes-Benz and an American sedan, combining the precision of the German with the light effort of the American car, giving Jaguars a gracefulness that no other luxury car can duplicate.

One of just 1,830 12-cylinder coupes built between September 1973 and November 1977, this highly original, automatic transmission example has enjoyed just two owners, both from the same family, from new. Finished in Squadron Blue with well-preserved, original beige leather interior, the car is presented in generally very good condition, having covered just 22,500 miles in total.

The SCM analysis: This car sold for $15,815, including buyer's premium, at Bonhams' Hendon sale, April 26, 2004.

The XJ6 was the solitary replacement for Jaguar's confusing saloon range in 1968, and promptly won most international "Car of the Year" awards. It was to be the last model designed by an independent Jaguar; the company was absorbed by British Leyland in 1972.

Wanting to give its marquee car its most potent powerplant, Jaguar fitted its 5.3-liter V12 engine into the XJ6 in 1972, giving rise to the XJ12. This model, too, won Car of the Year accolades. Only available with automatic transmission, the car rivaled the Rolls-Royce Corniche of the same era in refinement. Handmade Connolly seats, rich burl walnut finishing, and thick Wilton wool carpets spoiled its occupants. The design was muscular yet understated, only hinting at the car's ability to cruise at 140 mph.

Realizing a concept envisioned by Sir William Lyons as early as 1967, a coupe version of the XJ12 was made available in 1974, noted by a "C" suffix on its name. With a pillarless design, the car looked even more striking than the sedan, though many felt its Everflex (a fancy English name for vinyl) top detracted from the car's clean lines. Due to a slightly shorter length and decreased weight, the car was more agile than the saloon, and a skosh faster as well. Until the arrival of the XJS the following year, the XJ12C was touted as the fastest and quietest four-seater in the world.

With high hopes for a boost in sales and morale (both of which were sagging after the BL consolidation), Jaguar called on Ralph Broad and Broadspeed to prep XJ12Cs for competition in the European Touring Car Championship for the '76 and '77 seasons. Despite dramatic changes to make the cars competitive, the XJ12C battled weight and unreliability, and never managed to win a single event. BMW's 650

The fastest vinyl top in the world.

CSL proved to be too competent an opponent, and much to the company's chagrin, Jaguar pulled the 12C out of racing.

The coupes didn't fare any better in the marketplace. Smaller and more expensive than saloons, most buyers opted for either space or sportiness in lieu of a combination of both in the XJ12C. The car didn't weather the 1970s gas crisis well, either. As a result, only 1,832 models were sold, and the line quietly disappeared after the 1978 model year. Meanwhile, its saloon-bodied stablemate continued to be produced until 1997.

On the whole, the coupes have little upside and trade in a thin market, meaning expensive repairs are ignored. Replacement body panels and glass are almost nonexistent, and the engine is remarkably expensive to fix. The example shown here is in unusually good shape inside and out, however, showing only slight wear to the interior and no corrosion in the doorsills—a common sore sport in the XJ series. The car appears to have been owned by a family fond of the Jaguar marque, and they pampered it, as is evidenced by the low mileage.

If the car indeed is deemed to be in sound shape once the new owner has a mechanic peek under the hood, a shade under $16,000 doesn't seem like all that steep a fee, even if it is at least $6,000 over the going rate. After all, this car is a bit of an oddity in the Jaguar canon, guaranteed to draw attention at the club meet. It's chassis/engine combo was among the best of the industry during its time, and has been taken care of by two presumably fastidious owners. And, it assuredly is, as one enthusiast magazine put it, the fastest vinyl top in the world.

Perhaps not the coolest claim to make, but $15,800 can't buy many others.

(Photo and description courtesy of the auction company.) ◆

Years produced: 1975-78
Number produced: 1,830
Original list price: $15,650
Valuation: $10,000-$16,500
Tune-up/major service: $800
Distributor cap: $50
Chassis #: Plate on A-pillar
Engine #: Plate on engine
Club: Jaguar Club of North America, c/o Nelson Rath, 1000 Glenbrook, Anchorage, KY 40223
Web site: www.jcna.com
Alternatives: Rolls-Royce Corniche, Ferrari 400i, Mercedes-Benz 450 SLC
SCM Investment Grade: D

1988-91 XJ-S V12 Convertible

The car could go all day at three-digit speeds, carrying its occupants in reasonable comfort...but it pulled like a pig on tight corners, and often got single-digit mileage in a gas-crisis era

by Gary Anderson

When does a car cross the line from used car to classic? If you can figure that out, you may be able to buy that older car you've always admired at the absolute bottom of the market—after it has ceased depreciating and before it has started to accrue a collector's premium. We think the Jaguar XJ-S convertible with the V12 engine, especially those built between 1988 and 1991, is at that point now, and merits consideration.

Surprisingly, for a car that got no respect when it was first introduced, the Jaguar XJ-S was produced longer than any other car Jaguar has built to date. Over twenty years, from 1975 to 1996, Jaguar built over 115,000; first in the "flying buttress" style grand touring coupe and then, after 1988, in both coupe and convertible styles. The car was originally equipped with the V12 engine carried over from the Series III E-types; after 1991 it was available with Jaguar's six-cylinder engine as well.

When introduced, the XJ-S was criticized because it wasn't what the press expected as the successor to the sleek, fast, two-seat E-types, and frankly because it wasn't very good. Designed as a cruiser on the new four-lane roads in England and Europe, the car could go all day at three-digit speeds, carrying its occupants in reasonable comfort. But it was only available in a controversially styled coupe, had dead-feeling power steering, floated over bumps, pulled like a pig on tight corners, and often got single-digit mileage in a gas-crisis era. It was also an era of labor difficulties in England and Jaguar's build quality seemed to get worse every year.

So why did Jaguar continue to produce the XJ-S? Quite simply, they needed a sporting model to maintain their image and they couldn't afford to design a replacement. So instead, they kept on producing the XJ-S, fixing a thing or two each year until they finally got it right.

Did they get it right? We think they did. When they finally got around to making their own convertible in 1988 (coupes had been converted for many years, and there was an H&E conversion done in Cincinnati in 1986 and 1987 with Brown Lane's blessing) it was a very nice car. Over the years, they had updated the silky-smooth V12 to get decent mileage without sacrificing torque or top speed, sorted out most of the handling problems, and upgraded the interior trim to reflect the Jaguar image. The convertible continued to be produced until 1996, when it was replaced by the XK-8. In a way it still lives on, since its floor pan still underpins the new Aston Martins.

We believe that the entire line of factory convertibles has the potential to become classic. A "classic," at least according to this writer, has styling that will continue to attract admiring glances, performance that makes driving a pleasure in itself, reasonable dependability and parts availability so that it can be enjoyed without excessive expense, and won't depreciate further.

"Classic" defined: style that attracts attention, performance that makes driving a pleasure.

If you buy carefully, we think the early-style convertibles now meet these standards.

You should be able to find a car that has been owned by a Jaguar enthusiast who is now trading up to an XK-8, one that was conscientiously maintained by the dealer and maybe had even shown in the occasional Jag club concours. And you still shouldn't have to pay more than $25,000, and often even less. You might look for the "Collector Edition" produced in 1991 only; it has a nicer interior, but isn't worth a significant premium.

You can keep an eye on the second version convertibles (1991-1996) but they're really not cheap enough yet. They still show up on Jaguar dealer lots, complete with warranties in the Jaguar Select Edition program, which means they're still depreciable used cars. If you want to experience a V12 engine for less money, you might look at the earlier coupes. Regardless of which XJ-S you look at, buy one that is in exceptional condition; don't settle for less. The exterior should be rust-free and the interior needing only a little Hide Food. Make sure every single electronic accessory works, because they're a pain to trouble-shoot. Above all, these cars are not candidates for restoration—you wouldn't spend much less to restore a basket-case XJ-S than you might for a similar Ferrari.

From the March 2000 issue of *SCM.* ◆

> "The rear-end styling was tweaked a little... rear seats were added at the request of Princess Di, who threatened to buy a Mercedes otherwise."

Years produced: First series convertibles (1988-1991); all XJ-S (1975-1996)

Number produced: First series convertibles (13,197); all convertibles (31,752); all XJ-S (115,200)

Original list price: $41,500

Valuation: $7,000-$15,000

Tune-up/major service: $300-500

Distributor cap: $99.50 (may be difficult to find)

Chassis #: Plate on firewall and on dash at base of windshield

Engine #: Plate on engine

Club: Jaguar Clubs of North America, 888.258.2524

Web site: www.jcna.com

Alternatives to consider: Mercedes 560SL, Porsche 930 Turbo Cabriolet, Jensen Interceptor Convertible

1988 XJ-S Convertible

Styling, with its infamous "flying buttresses," offended Jaguar purists. Nonetheless, the car did posses a quiet ride, superior handling and a luxurious interior, and initial tests reported that the XJ-S could "run the pants off a 450 SLC"

by Brian Rabold

Chassis number: SAJJNADW3DA151528
Engine number: 8S059662HA

A Jag this capable, for under $12,000, sounds like a bargain, but...

Throughout the 1950s and 1960s Jaguar had, in the XK series and later the E-type, produced coupes and roadsters of unsurpassed performance and glamour. When the sleek E-type was finally retired, Jaguar replaced it with another sports model. Introduced in 1975, its successor was the V12-engined XJ-S, an effortless grand cruiser.

There was no lack of performance with the XJ-S, but the emphasis was always on its ability to cover great distances at cruising speeds up to 140 mph, while cosseting its occupants in near silence. More softly suspended than its predecessors, sumptuously upholstered, and by far the most expensive Jaguar of its time, the XJ-S fully deserved to be called exclusive.

"When all is said and done, enough money to buy a perfect, no-stories XJ-S will have been spent. The lurking question, of course, is why buy the dingy version in the first place?"

Visual condition throughout for this example is fair for its age. The driver's seat has some wear on the entry side and the seats could use a thorough cleaning. Presumably due to exposure at its residence in the South of France, the lacquer finish to the wood trim has started to discolor and lift. The bodywork is good in general except for the passenger side where some small dents are evident.

Christie's has been able to run the car and the engine started promptly and sounded well. When moving the car, however, we did notice that the power steering system makes considerable noise and most certainly requires attention prior to use. The electric roof was also inoperative. The odometer currently displays 15,838 miles, which is the same figure it showed in

July 1999. Thus, we assume that the odometer is not functional.

The SCM analysis: This two-owner car sold for $11,722, including buyer's premium, at the December 2, 2003, Christie's auction held in London.

Ad copy for the XJ-S proclaimed the car's debut as "a black day for Modena, Stuttgart, and Turin," though neither Mercedes nor Ferrari likely rue its arrival. For while Jaguar's XJ-S was never designed to replace the venerable E-type, the public couldn't resist the urge to compare the two, and the model never successfully escaped from the XKE's shadow.

Although propelled by the same all-alloy V12 engine found in Series III XKEs, the two models were distinctly different. The E-type was sporty and sexy, while the XJ-S was a true GT, offering occasional rear seats, a trunk designed to carry as much as a luxury saloon, and a price twice that of the Series III E.

Styling, with its infamous "flying buttresses," offended Jaguar purists. Nonetheless, the car did posses a quiet ride, superior handling and a luxurious interior, and initial tests reported that the XJ-S could "run the pants off a 450 SLC." The XJ-S boasted a top speed of 150 mph and a 0-60 time of 6.8 seconds, making it the fastest four-seater in the world upon its debut.

Tatty interior, broken odometor and chipped paint all point to neglect.

Early models suffered from build problems though, particularly in the electrical systems, which lingered into the '80s. However, most of the headaches had been sorted out by 1988, the launch of the factory convertible. In addition, the much-loved 5.3-liter V12 received improved fuel economy and a lower torque curve when it was reborn as the HE (high efficiency) in 1981. As a result, the first series XJS convertibles are a delight to drive.

Quiet, comfortable, and luxurious, they cruise the highway at twice the legal limit without provocation. This, paired with the trunk's spaciousness, makes the car ideally suited for extended trips to Vegas or Palm Springs.

A Jaguar this capable, for a shade under $12,000, sounds like a bargain. But we do not live in a perfect world, and whoever bought this car is not driving a perfect Jag. A good example usually has some form of service history. Unfortunately, the only records this car has are of neglect, embodied by poor cosmetics and general disrepair. A broken odometer, a tatty interior and scuffed-up paint can all be endured if the new owner so chooses. More difficult to ignore, however, is the power steering, which is a common problem with these cars. A bill of $5,000 wouldn't be unexpected to make things right, and that's just for what the auction company admits is wrong.

Then there's the power top. It is currently buggered by electri-cal gremlins, meaning the buyer is paying for a convertible but driving a coupe with body flex.

Maybe it will be an easy fix and no more problems will be revealed in the process. The new owner will still likely shell out another $1,000, raising his investment to around $18,000.

A more likely scenario is that all the tinkering with the power steering and top will uncover some other hidden sin that can only be solved by a bigger cash infusion. When all is said and done, enough money to buy a perfect, no-stories XJ-S will have been spent. The lurking question, of course, is why buy the dingy version in the first place?

If the buyer gets lucky with the necessary repairs while resisting the urge to make this cat right in all areas, he should be pleased. If not, though, he'll have to chalk the experience up as a valuable and expensive lesson in Jaguar ownership and apply his hard-earned knowledge to his next purchase.

(Photo and description courtesy of the auction company.)◆

> "While Jaguar's XJ-S was never designed to replace the venerable E-type, the public couldn't resist the urge to compare the two, and the model never successfully escaped from the XKE's shadow."

Years produced: 1988-1991 (first series convertibles); 1975-1996 (all XJ-S)

Number produced: 13,197 (first series convertibles); 115,200 (all XJ-S)

Original list price: $41,500

Valuation: $7,000-$10,000

Tune-up/major service: $800-$1,000

Distributor cap: $25

Chassis #: plate on firewall and on dash at base of windshield

Engine #: plate on engine

Club: Jaguar Club of North America, c/o Nelson Rath, 1000 Glenbrook, Anchorage, KY 40223

Web site: www.jcna.com

Alternatives: Mercedes-Benz 560 SL, Porsche 930 Turbo Cabriolet, Jensen Interceptor Convertible

SCM Investment Grade: C-

1989 XJ-S Coupe "Ex-Frank Sinatra"

Where the XKE will always be a collector car sought after by serious individuals, the XJ-S will continue to languish unloved—unless it was once owned by a deceased singer who set the world on fire

by Bill Neill

Chassis number: SAJNA 5849KC150201

Almost $200,000 to sit in Old Blue Eyes' Jag.

With the XK series and later the R-Type two-seaters, Jaguar had, for two straight decades, produced sport coupes and open roadsters of unparalleled power and elegance. When at last the moment came to retire the sleek E-type, Jaguar Cars chose not to replace it with another sports model. The world had changed, and with it, the market for high performance cars. Introduced in the Fall of 1975, its successor was the V12-engined XJ-S, an effortless Grand Tourer. There was no lack of performance, with a top speed of 153 mph and a 0 to 60 mph time of 6.8 seconds, but the emphasis was always on its effortless ability to cover great distances at cruising speeds up to 140 mph, while cosseting its occupants in near-silence. Extravagantly upholstered the most expensive Jaguar ever produced (before the XK-8), the XJ-S fully was, by its very definition, exclusive.

It was the last Jaguar to benefit from the unrivaled partnership of Sir William Lyons, with his great instinct for line and value, and Malcolm Sayers, aerodynamicist and scientist. When the car was launched, the now retired Sir William observed, "We desired from the very first aerodynamics were the prime concern and I exercised my influence in consultative capacity... I took my influence as far as I could without interfering with [Sayers'] basic aerodynamic requirements."

Frank Sinatra was certainly fond of the XJ-S model; in 1976 he received one as a wedding gift from Barbara Sinatra which he kept until the early '90s. This particular example was also the property of Sinatra, who was the registered owner in Beverly Hills in 1989. It would appear that he used it very sparingly and we are told that he later returned the car to the dealership where he bought it from with the

Years produced: 1976-1996
Number produced: 4,458 in 1989
Original list price: $47,000 in 1989
SCM Price Guide: $8,000-$10,000
Tune-up/major service: $800-$1,000
Distributor cap: $100.46 (Lucas), $165.78 (Marelli)
Chassis #: top of dashboard
Engine #: on valley behind throttle tower near firewall
Club: Clubs of North America, 1000 Glenbrook Rd., Anchorage, KY 40223
Web site: www.jcna.com
Alternative: Mercedes-Benz 450 SLC, Chevrolet Corvette
SCM Investment Grade: D

stipulation that he could drive it under dealer plates every time he was in Palm Springs. When Desert European Motorcars bought the dealership, the car was part of the sale. They registered it again with the California Department of Motor Vehicles with the license plates FAS II. Before the car went on the showroom floor, the current owner acquired it. The owner has in recent years been living abroad and again has hardly driven the car. It has remained in storage in Palm Springs. At the California emissions test in January of this year, the mileage was recorded at 9,234.

The SCM *analysis: This car sold for $178,500 at Christie's Pebble Beach auction August 15, 1998, only three months after Frank Sinatra died at age 82. The amazing sale price was many times the presale estimate of $10,000 to $15,000. This is a low-mileage coupe, but the price achieved here is due to enthusiasm for its famous owner and not to the mechanical attributes of the car.*

Interestingly, the very same car was presented again for sale by Gooding & Company on August 15, 2004 with an estimate of $60,000 to $80,000. By this time, it had accumulated 11,000 miles. It finally sold for $57,200.

This example was painted British Racing Green with tan leather interior, according to the catalog.

The XJ-S is not considered highly desirable by collectors. Jaguar built it for 20 years, making it the company's longest-running model. With more than 110,000 of them rolling out of the factory, it's hardly a rare car today, and more of a commodity. Expensive when new, XJ-S models are now worth only a fraction of their

> "Distinctive and handsome in a brutish way, with the long hood of the E-type, it has none of the lightness and sportiness that makes collectors willing to part with $30,000 and more for E-type coupes in nice condition."

list price. Are potential buyers discouraged by their reputation for mechanical problems or turned off by the styling? A peek at the hoses and wires swirling around the engine stuffed under the hood could make anyone think twice. Indeed, the V12 had difficulties with overheating.

The 326-cubic-inch V12 engine in the XJ-S was carried over from the final series of the XKE. But the XJ-S doesn't cause collectors to fall down and worship it the way its predecessor does. It weighs 500 pounds more than the last XKE, and the XJ-S certainly looks like a cat that has spent too long at the feeding trough. Although it maintains the long hood of the E-type, it has none of the lightness and sportiness that makes collectors willing to part with $30,000 and more for E-type coupes in nice condition.

Perhaps it is unfair to expect more from the XJ-S. As the catalog description tells us, it was built as more of a boulevard cruiser than the kind of road-hugging machine that challenges the best sports cars from Italy and Germany. The four headlights provide a visual hint of its bulk and its EPA rating of 10 mpg gives some idea of its thirst. With massive roof buttresses sweeping back to the tail, it is distinctive and handsome in a brutish way.

In the American market, the XJ-S came with a Turbo-Hydramatic 400 transmission from General Motors. While it may have been a bulletproof unit suited for Chevy taxis pounding the potholes of New York City, this box would hardly be a source of pride to drivers with sporting pretensions. Wrapping your leather driving glove around the handle of an automatic transmission originating in a GM factory is hardly the kind of image that keeps Jaguar owners awake at night with thoughts of downshifting for a sweeping curve. (The XJ-S got a four-speed automatic in 1991.)

Owners seeking respect naturally compare their XJ-S to the XKE. After all, it is still a V12 coupe with the Jaguar name. But there the resemblance ends. Where the XKE will always be a collector car sought after by serious individuals, the XJ-S will continue to languish unloved. Unless it was once owned by a deceased singer who set the world on fire. In this case, the fact that Mr. Sinatra possessed this coupe is responsible for 90 percent of the price it brought at auction. Celebrity ownership does not usually increase a car's value significantly, but in this case it rang the bell to almost $200,000. Ring-a-ding ding.

(Photo and description courtesy of the auction company.)◆

> "Perhaps it is unfair to expect more from the XJ-S. As the catalog description tells us, it was built as more of a boulevard cruiser than the kind of road-hugging machine that challenges the best sports cars from Italy and Germany."

From E-Type to XK8

When I brought it home, the wife said it looked like a jellybean; I felt it more closely resembled an E-type

by Cameron Shehan

Though I've been behind the wheel of various and sundry Jaguars over the last thirty plus years (an XJ12 followed by several V12 E-types and XJ-S coupes), at one point I found myself using first a Z-28 and then a C-5 Corvette for my daily drivers and parts runners. This sudden change of venue happened one day when, having just had the air conditioning fixed on my XJ-S, I realized I was inexplicably sweating on a warm day. That was the last straw; the six cylinder XJs had never felt strong enough anyway, and so I felt it was time to switch brands.

For something completely different, I brought home the six-speed Z-28. This really fast car was a lot of fun—for a while. But doing all that shifting while driving around in urban traffic grew old; the Z-28 turned into the C-5 with an automatic. This was a really great car, also very fast, but after several years I gradually became overwhelmed with all the plastic surrounding me. It was time to give Jaguar, my first love, another shot. By now Ford has taken over the company and made many promises relating to quality improvement, so I felt a reconciliation was in order.

My needs at this point were speed, reliability, and an interior feel available only in England. As my new Jag was to be a winter car as well as a daily driver, that meant (for me) no soft top. I felt the XJs were too frumpy; and since there was now a V8 available, an XK8 coupe it was.

I contacted my friend Thom down in Southern California, a regular buyer and seller of cars at dealer auctions and specified my needs. My old chum's helpful reply was something along the lines of "You idiot, don't you know how few XK8s were made? You sure won't have much of a choice…and by the way, it's going to take more money than you think." I thanked him for his thoughtful opinions, but nonetheless pretty much ignored him. I stubbornly waited for my XK8 to come up for auction, and in time the right one came along, a 1997 XK8 Coupe, British Racing Green, with just enough miles to have depreciated about 50%. I brought it home in 2001.

So I get the thing home and Carolyn (my wife and advisor) says, "It looks like a jellybean." I told her that while it may bear some family resemblance to a jellybean, upon closer inspection one could clearly see that what it really resembled was an E-type, and that is a always a good thing.

One strange occurrence I noted with the XK8 (at least with this particular car), you must keep your foot off the accelerator during the starting process. If you touch it within a second of start up, it will flood and you won't be going anywhere for a while.

Like many Jaguar sports cars, the XK8 is not for large people;

Speed, reliability, and an interior feel available only from England.

> "It was time to give Jaguar, my first love, another shot. By now Ford has taken over the company and made many promises relating to quality improvement, so I felt a reconciliation was in order."

fortunately, I am not large. The car is a wonderfully comfortable road rider. When it came into my possession, the car had done 35,000 miles, and it did another 25,000 reasonably carefree miles before anything requiring attention transpired.

At about 62,000 miles, a front wheel bearing failed. I have worked extensively with various Jags models, from 1950s through '70s, and in thirty-five years, I never once replaced a wheel bearing. But the XK8 is a modern cat, and does not have the over-engineering typical of the old days. As is so often the case with repairs to late model cars, I had to take it in to have the wheel bearing replaced; to do so on the modern XK8 is beyond the capabilities of a hobbyist like me. There is a price to be paid for the comfort and convenience you get with these younger cats. 2,000 miles later, a warning message alerted me that the stability control system had failed. I was still able to drive the car under normal conditions, but this message became the default message, overriding any other potential warning: it had to be fixed.

My friends at Consolidated Auto Works informed me that they could fix the problem to the tune of four figures (I wish they'd told me to sit down first). The process required replacing several components, the names of which escape me. Modern cars contain many of these mysterious items, rendering incompetent many of us folks who used to be able to work on our own cars.

Keeping in mind this mysterious issue, I pondered upon the advisability of keeping a modern car beyond its warranty period. Suddenly I became aware of the fact that I had owned this car for three years, a long time for me to keep a driver.

And so the quest for a new cat began. ◆

First Impressions: My 2002 XKR

Jaguar says the improved comfort is due to its "super sport suspension" and "adaptive damping CATS". My expert explanation is this—it feels good

by Cameron Shehan

The author and his supercharged cat.

The agreed meeting place was just north of Sacramento, mid-point between my old college buddy, Thom and I. The plan was meet, swap cars and catch up. As a favor to me, Thom had agreed to bring me the 2002 Jaguar XKR I had just bought, and then turn around and drive my 1997 XK8 back to Riverside, California to run through the dealer auction. As we had each just driven over 500 miles that day, Thom from Redlands and me from Portland, we took in some dinner accompanied by a couple of cold ones, had some conversation and headed to bed.

It wasn't until the next day that I really got behind the wheel of my new (new to me, anyway) XKR. In keeping with my long-standing policy of allowing someone else take the first fifty percent of a car's depreciation, I bought the car used. My original intention was to get a 2001 with 35,000 miles on it, but such a kitty could not be found; I was looking for a coupe, and convertibles outnumber coupes by about twenty to one. So, the aforementioned mileage policy was amended slightly, and I set my sites on a 2002 XKR with 14,000 miles. Oddly enough, the newer car, with 20,000 less miles on it, cost only nine percent more. Which led me to ask my skeptical self, "What's wrong with this one?"

After a day of driving around picturesque Sacramento, the happy conclusion was that there was absolutely nothing wrong with this one, so I decided to take it home. I got myself comfortable behind the wheel, dialed my home address into the navigation system, and was politely informed that I had 550 miles and slightly over nine hours to go on my trip. The navigation system certainly is a cool toy; the instruction book was missing, but the system is easy enough to figure out without the book. Of course, the system made certain erroneous assumptions (such as me averaging only 60 mph). After all, I was cruising rural I-5. The system soon realized that the speeds would be somewhat higher and cleverly made the appropriate adjustment to the projected arrival time.

So the next step was to find the answer to this question: Just how fast is this car? Well, I can tell you one thing; it was not at all bothered by the steep hills of Southern Oregon's I-5, purring up incline after incline without laboring a bit. This is true of most modern cars, but with one big difference—the time it takes to pass other vehicles (after the trucks which have been blocking both lanes clear the way). I didn't time this activity officially; there was no time to consult my watch. My guess is it took about four seconds to go from 40 to 80 mph uphill. (I once, during a period of silliness, owned a 328 Ferrari. This XKR is faster.) But, as usual, there is a small cost for this power; the XKR appears to get about 2-3 miles per gallon less than the XK8 (about 22 mpg highway), but the fun is worth it.

The transmission is a significant improvement over that of the now-discarded 1997 XK8. During normal driving the gear changes are so subtle that you must watch the tach to know that it is happening. The kickdown shifts are sharp. This car shifts when you think it should, which I found reassuring.

The '97 XK8 was a very comfortable road car, but this one is better. Where this superiority comes from is a mystery to me. Carolyn, my advisor, explains this by saying that it is "tighter." Officially, Jaguar says the improved comfort is due to its "super sport suspension" and "adaptive damping CATS". My expert explanation is this: It feels good.

I have not yet driven the car in a stressful situation, such as through twisty bits or slalom cones, but I have every confidence in my XKR, and expect great things.

As for the latest techno-wizardry, the most remarkable add on gadget would have to be the rain sensing wipers, which, believe it or not, actually work. While motoring along, it began to sprinkle, gradually increasing to a torrential downpour, which then evaporated to nothing. Without my touching anything, the wipers began with a few intermittent passes, increased to a timely frenetic wiping, and then, right on cue, just stopped. How do they do that?

The silliest add on is the "boot spoiler" which at the trailing edge of the trunk, and is 1.75" wide and .75" tall. It's hard to imagine how this could have any effect under 300 mph. But I guess it looks cool, and psychologically makes you feel more aerodynamic.

I decided to conduct a few traction control experiments. With the traction control on, flooring the accelerator resulted in some power cutouts followed by forward movement at a scary pace. With the traction control off and with 9" of rubber on the road, you get instant smoke and no forward progress at all. It won't hook up until you let up on the gas. This is more power than any sane person needs, but I seem to need it.

As I pulled into my driveway, I decided that this cat's a keeper.◆

2004 S-Type

In the flesh, the S-type is every bit as beautiful and classic as in photos—and quite possibly, even more elegant

"Hey, this thing is fun in the slalom," one half of our AutoFile test team noted after a day in the new Jaguar S-type at Southern California's Pomona Raceway. His playground partner concurred. "Through the slalom, it was like a tight version of a muscle car. You can slide the rear end all over the place and the car doesn't roll and flop anywhere near as much as you might have expected."

Expected, he might have added, of a Jaguar, the British luxury marque that has been long on styling, leather and hardwood, but maybe a little soft on spring rates, lateral acceleration numbers and enthusiast hardware.

The new S-type, Jaguar's first midsize car in three decades, is a giant step in the right direction, and isn't it wonderful that a company's volume car also can be an enthusiast car?

Not to say that the S-type isn't still a true Jaguar. Although it shares its underpinnings with the new Lincoln LS, you won't confuse the two cars when you see them. The Jaguar has an unmistakably Jaguar body, especially in front, where the modern, aerodynamic interpretation of the classic Mark 2 features sculpted fenders and hood, with a leaping cat hood ornament that soars over a big, beautiful, vertically barred grille.

An unmistakably Jaguar body.

Only 40 percent of the chassis components are shared by Lincoln and Jaguar. Among the differences are unique-to-Jaguar suspension bushings, shock absorbers and springs (the S-type is the first Jaguar with upper and lower control arms in the rear suspension instead of half-shafts that also serve as upper links).

Only the S-type gets to use Jaguar's AJ-V8, a slightly detuned version of the 4.0-liter engine found in the XK8 and larger XJ sedans. In the S-type, the V8 provides 281 horsepower and 287 lb-ft of torque at 4300 rpm. Jaguar says 80 percent of that torque is available between 1400 and 6100 rpm, but the power doesn't really build until you're some 3000 rpm into the powerband.

There's also a V6 S-type with a 3.0-liter Ford Duratec V6 alloy block. But Jaguar supplies its own top-end for that engine, with variable-valve timing and a new intake that help produce 240 horsepower and 212 lb-ft of torque.

The S-type uses the Jaguar-style J-gate shifter with normal and sport modes to control its new five-speed automatic transmission. We find the J-gate to be an awkward setup. Lincoln offers a five-speed manual with the V6 engine; Jaguar does not.

At Pomona, we tested a V8 S-type that had the optional weather package: heated front seats, rain-sensing wipers and Dynamic Stability Control (it uses yaw and steering-rate sensors

> "The new S-type, Jaguar's first midsize car in three decades, is a giant step in the right direction; isn't it wonderful that a company's volume car also can be an enthusiast car?"

and a lateral accelerometer sensor to keep the car from spinning). But it did not have the sport package, which adds CATS (Computer Active Technology Suspension that uses vertical and lateral accelerometers to adjust spring rates to improve ride and handling qualities) and aggressive, 17-inch Pirelli P-Zero tires.

Our car wore 16-inch rims and M&S-rated Bridgestone Turanzas. "In view of the car's good controllability in skidpad and slalom, I'd really like to see what it can do with more performance-oriented tires," one tester said.

Even with mud 'n' snows, the S-type clocked 7.24 seconds (faster than a Honda Prelude SH) in the 0-to-60-mph sprint, and hit 91.6 mph by the end of the quarter-mile. Its average speed through the slalom was 41.7 mph (faster than a Saab 9-5).

Perhaps its most impressive numbers were in the brake tests. The S-type has 11.8-inch front rotors and 11.3-inch rears. Despite a pedal that felt soft under ABS pulsation, this 3770-pound sedan exhibited very little nose dive and consistently made 60 mph-to-0 stops in the 122-to-124-foot range (only about a foot more than a smaller, lighter, BMW 3-Series sedan).

Inside, the new Jag is larger than the 3-Series. It even feels larger than the other, bigger Jag sedan. The S-type has an un-Jag-like back seat, which means lots of room. Those up front will enjoy the comfort and room, too.

They'll also like the ride and handling, but we suspect they'll like it even more if they opt for the Pirellis.

Excerpted from AutoWeek. For subscription information, visit www.autoweek.com.◆

2004 X-Type

Castle Combe is a circuit where speeds can be high enough to command your full attention; instructors still urge caution on a turn where 1953 photos show Stirling Moss upside down in a Cooper

by Kevin A. Wilson

I t's only logical that you've got to sit behind the wheel and put a vehicle through its paces before you get the full equation; the same holds true for the Jaguar X-Type. And now that we've driven the car, can we solve for X? The answer turns out to be positive. Details in a moment.

First, a reminder of how the math works. X-Type, Jaguar's first foray into the 3-Series/A4/C-Class entry-level luxury segment, aims to double the marque's sales worldwide. It's the big roll of the dice that parent company Ford hopes will enhance its profit from the burgeoning demand for luxury cars. This doubling of sales in question would rest atop the earlier doubling of sales when the mid-level S-type was added to the mix.

All X-Types sold in the United States will wear the jumping Jaguar hood ornament called a "leaper" even when equipped as the Sport model. The Sport package also substitutes black or body-color for most of the chrome on standard cars. The buyer can choose between 3.0- and 2.5-liter V6 engines and opt for automatic or manual transmission.

Effort to fit all the traditional Jaguar design cues onto the entry-level luxury sedan sometimes makes for a busy-looking accumulation of lines, but certainly sends the "this is a real Jag" message. Our impression from behind the wheel was much the same: The X-Type is a real Jaguar, within reach of more Jaguar-aspirants.

One source of doubt about whether people would like X-Type has been knowing that the Jaguar's underpinnings are derived from those of the European Ford Mondeo, the latest generation of the car once sold here as the Ford Contour. Purists wonder if such a car can be a "real" Jaguar. This particular parts-sharing, it turns out, only gives the Jag its chassis "hard points" and its engine blocks, but not much else. Jaguarites say the chassis itself shares only six small panels with its blue-oval counterpart, and that their version has been reinforced significantly for stiffness and quiet. In fact, they boast, by the time the leaper hood ornament goes on the car, its static rigidity is 30 percent better than that of the nearest luxury segment competitor; by another measure, body stiffness is higher than the BMW 3-Series, a mighty fine measuring stick to use.

Point is, after all the emendations, the small Jaguar winds up being more different from its Ford counterpart than are the midsize S-type and Lincoln LS. Over several hundred miles behind the wheel of an X-type, the rigidity of the chassis, build quality and quiet cabin all impressed us as true near-luxury sedan stuff.

Torque steer is expurgated, turn-in response is crisp, balance nearly neutral and attitude easily adjusted via throttle pedal. You can pretty much throw it away in a turn and not get bit—we tried and couldn't induce any alarming degree of over- or understeer. Body roll is nicely controlled with even the base model (what the engineers call the "comfort" suspension) being somewhat

An elegant ride from any angle.

stiffer than you might expect of a Jaguar. The company says the X-Type should appeal to younger drivers, many who regard the XJ-8 and even S-type as "grandpa-mobiles," and the suspension reflects the youthful attitude.

As for the countersteering, the car actually recovers from lurid slides without dramatics, and if you get totally ham-fisted it pretty much scrubs off speed until it gathers its skirts and away you go. Castle Combe is a 1.85-mile circuit where speeds can be high enough to command your full attention, but none of the moderate straights let us reach the 146-mph top speed of the 3.0-liter. This was largely due to a kink in the front (called Folly, so we thought we ought to take the hint) en route to Quarry; a turn where old photos show Stirling Moss upside down in a Cooper in 1953, and instructors still urge caution.

The day before, we'd driven through England's Cotswolds and the Black Mountains of eastern Wales, along the shores of the Rivers Severn and Wye. This drive in right-hand-drive pre-production prototypes found us dodging farm tractors on narrow lanes and zooming along motorways, but we needed the track to explore the car at its limits.

Our first drive of the X-type tells us it's friendly, forgiving and yet enjoyable on narrow mountain passes or fast racetrack sweepers in ways that many a four-wheel-drive luxury sedan in this price class is not. And it's a comfortable tourer, with copious trunk space and livable rear legroom for two adults.

Despite its relatively modest overall dimensions, the X-type can claim the largest trunk space in the Jaguar range, and a back seat useful for adult-size passengers. And from most angles, it looks rather elegant.

Final judgments must be suspended pending track testing and experience of left-hand-drive, full production models on American roads, but the early drive suggests that shoppers doing their sums will find X offers a distinct answer to the entry-luxury sedan equation, a solution distinct from C, 3 or A4. It's starting to add up.

Excerpted from AutoWeek. *For subscription information, visit* www.autoweek.com. ◆

2004 XJR

Put XJ through its paces on long, sweeping roads or even in a meandering city center and you realize it is a driver's car with an unbeatable being of lightness

by Dutch Mandel

The XJR carries a framed mesh grille, 15-spoke wheels, and 390 horses.

The good people who build Jaguar cars have learned a thing or two. What was a so-called big car in a long queue of available high-end rides is today among the best contenders on the consideration list. A long, lovely, leisurely tour—or even a serious supercharged blast on a two-lane blue highway—proves Jaguar's new XJ sedan rivals the no-compromise, uber-sedans from Germany.

It also proves the XJ fits in the U.S. market—a market growing, in segment size and in buyers' physical stature—with room to accommodate comfortably driver and

> **"To see the changes in the new XJ requires a true Jag aficionado; its lines are subtle and it retains that distinctively feline face."**

passengers' heads, shoulders, feet, luggage and lifestyle.

Aluminum is at the core of every improvement associated with XJ. Its design is the better for it; this is a bigger car in every dimension, yet it weighs 200 pounds less than the car it replaces, as well as being up to 570 pounds lighter than competitors. Aluminum is at the nexus of its safety measures; more robust, lighter bits come together to cocoon occupants.

As for performance, XJ would be a much less competent ride and require a more potent, inefficient engine if it weighed even

5 percent more than it does, which is the minimum weight advantage it has over its competition. Aluminum keeps the body shell stiff and that means a more pleasing, sporting and quiet ride.

If you worry about XJ somehow shaking apart, understand that Jaguar employs the same manufacturing techniques as used in the aviation industry. Hushed robots deliver some 120 yards of adhesive and 3,200 self-piercing rivets into each XJ car's assembly in a virtually silent process. After walking through the plant, a visitor almost pines to hear in the distance the plink-plink of a ball peen hammer. The benefit is amazing, really, when the company quotes that portions of this car are 40 percent lighter (like the front and rear doors, the front fender) and 60 percent stiffer than the car it replaces. The stiffness and rigidity helps XJ to be among the world's safest vehicles, according to its development team.

To look at the new XJ and see how it differs from its predecessor requires a true Jag aficionado, because its changed lines are subtle and it retains that distinctively feline face. While the XJ's design is unquestionably derivative— something for which it has earned criticism—familial lines aren't a bad thing, says Ian Callum, Jaguar design director. Callum's predecessor, designer Geoff Lawson, had completed nearly 60 percent of the new car's design before Callum took over. Callum was able to make only minor changes without blowing the budget.

XJ's increased interior volume is immediately apparent as you slip into the buckets and behind the leather-wrapped wheel; shoulder, leg and headroom—even in cars with sunroofs—is on par with the competition. And trunk space is more than 30 percent greater than the old car. Some early criticism with X-type was that its interior didn't look like that of a proper Jaguar. This is not true of the XJ, a veritable forest of natural textures and finishes, from fine woods on the dash fascia and along the transmission tunnel to supple leathers throughout. Even the entry-level XJ—with mouse fur headliner—looks good with sufficient wood and enough leather to please any Anglophile. The instrument binnacle, clearly seen through the wheel, is laid out in traditional form and function with tach on the left, a large speedo gauge in the center and temp and electrics to the right, all appropriately placed.

> "Some early criticism with X-Type was that its interior didn't look like that of a proper Jaguar. This is not true of the XJ, a veritable forest of natural textures and finishes, from fine woods to supple leathers throughout."

Which is more than what can be said for the aging and ergonomically deficient J-gate automatic shifter. Like holding on to a distant notion that cod-liver oil is good for you, Jaguar insists on using this outdated, cumbersome automatic shifter in its cars. The J-gate transmission is a vestige of some archaic past that someone somewhere believes is essential to Jaguar's DNA. Sure, you can drive the car for a while and you do get used to its odd pattern, but there is nothing intuitive about it. The J-gate is not ergonomically useful and it consumes great portions of valued interior real estate.

Put XJ through its paces on long, sweeping roads or even in a meandering city center and you realize it is as much a driver's car, perhaps even more so, than the Mercedes S-Class, Audi's new A8 or even the BMW 7-Series. It competes well in terms of elegance, but ups driver quotient considerably. While the XJ8 and Vanden Plas models boast just 294 horsepower at 6000 rpm (and 303 lb-ft of torque at 4100), again thank aluminum for making it appear on the road as though it has power in spades. That is certainly the case with the supercharged 390-horsepower XJR. Not only does the R also boast some 400 lb-ft of torque, it will do a standstill to 60 mph in five seconds (compared to 6.3 seconds for the non-supercharged car). In this day of fuel-economy watching, XJR boasts a 17-city/24-highway mpg rating, equal to the last version of the normally aspirated large sedan that now earns an 18/28 rating.

On the road the XJ is stiff, and that rigidity means great things for the driver in terms of responsiveness. The turn-in is quick but not unsettling and the car tracks true. While the XJ requires lighter steering-wheel input than does the R model, it is not disconcerting or overboosted. We prefer the R's feel, and would opt for more power every day of the week, though a driver of either model would not be disappointed with either choice.

But we only had two days in the XJ. And while we put plenty of miles on the clock, it seemed insufficient in a way. Maybe it's yearning, but we're going to do something about that: we've requested a long-term tester. Truly amazing stuff when you consider its unbeatable being of lightness.

Excerpted from AutoWeek. *For subscription information, visit* www.autoweek.com.◆

1991 XJ6

If you liked the styling of this model, then it is worth your while to look for one in good condition. If the car hasn't fallen apart in the first 30,000 miles, then it should last until you're bored with it

by Gary Anderson

Dear Mr. Anderson: I was at a local auction last week and a 1991 Jaguar XJ6 crossed the block. It was light metallic burgundy with tan leather, 130,000 miles, straight, with one tooth broken out of the grille, but wouldn't start (a weak battery, we were told). It sold for just $3,750. Did I miss the deal of a lifetime or are the resale values of these cars just in the toilet?—**B. R., Portland, OR**

In short, no and yes. You didn't miss the deal of a lifetime and the resale values of the pre-Ford Jaguars are in the toilet. However, if you liked the styling of this model, then it is worth your while to look for one in good condition. It is true that Jaguar build quality had slipped seriously in the period leading up to the Ford acquisition. However, if you can find one that survived the 50,000 miles it took to sort these cars out, you can put your family into a graceful four-door luxury sedan with timeless styling for well under $10,000.

I strongly recommend the sedans built between 1987 and 1994. These can be distinguished by their headlights, missing the twin hooded headlights of the sedans that preceded them, a design feature that Jaguar returned to with the XJ8s. They were the last models to be built with the XK engine, the twin-overhead-cam straight six-cylinder engine that was introduced in 1948 and continued to be used until the introduction of the new AJV8 engines in 1996. The interiors are rich with leather and wood, and performance is quite adequate to most demands. If the car didn't fall apart in the first 30,000 miles, then it should last until you're bored with it (the one that cleared the block in your local

Just a classy ride, but an economical one. Strongly recommended—sedans built between 1987 and 1994.

> "It is true that Jaguar build quality had slipped seriously in the period leading up to the Ford acquisition. However, if you can find one that survived the 50,000 miles it took to sort these cars out, you can put your family into a graceful four-door luxury sedan with timeless styling for well under $10,000."

auction has probably fallen apart by now). The most common problems were with the hydraulic load levelers and thin brake discs prone to wobbly wear, both of which can be remedied with readily available aftermarket kits.

Your best bet in finding a nice one is to contact your local Jaguar club. The Jaguar clubs allow all years of cars to enter concours—all you need to do is find a member who is ready to sell the one he has been showing with pride. If you do, you're likely to find one with all the trim pieces in place, the Connolly leather supple with applications of saddle soap, and the finish rich with expensive carnauba wax. We've all had to learn to live with the fact that the used-car guide lists these as worth no more than $10,000, and they are not likely to ever be collectible. They've just become classy rides for not very much money.

From the December 2000 issue of *SCM.*◆

Sedans Cross the Block

#38-1950 JAGUAR MARK V DHC. S/N 647096. Black/red leather. Odo: 54,077 miles. A wonderful example of a car that rarely gets done to acceptable levels. Excellent paint and chrome, excepting one part of one landau iron. Very good panel fit; cloth top is dirty but will clean up. Excellent fit and finish to interior, and done well with proper style. Cond: 1-. **SOLD AT $49,140.** *The purchaser, "America's Most Wanted" host John Walsh, is now the proud owner of one of the nicest Mark Vs I have ever seen. Perhaps $500 away from having all the little bits cleaned and straightened out, this is one handsome and impressive big kitty. Price was full market, but no question, in this case, a bargain.* **Barrett-Jackson, West Palm Beach, FL, 3/04.**

"Extremely poor paintwork over outstanding bodywork. Overall, a sad kitty."

#81-1951 JAGUAR MARK DHC. S/N 640335. Eng. #T9870. Green/green. LHD. Odo: 900 miles. Despite having been last restored over 10 years ago, panels, paint, chrome, trim and wood all still good. Cond: 2+. **SOLD AT $53,858.** *With flowing wings, rear covering spats, not forgetting indy front suspenders and, for then, new-fangled hydraulic brakes, no wonder this William Lyons inspired beauty bettered guide price band by $3,760.* **H&H Auctions, Buxton, UK, 10/03.**

#43-1960 JAGUAR MARK II sedan. S/N P210581BW. Old English White/white leather. LHD. 3.8-liter V6, automatic. The "Golden Jaguar." All chrome is said to be 24-karat gold-plated. Replica of a car officially commissioned by Jaguar for introduction at the '60 NYC International Auto Show. Quite correct throughout. Poor fit to some seat trim. Cond: 1-. **NOT SOLD AT $25,000.** *Not sold at G. Potter King Atlantic City sale 2/2003 for $50,000.*

Disappointed owner says he has more than high bid invested in plating. Strangely likeable, appealing in the same way that James Bond films make sense—a suspension-of-reality car. **Kensington, Bridgehampton, NY, 7/03.**

#196-1961 JAGUAR MARK IX sedan. S/N 79378BW. Sherwood Green/light green leather. Odo: 61,245 miles. Reported "nut-and-bolt" $100k restoration in mid 1990s, driven 5,000 miles since. Strong presence. Paint finish high quality, some minor flaws. Panel and gap fit good, all four doors function well. Chrome good. Interior well done, leather nicely patinaed. Engine compartment and chassis clean and tidy. Cond: 2-. **SOLD AT $68,200.** *Last year for Mark IX, most developed of the big Jaguar sedans of the series. The new Mark X series went to a fully independent suspension, unit-body structure, and less appealing body style. Seller is an SCMer with full documentation of restoration Heritage Certificate; says he uses the car regularly. Awareness of restoration costs and no-stories status might have pushed the price to the stratosphere. Probably a Mark IX world record, if anyone is keeping track.* **RM Auctions, Amelia Island, FL, 3/04.**

"Be afraid, be very afraid."

> "Original leather has more cracks showing than a plumber's convention."

#071-1962 JAGUAR MARK II 3.8 sedan. S/N P219077DN. Light yellow/black leather. LHD. Odo: 15,538 miles. Floor-shift four-speed manual. Restored to a high level, with almost all chrome redone, high-quality paint, nicely refinished wood, fresh leather, and excellent panel fit. Undercoated. Right-hand headlight gasket is original and dry-rotted. A few minor paint nicks and chips from reassembly of doors and panels. Cond: 1-. **SOLD AT $38,325.** *Sold off the estate of the man who restored the car—or, rather, almost completed the car before he passed away. His six years of work (without the benefit of enjoying the car) was someone else's gain, as the price paid here wouldn't have paid for the restoration work. If someone had any inclination at all for a Mark II, this was the car to buy. Bought exceptionally well.* **Silver Auctions, Fountain Hills, AZ, 1/04.**

> "One of the nicest Mark Vs I have ever seen."

S-Types

#54-1965 JAGUAR 3.4 S-type sedan. S/N PLB3997BW. Eng. #7B4623/8. Blue/blue. RHD. Odo: 897 miles. 3.4-liter I6, 3-sp. Color-changed in bare-metal restoration. Paint, chrome, trim, veneers all excellent with only minor cosmetic wear. Has been converted to run on unleaded, changed to column shift. Alternator replaced generator, electronic ignition and fuel pump, oil cooler, modern power steering and brake units. Anti-roll bar, uprated suspension, wider wheels. Webasto sunroof fitted. Restoration started at 41,000 miles; less than 500 miles since. Cond: 1-. **SOLD AT $26,732.** *Restorations not done to original specifications don't usually bring full money, but this one was especially well done. Near top guide price paid here, a strong retail valuation, and great fun to drive, I'm sure. But say goodbye to that vintage feeling.* **Christie's, London, UK, 4/03.**

#108-1965 Jaguar 3.4 S-type sedan. S/N PLB 3997 BW. Eng. #7B 4623/8. Opalescent blue/blue leather. RHD. Odo: 889 miles. Automatic. Claimed to be genuine low mileage, having been stored for 30 years before 1997 restoration. Converted to run on lead-free gas. Wide chrome wires. All rust repaired with metal. Repaint from then still excellent, chrome pitted, retrim good apart from splits to driver's seat leather. Cond: 2+. **NOT SOLD AT $20,640.**

$25,800 being asked for looked far too expensive for Jag that seemed to be worth nearer $17,000. Obviously more than that has been spent on this car, but all that just becomes a gift for whomever the new owner is, not an investment that has any repayment potential. **Christie's, London, UK, 12/03.**

#88-1966 JAGUAR 3.8 S-type sedan. S/N P1878735BW. Black/red leather. LHD. Odo: 47,153 miles. Original leather has more cracks showing than a plumber's convention, now held together only by leather dye and paint. Wood is crazed, cracked, dry. Vinyl door panels quite good. Extremely poor paintwork over outstanding bodywork. A sad kitty. Cond: 5+. **SOLD AT $3,850.** *Once you have it at home, then what? Needs a full restoration for show use, perhaps a judicious $15,000 spent to make it a decent driver. Even at that point, dollars spent would far exceed expected sales price. Cheap, but no bargain.* **Kensington, Bridgehampton, NY, 7/03.**

> "Strangely likeable, appealing in the same way that James Bond films make sense— a suspension-of-reality car. Probably a world record, if anyone is keeping track."

XJs

#234-1987 JAGUAR XJ-6 sedan. S/N SAJAV1346HC464433. Silver/black leather. LHD. Odo: 94,678 miles. A coming-out party will be held shortly for all the rust that is bubbling all over the body under the fresh repaint. Most wood is delaminating. Front seat bottom stitching is coming loose. Seems to run out fine, driveline will make for a good kit car. Cond: 4+. **SOLD AT $5,600.** *Be afraid, be VERY afraid! A lifelong all-season Wisconsin Jaguar that is rapidly dissolving into a pile of iron oxide is hardly a car to be buying at retail plus. The seller must be very happy indeed.* **Mecum, Elhart Lake, WI, 7/03.** ◆

> "A lifelong all-season Wisconsin Jaguar that is rapidly dissolving into a pile of iron oxide is hardly a car to be buying at retail plus."

The Twenty Year Picture

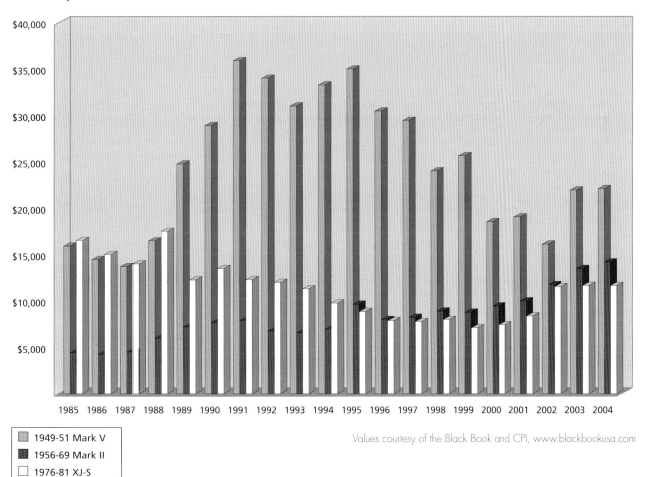

Legend:
- 1949-51 Mark V
- 1956-69 Mark II
- 1976-81 XJ-S

Values courtesy of the Black Book and CPI, www.blackbookusa.com

Section IV
Ultra Exotics

The XJ 220 is an impossibly low and long car. I saw my first one at an event in England, and was struck how much like a jet fighter it seemed. Yes, the story of this car is full of disappointments, but the end result is still a masterful piece of road-going equipment.

At an auction in Paris, I saw an XJ 220 offered for sale. It had covered about 30,000 miles, its nose covered with rock chips and some scratches to the front spoiler.

I envied the man who had spent those 30,000 miles behind the wheel of that car, on a continent where there are still places to cruise at 120 mph all day long without getting the local police all hot and bothered.

In the end, I'm glad Jaguar saw the XJ 220 project through to completion. As

the years pass, it continues to look more and more attractive. Whenever one shows up, it will always be accorded the admiration that a supercar deserves.—*Keith Martin* ◆

1990 XJR-15

As a collector car, the XJR-15 does not appears poised to set the world on fire; experts say it might become appreciated ten years from now, but for most collectors that is a long time to wait

by Bill Neill

Chassis number: 10
Engine number: XJR15-041

The history of Jaguar sports racing cars is somewhat legendary, with the C-type and D-type cars taking victories at the Le Mans 24 Hour race in 1951, '53, '55, '56, and '57. In the early 1960s the racing lightweight E-type also upheld the honors until Jaguar officially withdrew from racing, leaving the field to privateers to fly the Jaguar flag, such as Bob Tullius in the US, racing his much modified E-type, and Tom Walkinshaw in the UK, competing with an XJS in the European Touring Car Championship.

Tom Walkinshaw Racing (TWR) received factory support from 1983 and the following year they won the championship. In the early 1980s Bob Tullius and his Group 44 racing team, with support from the factory, decided to build and race a new Jaguar in the IMSA sports car category. Their success and foray to Europe and Le Mans in 1984 quickly garnered the attention of both Jaguar and Tom Walkinshaw.

With renewed factory support, TWR built and designed a V12 Jaguar to contest the World Sports Prototype Championship. They soon produced a winning combination and naturally their main goal was to beat arch rivals Porsche and Mercedes at Le Mans.

By 1987 the Jaguar XJR-8 was truly a world beater; they had a spectacular season, winning the team prize, and the team drivers filled the first four spots, headed by Raul Boesel. In 1988 they repeated this success with the new XJR-9 taking wins at Jarama, Monza, Silverstone, Brands Hatch and Fuji, and winning the World Team Championship again for TWR and Jaguar, giving Martin Brundle the Driver's Championship. More important than any of these, however, was the Jaguar victory at Le Mans after a break of over thirty years. This same season TWR bravely took on the USA/IMSA series with an XJR-9 and a major win was the Daytona 24 Hour race.

Early in 1988 Tom Walkinshaw had started thinking about building the XJR-15 and initially designated the project R9R with the intention of using the car as a test bed for the use of advanced composite materials in road cars. They used the chassis design of the Le Mans-winning XJR-9 as a base. However, the whole plan was put on hold when Jim Randle's design for the XJ 220 road car appeared and JaguarSport (the working relationship between TWR and Jaguar) decided to become heavily involved in it. But then, owing to high development costs (and takeover discussions with Ford), the XJ 220 project was shelved and TWR went back to developing the R9R.

The TWR team led by Andy Morrison recruited the respected designer Peter Stevens from Lotus and with engineers Eddy Hinley, Dave Fullerton and Jim Router created this fabulous "supercar,"

This supercar can outperform anything else with wheels, but not on US roads.

very much a competition car, but also able to be road legal. They kept the integrity of the Le Mans car by using a carbon fiber and Kevlar monocoque and body. Its 450-hp V12 engine remained a stressed member that carried the rear suspension and six-speed gearbox. The bodywork was completely new, aerodynamically efficient, distinctively Jaguar and stunning in person. In 1990 TWR announced the car to their clients as a new racing car built for a new series called the Intercontinental Challenge. As promised, the car was also road legal with sensible ground clearance, bumpers and traffic indicators.

Just 25 cars were to be built and orders flooded in immediately, despite the nearly $1 million price tag. They then decided to build 40. A month before the public launch, Jaguar too fully endorsed the car and its name was changed from TWR R9R to JaguarSport XJR-15 and 10 more were to be built for "friends of Jaguar."

The race series was held in a similar manner to the BMW M1 Pro-car challenge of the '80s, although no Formula One drivers were allowed to enter. There were three races to be held as support races to the 1991 F1 Grand Prix Championships at Monaco, Silverstone and Spa-Francorchamps with a $1 million prize for the owner of the winning car in the final race.

> "The catalog refers to the car's 'sensible ground clearance' but this may be pushing the description a little bit. The front spoiler looks about right for sweeping pine cones off your driveway."

Years produced: 1990-1991
Number produced: 50
Original list price: $1 million
Valuation: $150,000-$200,000
Tune-up/major service: $1,000
Distributor cap: $165.78
Chassis #: plate on bulkhead behind driver's seat
Engine #: stamped on top of bellhousing mating flange
Club: Jaguar Clubs of North America, 1000 Glenbrook, Anchorage, KY 40223
Web site: jcna.com
Alternatives: Mercedes-Benz CLK GTR, Porsche GT1, McLaren F1
SCM **Investment Grade:** D

This XJR-15, chassis number 10, is not believed to have taken part in the original race series. The car comes fitted with the desirable features of two seats trimmed in leather, five-speed gearbox, handbrake and speedometer and an on-board fire extinguisher system. It should be noted that this car is not currently US-road legal and is being sold on a bill of sale only. This stunning XJR-15 joined the Patrick Ryan collection in 1996 when he purchased it from another U.S. collector; it has hardly been used. It shows about 400 miles on the odometer, and for ease of use Pat replaced the racing carbon clutch with a conventional one.

Designed as part of the Jaguar competition series, this rare, all carbon fiber/Kevlar supercar would be a worthy addition to any Jaguar, supercar or sports car collection. The XJR-15 is a Le Mans winner design built for the road, yet equally at home on the track.

The SCM analysis: This car sold for $182,000, including buyer's premium, at the Christie's auction held August 19, 2001 in Pebble Beach, California.

The catalog goes on about the XJR-15 being a race car that is also road legal, only to conclude that this car is not legal on American roads. This takes away much of the fun of owning a supercar that can outperform anything else with wheels. Cars restricted to track use have a very specialized market. How can you share your super-duper car with your friends when you can't even show it to them? You can't meet them for lunch downtown without risking a ticket. You can't take anyone for a ride unless they meet you at the track, hardly a convenient arrangement.

If you owned an XJR-15, you'd like to be out on the highway making use of the claimed 0 to 60 time of 3.1 seconds, but you can't show Porsches your taillights when you aren't even allowed out of your driveway.

The Sultan of Brunei is said to own a couple of XJR-15s, but in his country they probably are street-legal.

Here in the U.S. it may be possible to get permission to drive the XJR-15 on public roads during rallies and other limited circumstances. The catalog description refers to the car's "sensible ground clearance" but this may be pushing the description a little bit. The front spoiler looks about right for sweeping pine cones off your driveway.

Certainly the XJR-15 deserves to be ranked with the supercars. With a 6-liter, dry-sump V12 engine rated at 450 horsepower, race track suspension, and AP Racing brake calipers, it definitely delivers the goods.

But there are several drawbacks. All XJR-15s are right-hand drive, limiting their appeal.

Originally, XJR-15s were supposed to be raced in the "Jaguar only" series by professional drivers, but it appears that only 16 or so of the 50 built actually participated. The car featured here, S/N 10, was apparently never raced. Although race versions had six-speed transmissions, street versions of the XJR-15, such as the car featured here, lost one gear. Because of the hard use race cars receive, non-raced XJR-15s will be worth slightly more today.

The catalog says the XJR-15's body is "distinctively Jaguar." Its designer, Peter Stevens, is also responsible for the McLaren F1, another racy shape to which this car bears some resemblance. Furthermore, the development of the XJR-15 was more of a TWR project than it was an effort by the Jaguar factory. (The last-minute name change from TWR

You can't show Porsches your taillights when you aren't even allowed out of your driveway.

> "The car is not legal on American roads which takes away much of the fun of owning a supercar that can outperform anything else with wheels. How can you share your super-duper car with your friends when you can't even show it to them?"

to Jaguar is an indication.) The XJR-15 may wear the Jaguar name on its nose, but to purists the only thing Jaguar about this sleek machine is its V12 engine.

The XJR-15 is a good example of the crippling depreciation that afflicts some high-performance automobiles. Offered for sale new at the nice round figure of $1 million in 1990, 13 years later this Jaguar sold for only 18 percent of its original price. And that's with only 400 miles of use. You could hardly ask for an odometer with a smaller number on it. Race cars often depreciate rapidly and their maintenance is rarely cheap.

It's interesting that Jaguar produced two mid-engine, two-seat supercars at about the same time: the XJR-15 and the XJ 220. Does it make more sense to buy an XJR-15 or an XJ 220? It depends on whether you want a street car or a detuned racer with headlights. The former was produced in more limited numbers and is powered by a V12 instead of a V6, but with less horsepower and a lower top speed. The XJ 220 gives its owner air conditioning, power windows and mirrors, and tilt adjustable steering wheel. (About 350 examples were built.) Plus you get tilt-up doors that lift during opening, a feature that has enthralled people since the Mercedes Gullwing.

With its firm seats and no-nonsense carbon fiber interior, the XJR-15's cockpit has more of a race car flavor. Think of the Ferrari F40. The XJR-15 is shorter and lighter than the XJ 220, which should make it easier to drive. Unfortunately for those who crave attention, the XJR-15's doors open outward in a conventional manner (like those of a Ford Focus).

As a collector car, neither the XJR-15 nor the XJ 220 appears poised to set the world on fire. (The $182,000 price of the XJR-15 shown here is only about $15,000 more than an XJ 220 that was auctioned in Monaco the same year by Bonhams.)

Although only a few dozen were built, XJR-15s appear at important auctions and usually sell for well under $200,000. RM Auctions offered two XJR-15s at their 2003 sale in Monterey, California, and one went for $154,000. Experts say the XJR-15 might become appreciated ten years from now, but for most collectors, that is a long time to wait.

(Photo and description courtesy of the auction company.)◆

Elton John's 1993 XJ 220

The buyer of this one at Christie's paid a substantial premium for Elton John's sunglasses resting on the dash for its first 852 miles

by Gary Anderson

Chassis number: SAJJEAEX7AX 220882

Jaguar's answer to the Ferrari F40 and Porsche 959.

T here's a tightly wrought intensity to the XJ 220's curvaceous silhouette; it screams haunched aggression. But this isn't some primped, perfumed and preternatural piledriver, just a polite, effortless and hugely capable machine that's disturbingly physical in its message. Drive one hard and your metabolism takes a battering; the sheer drama of being able to reach 100 mph in under eight seconds while detonating huge shards of sound from its twin-turboed 3.5-liter V6 leaving the driver strangely detached from the surreal madness of it all." (—Richard Heseltine, *Classic and Sportscar*, October 1999)

In the mid-'80s, when the supercar was born, Jaguar didn't have a car to compete alongside the fabulous Ferrari F40 and Porsche 959, even though it had the same racing heritage. Jim Randle, the head of Jaguar's Engineering depart-ment, had an idea for such a car but active pursuits distracted the company from being in the supercar league.

In 1988, after four years of development, Jaguar announced that they too would be using the knowledge gained in racing to launch their own supercar, and an amazing

> "There's a tightly wrought intensity to the XJ 220's curvaceous silhouette; it screams haunched aggression."

Years produced: 1992-94
Number produced: 281
Original list price: $625,000
SCM Price Guide: $125,000-$150,000
Tune-up/major service: $1,500
Distributor cap: $40
Chassis #: radiator support in front compartment; next to engine in rear compartment
Engine #: front of block
Club: Jaguar Clubs of North America, c/o Nelson Rath, 1000 Glenbrook, Anchorage, KY 40223,
Web site: www.jcna.com
Alternatives to consider: McLaren F1, Lamborghini Diablo, Ferrari F50

prototype of the XJ 220 appeared at the Birmingham Autoshow. The design featured a V12, fuel-injected, 48-valve 530-bhp engine and four-wheel drive.

When Jaguar was bought by Ford in 1989, Ford decided that the project should be put into production by Tom Walkinshaw's JaguarSport division. To assure practicality as a road-going customer car, Jaguar stated that 530 bhp would come from a twin-turbo 3.5-liter V6 engine that had been developed in the Group C XJR-10 and 11 race cars, with two-wheel drive. Production began in 1992.

Built on a chassis of aluminum honeycomb, the finely sculpted bodywork of lightweight aluminum was finished in one of five metallic colors: silver, gray, green, maroon or blue. The hugely powerful twin-turbo V6 engine could be viewed through a glass panel, and its design configuration limited the luggage space at the rear of the body to just enough for a briefcase and tool kit. However, the cabin was designed to be purposeful yet spacious. There was ample head room for even the tallest of pilots, and creature comforts extended to air conditioning, full leather interior and stereo.

Tom Walkinshaw's own XJ 220, order 001, was loaned to *Autocar and Motor* in June 1993, for the first, and they noted, only independent road tests of results that could be compiled. Their figures were an astonishing 3.6 seconds for 0-60, continuing on to 100 mph in a further 2.7 seconds, and the acceleration between measures well over this level were equally amazing—130-150 mph in 4.2 seconds, for example. Testing the car for JaguarSport at the banked Nardo circuit in Italy, Phil Hill clocked a maximum speed of 213 mph in the car.

In virtually every respect, the press report was complimentary. Rear view vision was not the strongest point of the car and the original price of $625,000 had its downside, but perhaps the most fascinating aspect was its pure driveability. It would later be eclipsed by the McLaren F1, but for a brief period the 220

"This isn't some primped, perfumed and preternatural piledriver, just a polite, effortless and hugely capable machine that's disturbingly physical in its message. Drive one hard and your metabolism takes a battering; the sheer drama of being able to reach 100 mph in under eight seconds while detonating huge shards of sound leaving the driver strangely detached from the surreal madness of it all."

reigned supreme, as the supercar by which all others should be judged.

This car sold for $330,998, including buyer's premium, at Christie's Elton John sale on June 5, 2001.

The XJ 220 probably would have been the epitome of desire in 1984, when a group of enthusiasts within Jaguar started a skunkworks project to develop a mid-engine, four-wheel-drive, V12 Le Mans racer for the road. Even in 1989, when Ford approved it, subject to use of the simpler TWR V6 engine that won at Le Mans and Daytona, it seemed like a good idea. Unfortunately, the car was finally introduced in 1992 in the middle of a disastrous economic environment. Even with monstrous performance and excellent road-going manners—the only complaint from owners today is that the heat through the raked windscreen can overwhelm the air conditioner on a hot day—the car couldn't justify its asking price of $625,000.

Two years ago, $275,000 would have bought you a brand-new, never-used, completely DOT/EPA-legal XJ 220 that you could have driven for up to 2,500 miles a year, imported under an exemption originally engineered for Bill Gates and his friends to import McLaren F1s. Now, the few XJ 220s that remained unsold in 1996 out of the 281 originally built have all been purchased. If you want one, you'll have to buy it at auction. If you want to use it in the States, make sure it has the required—and costly—paperwork and modifications to make it legal here. Also be aware that spare parts can be impossible to find.

Bonhams & Brooks recently sold a Euro-spec example in Monaco for $167,421. The buyer of this one at Christie's paid a substantial premium for Elton John's sunglasses on the dash for the first 852 miles. The right price, especially for one that has been legally imported into the United States, is probably somewhere in between these two extremes.

(Photo and description courtesy of the auction company.)

From the September 2001 issue of *SCM*.◆

1997 XJ 220 Two-Door Coupe

For a time there was a fair amount of embarrassment associated with the XJ 220s; speculators had plopped down deposits while the market was rising, and scurried like hunted weasels as the market collapsed

by Keith Martin

Chassis number: SAGGEAEX8AX220686

For the Jaguar enthusiast, this is the marque's finest two-seater coupe.

The magnificent looking and lavishly specified Jaguar XJ 220 coupe is absolutely the modern day successor to the multiple Le Mans-winning C-type and D-type Jaguars of the 1950s, and is derived directly from the double-Le Mans-winning TWR Jaguar Group C cars.

This particularly desirable example of the most rare and exotic modern classic was only delivered to its original owner this past June, and it was driven by him to Le Mans for the 24 hour Grand Prix d'Endurance race. The car has fewer than 1,800 km recorded. The owner offered it at a most realistic level representing considerable savings from the list price for what is, for all intents and purposes, still an as-new motor car.

It is left-hand drive, French registered, and, being a late number from the limited production run, it benefits greatly from having larger brakes fitted than earlier examples. The car is finished in factory Spa Silver with interior beautifully trimmed in Smoke Grey leather.

The Jaguar XJ 220 coupe is assembled around an up-to-date, bonded and riveted monocoque chassis, formed from corrosion-proof lightweight aluminum sheet with internally stiffened aerospace-grade aluminum honeycomb sections in areas of high stress.

The power unit is a race-derived Jaguar all-alloy four-cam V6 unit of 3.5-liter capacity, with separate turbochargers coupled to each 12-valve headed cylinder bank. Transmission is via a tailor made five-speed and reverse transaxle with synchromesh on all forward ratios, a spiral-bevel final-drive and VC limited-slip differential.

Also race-derived is the suspension of the XJ 220—suitably modified for optimum comfort plus control under road going conditions. Steering is by direct rack-and-pinion, and the brakes are power-assisted, outboard mounted and ventilated discs. The distinctive high performance lightweight

"0-100 mph is said to occupy just 9 seconds. Maximum speed is in the order of 220mph, and the XJ220 overall is absolutely one of the world's most illustrious supercars of the 1990s."

road wheels are 17-inches in diameter at the front, 18-inch at the rear, wearing ZR-rated radial-ply tires.

The performance figures include the shattering 0-60 mph acceleration time of 4.0 seconds, and 0-100 mph is said to occupy just 9 seconds. Maximum speed is in the order of 220mph, and the XJ 220 overall is absolutely one of the world's most illustrious supercars of the 1990s.

Amongst this rare breed, the example now offered here is virtually brand new. For any Jaguar enthusiast, this is a rare opportunity to acquire what will surely in future years be regarded as the marque's finest two-seater coupe.

This may be the first XJ 220 to change hands in a public arena. The new owner paid $193,993 for the car at the Robert Brooks September 8, 1997 auction in Paris.

For a time there was a fair amount of embarrassment associated with the XJ 220s; speculators had plopped down deposits while the market was rising, and scurried like hunted weasels to get out of their contracts as the market collapsed. We'll revise our Price Guide *to reflect this sale. We don't believe that XJ 220s, over time, will ever be more than an oddity in the collector car world.*

(Photo and description courtesy of the auction company.)
From the November 1997 issue of *SCM*.◆

Section V
Collecting Thoughts

This chapter is about really using your Jaguar. Whether it's showing it off at the local concours, tearing by an Italian Piazza on the Mille Miglia, or just making sure you have the right classic car insurance no matter what you do, you'll find stuff of great use in these next pages.

While we at *Sports Car Market* magazine spend a lot of time analyzing the market, pointing out the good buys and the bad, along with which models are most desirable and which you should stay away from, in the end all of us here are car enthusiasts just like you. So, after sitting in front of a blinking computer screen

crunching numbers and doling out do's and don'ts, all we really want is to get behind the wheel of a classic car and head out onto the open road.

We hope you've enjoyed your journey through the Jaguar experience in these pages. And if you don't have a Jag, perhaps you'll find yourself one step closer to owning one. If we've helped you think about what you want in a Jaguar a little more critically, and provided some tools that will assist you in making an informed decision, then our mission is accomplished. Of course, we hope you've had a little fun along the way as well. Happy motoring.
—*Keith Martin* ◆

Mille Magic

It's one of the most arduous historic motorsport events in the world—the Mille Miglia recreates the legendary 1,000-mile Italian car race using a spectacular array of machinery from the 1920s to the late '50s. Phil Weeden was there and kept a diary during Jaguar's 2004 campaign

It must have taken all of about 30 seconds to decide whether or not to attend this year's event, following an unexpected invite from the Jaguar Daimler Heritage Trust's Tony O'Keeffe.

Aside from the Le Mans classic and a couple of rallies staged in the US, there is seldom an opportunity for some of the finest historic race cars to venture out on to the open road. The Mille Miglia is probably the most demanding of all these events and yet it never struggles to draw the entrants. With space for just 374 cars and applications regularly exceeding 800, nothing but the finest breed of classic is accepted. To that end, we are pretty fortunate to see quite a few Jaguars in a line-up that, naturally enough—being in the Italy—consists of many a Ferrari and Maserati. The factory effort consisted of the famous NUB 120, XK-120; the 1956 long-nose works D-type (XKD 605); the D-type owned by Gary Bartlett (XKD 530); a 1953-Mille Miglia C-type (XKC 045) and a splendid example of an XK-SS (no 707). Racing Green Cars also entered its XK-SS (no 701), driven by Mike Salmon and Graham Love.

I had been warned that sleep wouldn't be on the agenda, but fun and long-lasting memories would. Whatever happened, it was going to be an extraordinary adventure.

Tuesday 4 May

We arrived at the Locando del Lupo Hotel, some 45 minutes from Milan's Malpensa airport. What then followed was a pretty taxing drivers' briefing. With references to CO, PT, VT and CT, it meant sweet FA to me, but I was assured it would all be OK!

It becomes glaringly obvious that we're in for a treat, as the police involved in the event turn a blind eye to speeding and most fracturing of local motoring laws, which was surely going to make for some entertaining driving.

Over lunch, it wasn't long before the inter-Jaguar rivalry was heating up. Side bets were being taken and various tips slyly passed around like they were top secret military information.

There was talk of clutch burnouts, carbon monoxide poisoning and overheating—all of which did nothing for the confidence. How would these old racers ever make it to the finish line?

Wednesday 5 May

After a late breakfast, the cars were fired up for the first time after a heavy night's rain. John May, a guardian of NUB 120 for several years now, was busily wrapping the distributor in bin liners to protect the engine's electrics from the rain. These early alloy cars just don't hold back the elements as well as the later steel ones do. The driver and passenger in NUB looked set for a soaking —and that was with the hood up!

Our next stop was Brescia. I accompanied Jaguar's Cecile Simon in a 2004 XKR convertible. Our concession to the classics was to have the roof down—but we also cheated and had the heaters and electric seats on. We were exposed to the elements but we were toasty warm inside. This and the sight of five fabulous "golden oldies" in front made for a quite surreal experience. I was

in heaven, and drank the day like it was my first bottle of water for a week.

So far it had been all rather leisurely. By tomorrow night, though, the real challenge would be about to commence.

Thursday 6 May

Definitely a day of extremes: we were up crazily early in order to get the cars down to scrutineering. I had the privilege of driving the XK-SS. A little fearful of burning out the racing triple-plate clutch, my progress was hardly swift, but I loved my brief time at the helm. It certainly gave me an appetite for more.

We arrived at 7 am in Brescia's town square, jubilant on discovering that we were just six from the front of the queue. When the inspections began at 9 am, we wouldn't be far behind. Until, that is, we peered round the corner and saw a trail of about 50 Mille cars disappearing off into the distance!

The atmosphere at scrutineering was carnival-like, with people staring in admiration and awe at what must have been over half-a-billion Euros worth of motor cars.

That's the trouble with these old race cars —no roof! JDHT's Richard Mason provides welcome shelter for Bob and Tracey Dover

Push! In the queue for scrutineering, we didn't want to keep starting the engine and killing shortly after. It would have done no favors for the battery, spark plugs or clutch.

After that spectacle we had nothing to do but wait until we headed to the old Monastery—soon to be the Mille Miglia museum—for dinner. In the meantime, the teams sorted their maps, timings and strategies. This may have been fun, but everyone seemed unquestionably serious about doing well.

After a light dinner (too nervous for a heavy meal) we headed down to the start line. More waiting. But this time the excitement was at fever pitch. The streets were lined with motorsport fans, all hoping to catch a glimpse of their favourite Ferrari, Maserati or, of course, Jaguar. NUB 120 pulled up to the queue for the start to exclamations of "Bella, bella, bella!"

After much crackling of deep, burbling exhausts, the first of our Jaguars set off—Gary Bartlett leading the charge in XKD 530. It was then our job as the support team in five new X-TYPE estates to get under way to follow these thundering classics out from the centre of Brescia.

The drive to Ferrara ended similarly to the way it began, with ecstatic crowds waving on the cars, despite the fact that it was now well past two in the morning. We climbed into bed some time after three, having hastily plugged in phones, digital cameras and computers. They weren't all going to be fully recharged by the morning, but then neither would we be; there wasn't a lot we could do about it in the two-and-a-half hours of slumber time.

Friday 7 May

Did I sleep, or was it just an elongated blink? I couldn't really tell. We were back with the cars early enough to allow John May to carry out some checks and minor jobs to NUB 120 before it embarked on a day's driving, consisting of over 600 km of some highly-challenging roads.

The day was long, but huge fun. Over 12 hours on the road in our fully-laden X-TYPE estate, covering in excess of 400 miles —this was no ordinary day.

We arrived in Rome late into the evening to more scenes of automotive adoration. While the support cars headed straight to the hotels and the finish point for the evening, the competitors were treated to a police escort into the heart of Rome, with hundreds of people lining the streets to observe a live automotive history book unfold before their eyes.

Saturday 8 May

As the sun rose over Rome, the volcanic burble of high-octane exhausts was filling the morning air. This was the final day of the Mille and arguably the toughest, with the longest stint and some testing roads up through mountains and into Bologna and Florence before heading back into Brescia. After two tiring days, everyone was feeling the pressure.

The first half of the day I was again chasing the Jaguars in our X-TYPE estate 2.5 V6 support vehicle. With tools and luggage loaded in the back—seats down—this was going to be a formidable test for Jaguar's new estate model. And boy did it prove itself. Aside from a temperamental satellite navigation system, which seemed to confuse everyone who tried to follow it, these cars seriously impressed.

After a number of untimely events, which I won't go into here, I was about to experience the Mille from the passenger seat of Gary Bartlett's D-type. Having piloted the XK-SS (albeit briefly) and put the X-TYPE estate through its paces, this was to complete the Mille experience. Talk about save the best until last. For 200 miles or so, we explored some of Italy's finest roads, witnessing some stunning scenery. When we were on the quieter stretches, we felt at one with the car, so physically connected are you with the D-type. Viewing the road ahead across a bonnet of timeless Marilyn Monroe-like curves, with a roaring XK engine making its sounds (and heat) known through the subtle louvres, it was a profound experience.

This was matched only by the elation one felt as we arrived in places like Florence with people lining the city square waving and cheering. Even though the Italians' hearts are clearly with cars of a red hue, the smiles and cheery faces showed a passion for the Jaguars, especially sports cars like the "D".

One final complication was to delay our return to Brescia. As the sun set visibility was deteriorating dramatically—and this was with the lights on. Or so we thought. Our support vehicle, driven by Melvin Floyd and Tim Card, was right behind us. So when

Checking the fluid levels on Gary Bartlett's XKD 530. The weather and testing driving conditions didn't deter this D-type; other than faulty headlights, it didn't skip a beat for the entire run.

we pulled over and discovered that we had no headlights, the chaps perfected a "get us home" fix which boosted the lights to a level they had not been for a long time. There may be a deeper rooted problem with the wiring behind the dash, which will inevitably require further investigation when the car gets back to CKL's East Sussex workshops.

We leapt back on to the open road for the home straight. It was a quick run back and huge fun. Despite the wondrous noise, the heat from the exhaust and cramped conditions, there were times of peace as we drove beneath a blanket of a clear night sky with a scattering of stars lighting our path home. It was simply magical.

We were late into Brescia but that didn't stop a few die-hard fans welcoming us back. We were all tired and yet so ecstatic. We had made it back and enjoyed every single mile. Those roads, the cars, people and places are indelibly stamped on my mind.

More information on the event can be found on www.millemiglia.it. From the July 2004 issue of Jaguar World Monthly. ◆

The results

By the end of the first night's driving, SCMer Gary Bartlett and his co-driver, Steve Cashdollar, were a heady 19th, with Roger Putnam and Jerry Juhan in NUB 120 behind in 54th. Stuart Dyble and Matt Franey were a bit further back in 124th, with Bob and Tracey Dover in 201st. Tony O'Keeffe and Victoria Macmillan-Bell were still finding their stride back in 315th. However, all this was to change.

After day two, Bartlett and Cashdollar were fronting the official Jaguar charge in 85th place, but this time the Dovers had played catch-up and were just nine places behind. O'Keeffe and Macmillan-Bell had made impressive gains and were up to 155th, while Dyble and Franey had slipped back to 170th. After a disastrous day, missing various checkpoints, Putnam and Juhan in NUB 120 had slipped to the back of the field in 339th.

At the end, the American Jaguar duo, Bartlett and Cashdollar consolidated their lead, moving up to 78th. Dyble and Franey had made up incredible ground to finish 115th, scooping the best British team prize in the process. Just five places behind were Bob and Tracey Dover while Tony O'Keeffe and Victoria Macmillan-Bell finished 162nd.

In the marque standings, Jaguar made an impressive improvement over last year, rising from 14th to eighth.

The day before the race, the Jaguar big cheeses stopped off for some... well, big cheese. Parmesan was the order of the day. Not much room for it in a C-type, though.

Two C-types, One Chassis Number—Let the Games Begin

The key question was obvious: If the car was the genuine XKC 023, where had it been hiding for the previous thirty-odd years, before turning up in Italy?

by Martin Emmison

Once completely dismantled, XKC 023 was brought back to life.

With any collectible there is always an issue of authenticity, whether art, antiquities, baseball cards or automobiles. In the collector car world, relatively minor disputes over correct engine numbers and the use of NOS versus reproduction parts are common.

Every once in a while, however, we come across a case of identity theft, in which a replica hijacks a genuine collector car's chassis number. I described the process in general terms in "The Fake and The Fall Guy" (*SCM* December 2003), but what follows is the outline of a real case, in which two cars have both claimed to be the same original Jaguar C-type. Each owner is maintaining his own conflicting version of the car's history—it will become clear which one I represent.

The story begins in October 1952 at Jaguar's factory in Coventry, England. A "customer" (as opposed to factory team racing) C-type sports racing car, chassis number XKC 023, engine number E-1023-8, was shipped to Portland, OR, for delivery to its first owner, Joe Henderson. The car's subsequent racing career was confined to the West Coast, where its closest brush with fame came from its second owner, Jack Douglas.

Douglas was a comedy writer for Bob Hope, among others, and he was friendly with Mitzi Gaynor, the star of *South Pacific* and other Hollywood films. The photo of the two shown on the next page was almost certainly taken before the sports car race at Torrey Pines, CA, on July 10, 1955. If so, Douglas' pudding basin helmet is significant, because he rolled XKC 023 in the race, and lived to tell the tale.

Douglas had the car repaired, and sold it to another California racer named Ces Critchlow. After a few successful races, Critchlow rolled the C-type again, this time at the Paramount Ranch Races on November 18, 1956.

Sometime after the crash, XKC 023 suffered the indignity of having its twice-damaged alloy body removed. It was replaced by an ill-fitting fiberglass Devin body at Horvath Motors in Costa Mesa, CA, where Critchlow worked. He was

soon drafted into the U.S. Army, and the car spent two years in a corner of the workshop, with the remains of its original body sold off. The C-type soon slipped quietly into that murky state of unloved afterlife that often befalls retired racing cars.

MISSING, PRESUMED LOST

In most Jaguar circles, XKC 023 was a mystery car—or as they say in wartime "missing, presumed lost"—which explains why more than one car emerged that claimed its identity. But I won't waste space here recounting the story of the imposter that had only the original cylinder head, nor of the "XKC 023" built around certain parts from the original discarded body. Both of these were sold recently for replica prices, and are no longer pretenders to the crown. I will concentrate instead on another would-be XKC 023, which is currently owned by a German industrialist who maintains that his car is the real one.

In the late 1980s, this car, then owned by the Italian Jaguar enthusiast and motoring artist Francesco Scianna, was entered in the 1988 Mille Miglia and some similar European events. The car indeed appeared to be XKC 023 at the time, with that number stamped on the chassis on top of the front shock absorber tower, and the chassis and engine numbers stamped on a chassis plate affixed to the car. The car even carried temporary FIA papers, which enabled Scianna to enter it in the events.

The car carried the registration mark "TGH 210," suggesting that Scianna's C-type was British registered. Had anyone

Mitzi Gaynor and Jack Douglas at Torrey Pines.

The C-type after being rolled in November 1956.

searched the UK registration records between 1988 and 2002, however, they would have found that no vehicle was so registered because that registration mark had officially lapsed from disuse in 1983, when computerization of the UK's vehicle records was completed.

Scianna sold the car some time after 1988, and its next owners were Italian, each of whom presumably believed it was authentic. After all, the car had the benefit of papers issued by the Italian organization ASI (Automotoclub Storico Italiano), and ran again in the 1994 Mille Miglia, all of which reinforced its apparent identity as a genuine C-type.

The car was offered for sale as XKC 023 at the Essen Classic Car Show in the mid-1990s, when a prospective buyer who was suspicious of its origins sent some photographs of the car, including a copy of its 1950s-style British logbook, to C-type expert Peter Jaye in England.

As the collector car movement had gathered momentum in the 1980s, a number of British companies began building C-type replicas. Some were very good, some only approximate. None, however, were more faithful to the original in the materials used and millimeter-perfect measurements than those manufactured by Jaye, who also traded in replacement parts for the original cars. He confirmed that the car offered at Essen was one of his replicas and expressed his view that its logbook was false.

An inspection of the C-type was then commissioned by an Italian dealer who had the car for sale. Lynx Engineering, another manufacturer of replicas that is well known in England for their work on original C- and D-types, reported that the chassis was in fact built by Peter Jaye, and the body by RS Panels. At this point, it became widely publicized that "TGH 210" was not the genuine XKC 023.

THE REAL 023 COMES BACK TO LIFE

Back in the United States, Terry Larson, the Arizona-based expert, restorer and dealer in C- and D-types, was researching

his book, The C-type Register. For some years he had been trying to trace what happened to the real XKC 023. He had heard about "TGH 210" from Peter Jaye, among others, but hadn't found out what happened to the original car. At least not until he was contacted by Tom Groskritz, another Jaguar racer and authority on C- and D-types, who happened to have snapped a shot of Ces Critchlow surveying his damaged C-type after the crash at Paramount Ranch back in 1956.

Groskritz put Larson in touch with a man named Frank Schierenbeck who claimed to have the real XKC 023. Larson spoke with him on the phone, and the history of the missing C-type was revealed.

Indeed the car had spent most of the late 1950s hidden under a tarpaulin, until Schierenbeck liberated it in 1962 for $1,000 in cash and an overhaul of a Ford pickup. Schierenbeck owned an import service shop in Santa Ana, CA, and was well known for his work on Jaguars. Briggs Cunningham was one of his customers.

Schierenbeck kept the car for 35 years, initially registering it for road use and entering it in local sprints in Southern California, on one occasion achieving a recorded speed of 165 mph. At a later point XKC 023 was dismantled, and Schierenbeck moved to Oroville, a rather remote part of Northern California. The disassembled car went with him, but he never got

Revealed under the weld: Positive proof of identity.

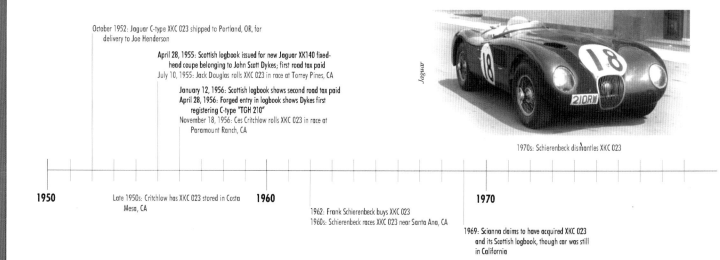

October 1952: Jaguar C-type XKC 023 shipped to Portland, OR, for delivery to Joe Henderson

April 28, 1955: Scottish logbook issued for new Jaguar XK140 fixed-head coupe belonging to John Scott Dykes; first road tax paid
July 10, 1955: Jack Douglas rolls XKC 023 in race at Torrey Pines, CA

January 12, 1956: Scottish logbook shows second road tax paid
April 28, 1956: Forged entry in logbook shows Dykes first registering C-type "TGH 210"
November 18, 1956: Ces Critchlow rolls XKC 023 in race at Paramount Ranch, CA

1970s: Schierenbeck dismantles XKC 023

1950

Late 1950s: Critchlow has XKC 023 stored in Costa Mesa, CA

1960

1962: Frank Schierenbeck buys XKC 023
1960s: Schierenbeck races XKC 023 near Santa Ana, CA

1970

1969: Scianna claims to have acquired XKC 023 and its Scottish logbook, though car was still in California

around to putting it back together and hardly anyone knew that he still had it. Except for Groskritz.

Fortunately, not just Groskritz, but Critchlow and a mechanic named Mike McEniry are still with us, and were willing to confirm the history of the car. McEniry worked on the car during Critchlow's ownership, and recalled that they welded up the spider gears in the differential to give the car more bite out of the corners.

In late 1997, Schierenbeck consented to a visit from Larson and he caught his first sight of the scattered parts comprising XKC 023. Recounting the discovery, Larson said: "We're not talking a few little bits, we're talking about everything you need to drive down the road." Moreover, he found the original identification "XKC 023" stamped on the front crossmember, one of two places where chassis numbers had been originally stamped by the factory.

ONCE HIDDEN, NOW REVEALED

On investigation Larson also noticed that one of the mounts for Critchlow's Devin body had been welded over the spot on the shock absorber tower where the original chassis number should be stamped. This had remained untouched for 40 years, so when they cut the weld and folded back the body mount, the process was meticulously recorded on film. What appeared was the number "XKC 023," as stamped by the factory, final proof indeed that this was the original chassis. Clearly, these were the parts of a complete car: the original chassis, the original engine block stamped E-1023-8, and the original gearbox and rear axle with the correct numbers.

There were many other important parts, even the original footwells, and the transmission tunnel with its original "Harduras" trim intact. All were original to the car, with the exception of the missing body (which was later acquired and reunited with the car). Larson bought everything, and rebuilt the car for his (and my) client, Christian Jenny. When rebuilding the differential, the spider gears were found to have been welded up, as recounted by McEniry.

The discovery and restoration of XKC 023 was well publicized, with articles published in AutoWeek in April 1999, in Jaguar Journal in May/June 1998, and elsewhere. As a result, a number of other people contacted Larson to provide more information and photographs about the car's early racing history.

After all of this, one might expect the story to end here—but it doesn't.

BOB'S VERY OWN "C-TYPE"

Around the same time, a European dealer acquired the Jaye replica. This dealer, "Bob," was intent on selling the car, so in his version of the truth, the "second car" discovered in California and restored by Larson was dismissed as looking "like a replica." Early in 2001, a prospective buyer was found, a German.

The German made contact with Christian Jenny, and asked his views about the situation. Not unnaturally, Jenny explained the provenance of his C-type. In various phone and e-mail communications, he provided evidence that he owned the genuine XKC 023, and warned the German in clear terms against buying the car. Nonetheless, the German did so in 2002, paying a reported €125,000 (roughly $125,000 at the time), a mere fraction of the value of a genuine C-type, which would normally have sold then for between $750,000 and $900,000.

Once he had bought the Jaye replica, the German wasted little time in his efforts to establish its claim as the genuine XKC 023. He submitted an entry for the 2003 Mille Miglia, which, amazingly enough, was accepted. In March 2003 he applied to the Jaguar Daimler Heritage Trust in Coventry (JDHT) for a Heritage Certificate under chassis number XKC 023, which to their subsequent regret they issued. However the JDHT certificate was endorsed with the words: "Please note that we do not believe this car was ever registered in the U.K."

Jaguar

Early 1980s: Peter Jaye builds replica C-type

1994: "TGH 210" runs in Mille Miglia again

1997: Terry Larson visits Schierenbeck and discovers dismantled XKC 023

1998: Larson buys XKC 023 from Schierenbeck for Christian Jenny and begins restoration
1998-1999: Discovery of XKC 023 widely publicized
Late 1990s: European dealer acquires "TGH 210"

1980

1990

2000

2004

1988: Francesco Scianna enters replica C-type in Mille Miglia as "TGH 210"

March 2003: German applies for Jaguar Daimler Heritage Certificate
2003: German runs "TGH 210" in Mille Miglia
2003: Jim Whyman proves logbook has been forged

2002: German buys "TGH 210" from European dealer for $125,000

2001: German contacts Jenny to inquire about legitimacy of "TGH 210"

The German then applied to the British registration authorities to have TGH 210 reactivated. The British system allows owners of vehicles whose numbers lapsed through disuse in 1983 to reclaim them, if they can provide documentary evidence to show a clear link between the car and the number being claimed. A new registration document for TGH 210 was issued to the German at a British address in May 2003, quoting chassis number XKC 023, engine number E1023, and a date of first registration of April 28, 1956. Clearly the documents that were submitted in support of the application had shown this information, though certainly the endorsement on the JDHT certificate about the car never having been registered in the U.K. should have precluded the reissue of the number.

The next move was to apply for a FIVA Identity Card, to open the way for TGH 210 to participate in the major European road events. When the German submitted his application to the German FIVA authority, he submitted various documents to support his claim, including copies of the old British logbook that came with the car and the JDHT Heritage Certificate.

But when submitted to FIVA, that certificate was missing its endorsement, which noted that it was believed that the car had never been registered in the U.K. Remember the famous saying that there are no problems, only solutions? The solution to the troublesome endorsement was simple—it had been removed.

The German FIVA authority, however, referred his application to its British counterpart, presumably because the British were thought to know more about the history of competition Jaguars. The papers landed on the desk of Jim Whyman, secretary of the Federation of British Historic Vehicle Clubs, who was able to call on various experts to investigate the history of TGH 210. The key question was obvious: If the car was the genuine XKC 023, where had it been hiding for the previous thirty-odd years, before turning up in Italy?

In Scotland, according to the German's papers. After its inversion at Torrey Pines in July 1955, XKC 023 was said to have been shipped back to the U.K.—not, as would have been logical, for repair by Jaguar Cars Limited, but by its supposed new Scottish owner, John Scott Dykes. He is said to have repaired the damaged C-type in his repair shop in Kilmacolm, a small town in Renfrewshire, due west of Glasgow, and then to have registered the car for the public road. After a series of further Scottish owners, the car was supposedly acquired in 1969 by Francesco Scianna, then living in Newbury,

Berkshire, England. As part of his research, Jim Whyman sent an e-mail to Scianna seeking confirmation of all this, but never received a reply. However, Scianna did write to the German maintaining his position that the car he had owned was the real XKC 023.

A BADLY FORGED LOGBOOK

The only supporting paperwork for this alleged Scottish history is a 1950s-style log book, which has been used by successive owners over the years in attempts to prove that the car is authentic. Peter Jaye saw a copy, as did Lynx, Terry Larson, and a number of others. No one that we are aware of, except its various owners, has seen the original of this logbook, so a photocopy of it is pictured here.

Jim Whyman conclusively proved that this logbook is a forgery. His research, with assistance from Jaguar's chassis book for 1955, showed that the car for which the logbook was originally issued was an XK140 fixed-head coupe, supplied new on April 28, 1955 to John Scott Dykes of Greystones, Kilmacolm, Scotland.

The original logbook was issued by the County Council of Renfrewshire on the first registration of a new vehicle. In its original form, the logbook would have identified the make, model, chassis and engine numbers, color and registration mark of that new vehicle, its first and subsequent owners, and their payments of the British road tax, recorded on each occasion by a circular date stamp. But this log-book appears to have been doctored, with the details of the original vehicle and its registration mark erased and the identity of XKC 023 and TGH 210 inserted by an inexpert hand.

There are a number of obvious anomalies. "B,R, Green" is nonsense, as the color would simply have been entered as "green"; it is also unlikely that the type or model of the car would have been described as "XKC."

More significantly, the date of first registration has been entered by the forger as April 28, 1956, and the round stamp against the entry of Dykes as the first owner has been changed from "55" to "56," whereas the first official stamp in the top right hand corner recording payment of road tax for the original vehicle is dated April 28, 1955. The second road tax payment is quite clearly stamped "12 JAN 56." It would hardly have made sense for Dykes to have paid road tax for a full 12

months before his car was first registered.

Even better, Jim Whyman tracked down Dykes' widow and daughter, who confirmed his enthusiasm for Jaguars, but had no recollection of his ever owning a C-type. They even supplied photographs from 1955 of the family's XK140 which was registered JHS 50.

It was thus an elementary mistake for the forger to have chosen an April 1955 logbook to support the supposed Scottish history of a racing car that he must have known was rolled in America in July 1955, even if he could be forgiven for not knowing about the car's subsequent accident at Paramount Ranch the following year.

TOWARDS RESOLUTION

So, where do we go from here? Christian Jenny, owner of "the real" XKC 023, has made a formal offer that the two cars claiming the same chassis number be examined at a neutral location by independent experts, to which we have not received a response. Of course, our hope is that this inspection would cause the German to stop claiming that his car is XKC 023, and to surrender the logbook to the British registration authorities as and when they revoke the TGH 210 registration for his car.

It's obvious that the German did not forge the British logbook—that was done many years ago, and he merely acquired the logbook along with the car. We might also hope that he would surrender the JDHT Heritage Certificate, and remove the improper "023" stampings from the chassis and engine, to prevent any future buyer from being deceived as to its provenance.

Sotheby's recently announced that a painting by Vermeer that had some questions about its authenticity had, after ten years of research, been declared to be the real thing. Jenny's XKC 023 has been scrutinized by the leading C-type experts in the world, for over five years, and been pronounced by all to be the real thing. Isn't it time for all parties involved to acknowledge the reality that there is only one C-type that can properly wear the stamped mantle of 023, and that the other is just a pretender to the throne?—Martin Emmison

Martin Emmison (memmison@gdlaw.co.uk) is a British lawyer representing Dr. Christian Jenny, the Swiss owner of the Jaguar C-type that was found in California in 1998 and restored by Terry Larson. The views expressed in this story are his and have not been independently verified by SCM.◆

> "It's obvious that the German did not forge the British logbook—that was done many years ago, and he merely acquired the logbook along with the car. We might hope that he would surrender the JDHT Heritage Certificate, and remove the improper '023' stampings from the chassis and engine, to prevent any future buyer from being deceived as to its provenance."

A "Bought by Phone" Nightmare

When the delivery truck pulled up, I was waiting with camera in hand to document this momentous occasion. But as the car rolled off the truck, my heart sank and I broke out in a cold sweat

by Ron Avery with Kathy Karapondo

This tale comes to us from SCM subscriber Ron Avery, who found the experience of buying a car sight unseen to be an enlightening, though altogether a quite painful one. All names (except for Avery's) have been changed to protect the innocent... and the not-so-innocent.

During the past twenty years, I've become quite a car enthusiast; I've bought and sold a good many cars of varying price ranges. My main interests have been Alfas, Ferraris and Jaguars.

Since my father passed away last year, I had been thinking about expanding my car collection to include the cars he owned throughout his life, cars that we had enjoyed together. I currently own a 1984 308 GTS, similar to my father's.

I had always admired his Series I E-type coupe, and had been saving for ten years in order to buy one. In order to make a smart purchase, I read many books on the subject, devoured anything that appeared in *SCM*, joined the Jaguar Club, and spoke with many club members, mechanics and restorers.

While surfing the Internet, I came across a 1967 Series I 4.2 coupe located in Denver. I found it on a classic car dealer's Web site; let's call it "Beelzebub Classic Cars." The ad read: "Like a dream." The price was $27,500.

I contacted "Bob Goodguy," certified mechanic and board member of the Jaguar Club of Denver, and asked him if he was familiar with this car and the company offering the car. He was, and said he'd checked out this particular car for another client several months earlier. In his opinion, the car was worth only around $17,500, and was not as nice as Beelzebub Classic Cars claimed. Bob felt the paint job was sub-par, and did not like the fact that the car had a dented floor on both the passenger's and driver's side from being improperly jacked. Bob's assessment was that this car was overpriced by about $10,000. I decided against the purchase, but decided to call the owner of Beelzebub, "Lucifer Jones," and left him a message stating why I was not going to buy the car.

A picture speaks a thousand words—and hides a multitude of sins.

> "Still skeptical, I asked Lucifer Jones what would happen if the car didn't check out. Would there be any guarantee? He said, 'What's not gonna check out?' "

A few days later, Mr. Jones called me, very upset with Bob Goodguy's opinion of the car. Mr. Jones stated that the value of the car was fair and the paint was good, though not show quality. He said that he had a good reputation, and had been in business for 15 years without any problems.

So I contacted "Jon Jag," a Jaguar restoration specialist in Los Angeles who has advised me on other vehicle purchases. He informed me that he knew Lucifer Jones and had sold him cars over the years. He said he'd bought parts from Mr. Jones before, but never a car. Jon called Mr. Jones on my behalf to discuss this particular car.

Jon called me back in twenty minutes and said that according to Mr. Jones's description, the car sounded as advertised, though he felt the price should be closer to $22,000.

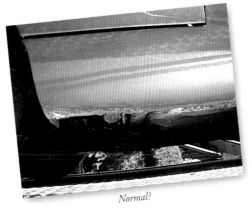

Normal?

And acceptable?

Needs paint.

I called Mr. Jones with detailed questions about the condition of the car. When asked about the radiator fan, he said that it was not stock, but worked great. He said he had driven the car himself around Denver, and it never got hotter than 70 degrees Celsius. He told me that the wire wheels were in good condition, with no rust, but could use a cleaning. After several more questions, he agreed to lower his price from $27,500 to $25,100. Mr. Jones stated that he could not come down any further in price, as he had spent $2,000 on new leather seats, new carpet, etc. Still skeptical, I asked Lucifer Jones what would happen if the car didn't check out. Would there be any guarantee? He said, "What's not gonna check out?"

At this point the red mist of desire that all SCMers are all too familiar with set in. I really wanted this car, and decided to disregard the on-site examination by Mr. Goodguy. I took a giant leap of faith and agreed to purchase the vehicle from Mr. Jones for the amount of $25,100. I would also pay for shipping expenses from Denver to Los Angeles ($951.92).

After I received the photos and a compression report from Mr. Jones the next day, and thinking of all those great times driving with my father in his E-type coupe, I wired $25,100 to Beelzebub Classic Cars.

The night before the car arrived, I was so excited I couldn't sleep. When the delivery truck pulled up, I was waiting with camera in hand to document this momentous occasion. But as the car rolled off the truck, my heart sank and I broke out in a cold sweat.

The car was not "clean" with "never any rust" as quoted on the Web site. There was rust galore. There was also lumpy paint, lots of Bondo, missing screws, incorrect replacement screws, and all of the chrome was bad—not just

"The man's story was nearly identical to mine: car bought sight-unseen, a huge disappointment when the car arrived, and a refusal to refund the entire amount by Mr. Jones. After paying shipping and accepting a lesser refund, this poor guy joined my sadder-but-wiser club. Misery loves company, they say."

the bumpers, as I had been told. I felt like I had been cheated and lied to.

I felt sick as I took the vehicle in for inspection to "Bill Bootstrap" (owner of "Bootstrap Jaguar"). During the ten-minute drive, I noticed that the car was running hot (around 90 degrees Celsius). After a brief inspection of the car and a short drive, Mr. Bootstrap informed me that in his opinion, my $25,000 car was worth little more than $10,000. He said that the entire car would have to be re-chromed—not just the bumpers and taillights, as Mr. Jones had told me.

He also said that the new leather seats were actually vinyl. The list went on and on… broken

Needs chrome.

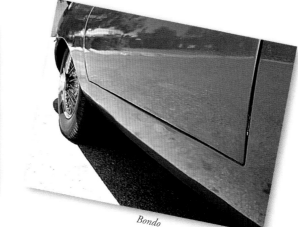

Bondo

Rust

Paint chip

hinges, torn metal, leaky transmission and brake cylinders, loose rear-view mirror, cheap paint job, and Bondo, Bondo, Bondo. There was even rust on the inside of the doors. It was becoming clearer and clearer that this once-fine car had not been well cared for at all—and I'd been had.

I called Mr. Jones several times that day. He was a bit more difficult to reach now that he had my money. He relayed through his assistant that he would be in meetings all day, and would return my call later. After several more calls, I finally reached him at home. I let him know how disappointed I was and that I wanted a refund.

He disputed my claim that the car was in poor condition, and said the amount of rust on the car was "normal and acceptable" (even though his Web site had said there was "never any rust"). He also said that if Bill Bootstrap could not tell the difference between leather and vinyl, then he sincerely doubted his expertise. He kept repeating, "It seems like you just don't like the car."

I asked for my $25,100 back and offered to pay the shipping. Mr. Jones finally countered with a $24,000 offer for the car, but I would have to pay shipping. I felt I had no other options. I reluctantly accepted his offer and shipped the car off, over $3,000 poorer, but much wiser.

About a month later, I received a puzzling call from a gentleman on the East Coast, who told me he found my insurance card in the console of his recently purchased Jaguar Series I E-type coupe. We quickly came to the conclusion that Mr. Jones had sold him the car while it was still in my possession, telling him that it was on his lot.

When Mr. Jones was asked why my card was in the car, he replied that when my financing had fallen through due to bad credit, he had repossessed the car (ironic, since Mr. Jones will not release a vehicle until it's paid in full). In order to pull off this shell game, Mr. Jones had even applied for a new pink slip, since I had the original. (The reason he gave on his application, under penalty of perjury, was that the pink slip had been "lost.")

The man's story was nearly identical to mine: car bought sight-unseen, a huge disappointment when the car arrived, and a refusal to refund the entire amount by Mr. Jones. After paying shipping and accepting a lesser refund, this poor guy joined my sadder-but-wiser club. Misery loves company, they say.

I am sharing this story because I don't want this to happen to anyone else. In retrospect, I think I knew the car was a bit over-priced, but the fact that it was the same color and type as Dad's helped push me over the edge of reason and good sense. Against my better judgment, I bought a car based on emotion, hoped for the best, and got the worst. But I learned my lesson. I will never, ever, buy another car without laying my own two hands on it.

But there is a happy ending to this story. Two months after my ordeal, I did find another Jaguar E-type, only two hours away from my home. Before the purchase, I had it inspected by a marque expert, just as before. But this time, I also looked it over myself and took it for an extended test drive. I'm happy to report that I am now the proud owner of a cherry-red 1965 E-type Jaguar, pretty much like Dad's.

From the March 2004 issue of *SCM*. ◆

Eight E-Type Myths

You have to decide what kind of Jaguar owner you will be...if you're not the kind of person who delights in every free moment prepping your car for the next Jaguar Club concours, you don't need a concours-level XKE

by Gary Anderson

Buying an E-type can be a tricky affair. As with any old car, there are plenty of potential financial pitfalls. Knowing what to watch for can save you thousands of dollars and lots of time. Before rushing into a perilous purchase, look at several cars, take your time and find the one that's right for you. More than 70,000 XKEs left the factory, so buyers can afford to explore their options. Learn about the marque and model, and get help in evaluating it and fixing up the few things that may be wrong. If you do, you'll be rewarded with a car that looks great, attracts admiring glances everywhere you go, and gives you a marvelous feeling as it swiftly takes you down the interstate or propels you around the curves of a country road.

Series Is are worth the most.

When shopping for a Jaguar XKE, like any number of other cars, there are plenty of things that require vigilance. Included in this are disingenuous sellers who will try to hook you with sales pitches that are full of information that is just plain wrong.

Below are eight of the more common creative interpretations of Jag-selling reality we've come across, and our responses.

1. Series I, II and III E-types are all equal when it comes to value.

Certainly all E-types are collectible, but their desirability, and hence their values, vary greatly. Because collectors consider it to be the "purest" of the breed, the Series I (1961-67) has the greatest value even though minor improvements made when the Series II (1968-71) was introduced (such as an improved cooling system and more comfortable seats) make it a better driver. The value of the Series III (1971-74), with the power of its V12 engine and inevitable comparisons with V12 Ferraris, falls in between the Series I and Series II.

2. Series II and III Jags with automatics are highly desired.

This is a sports car. Sports cars are defined by their manual transmissions. On the other hand, there's a proper price for everything, and if your better half doesn't appreciate the finer points of double clutching, an automatic priced about $10,000 might be just fine. But, before

> "When shopping for a Jaguar XKE, like any number of other cars, there are plenty of things that require vigilance. Included in this are disingenuous sellers who will try to hook you with sales pitches that are full of information that is just plain wrong."

you buy, make sure that the auto box is in good operating order. Some nice transmission conversions are available (such as the typical five-speed Ford Mustang box with competition gears) that replace the often-temperamental four-speed gearbox. These conversions can be cheaper than the cost of a transmission rebuild, but an original transmission in good condition is still best in terms of value.

3. You can use the same E-type Jag for show and go.

Before venturing into the market, you have to decide what kind of Jaguar owner you will be. There are the concours competitors and then there are the owners who enjoy driving their cars. If you're not the kind of person who is going to delight in spending every free moment prepping your car for the next Jaguar Club concours, then you don't need a concours-level XKE. To win a concours trophy in the Jaguar Clubs of North America, you need an XKE that not only has matching numbers on all components, but exactly the right marks on every nut and bolt. The car also has to be spotless, which means you'll have to trailer it to the meet behind your Chevy Suburban.

If driving the Jag on a twisty, dusty country lane is more your idea of fun, then you don't need to spend the low six figures that a JCNA 99-point car can fetch in today's market. You can probably find a car to enjoy for half that or less.

In terms of an investment, keeping the 3.8 engine is a wise decision.

6. Clutch slips? Don't worry.

Clutches on Jaguars shouldn't slip. Certainly the problem will never be as simple as a slave cylinder. And that innovative monocoque tub, copied from the racing D-types, around which the Jaguar chassis is hung comes with a price. To service the clutch, the entire engine and transmission has to be dropped out from beneath the car since there is no access from above. This is not an inexpensive job.

7. Any body shop can take care of that pesky bonnet fit problem.

An all-too-typical occurrence is the bonnet fit problem. The only outward symptom may be an inconsistent gap between the rear edge of the bonnet and the front edge of the car. This can be caused by several different problems—or a combination of many—all of which are expensive to fix. The one-piece, forward-opening bonnet of the XKE is its most distinctive styling feature. However, it is the most vulnerable and most complicated piece of metal on the car. Series I cars in particular were easily damaged. If not carefully opened, the front of the bonnet could hit the ground, denting the bonnet or, even worse, bending it out of alignment. Early cars have absolutely no bumper protection so, consequently, the bonnets frequently took the brunt of careless drivers. They were almost as often badly repaired.

4. Replacing the 3.8-liter engine with a later 4.2 engine enhances an early car's value.

Any engine swaps in any collectible category marque invariably reduce the value of that car. However, if the asking price is around half the value of a comparable original-engine car in the same condition, and you don't intend to show the car in competitive Jaguar concours events, then there's no reason to shy away from the cross-generational hybrid. On the other hand, if it's a 350-c.i. Chevy V8 nestled under that curvaceous hood, you're not likely to be welcomed into most Jaguar circles.

5. Servicing the E-type's racing-style discs is no big deal.

It's not difficult to change pads, but if you have to replace the rotors or service the calipers on the rear brakes, be prepared for a large charge. To get at the brakes, the rear suspension has to be dropped after first removing the exhaust system. If, like many well-used cars, your exhaust is rusted into place, you've got two large problems rather than only one small one. And that, friends, is a very big deal.

> "Any designer will tell you that the coupe (with the exception of the ungainly later 2+2 body style) is the most elegant version of the Jaguar XKE design. However, designers and enthusiasts don't always think alike, and in the contemporary vintage car world when collector cars are only driven on sunny days, a convertible will always be worth more than a coupe."

Like most other collector cars, XKE buyers pay more for wind-tousled hair.

8. A coupe is worth just as much as a convertible.

Any designer will tell you that the coupe (with the exception of the ungainly later 2+2 body style) is the most elegant version of the Jaguar XKE design. The coupe was the original show car when the model was introduced in Geneva in 1961. However, designers and enthusiasts don't always think alike, and in the contemporary vintage car world when collector cars are only driven on sunny days, a convertible will always be more desirable and worth more than a coupe.

From the September 2002 issue of *SCM*. ◆

Preparing Your Car for Concours

At Pebble Beach, I once watched the owner of a beautiful black Ferrari put a big splotch in the center of his hood with an untested polish; it was like watching someone fingerpaint over the Mona Lisa

by Richard Griot

When Keith Martin asked me to write about preparing your Jaguar for a concours event, and to keep it under 1,600 words, I thought, "Where do I start?"

That's a question you might ask yourself when detailing an entire car. When faced with such a big job, the natural tendency may be to procrastinate; but don't even think about detailing your car the night before an event. Give yourself a few weeks, and break it up into manageable tasks. Just start cleaning here and there; detailing your car little by little (maybe that's why we call it detailing). If you get started early, you'll sleep better beforehand, you'll be much more relaxed, and actually have fun at the event. And, most likely, there won't be an area of the car that you pray the judges don't discover.

Save yourself hours of work, and get a scoring sheet ahead of time from the event organizers. This will tell how many points are divided up between paint, interior, engine, etc. Some concours events don't even look at the engine compartment, so there is no need to get fanatical cleaning under the hood.

To get you started, I've compiled some tips on how to get the best results when preparing for concours. And while there are several good quality car care lines, I, of course, am partial to Griot's Garage Car Care Products (I hear the owner is a heck of a guy). You can find all the products mentioned here at www.griotsgaragecatalog.com. And, once bitten by the concours bug, you can refer to the Griot's Garage "Detailers Handbook" for that extra edge when eyeing that "Best of Show" trophy. You can buy a booklet, or just download it for free at http://www.griotsgarage.com/pdfs/DetailersHB_BW.pdf .

First, the difference is in the details. It's not what you do, but how you do it that will make the difference between "nice" and "wow." Always wash your Jaguar in a shaded area, making sure the vehicle's surface is cool; soapy water will dry on hot paint and spot. If you've been out driving, wait an hour or two

The difference is in the detail

> "Save yourself hours of work — get a scoring sheet ahead of time from the event organizers. Some concours events don't even look at the engine compartment, so there is no need to get fanatical cleaning under the hood."

and let the car cool down. Spraying cold water on hot wheels and brake rotors can damage them. Use a gentle car wash product (such as Griot's Car Wash) that is safe for all surfaces. Avoid harsh dishwashing liquid, as this will strip the wax off, and always follow the mixing directions; using more car wash than is recommended could result in streaking.

The most efficient way to clean your Jag, or any vehicle, in the following order: top, front hood, front fenders, doors, rear deck, rear fenders and the rear. This is usually going from the least dirty parts to the dirtiest. If the car is very dirty, you may want to renew your car wash and water. Save the tires and wheels for last since they are usually the dirtiest areas.

After you've washed your vehicle, run your fingers and palm gently over the paint. The surface should feel as smooth as glass. If it feels rough, or if you hear a "friction" sound, the surface still has contaminants, which need to be removed. Oils, dirt, brake dust, tar, and acid rain deposits from the environment form tiny particles that can stick to your paint. Over time, they build up and form an invisible layer (although you can see it with a 10-time magnification loupe).

Don Brister

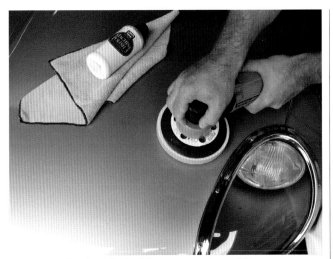

A good random orbital polisher can save you hours of elbow grease.

This is what you are feeling and hearing when you touch the surface. Even though you've washed the car, these contaminants won't come off with car wash alone. The best way to remove them is to use Griot's Paint Cleaning Clay.

This step is imperative before you lay down a coat of wax. Paint Cleaning Clay is easy to use; to get the most out of it, knead it into a ball and pat it into a flat pancake shape. Paint Cleaning Clay requires a lubricant, like Griot's Speed Shine; it's vital to the successful claying process, and allows the clay to glide across the paint. Working in small areas (around two square feet), start by spraying a two-foot section as well as the clay in your hand with Speed Shine. Now wipe the clay back and forth over the surface, making sure you keep your speed up. You don't need to rub hard; just a few passes will do it. If the clay starts to stick to the paint, it's an indication that you need more Speed Shine on the paint. For larger specs of tar or overspray, you may need to make more passes and press down a little harder. You'll feel the clay starting to glide more easily over the surface the cleaner it gets. Wipe the area dry with a clean 100% cotton cloth or micro-fiber towel. Now, run your hand over the surface again—your paint's surface should feel silky smooth.

After your paint is completely clean, it's time to evaluate the surface. Swirl marks will make the paint look poor out in the sun, but they are extremely hard to remove by hand. New polish technology and selected orbital polishers can now produce perfect results without risking burning through the paint. If you want to have a chance at winning, removing the swirl marks and enhancing your paint to perfection is a must. Judges love paint that is well cared for, and has fantastic color, depth and clarity.

The best way to polish out scratches or remove oxidized paint is with a random orbital machine and a thin foam pad. This is where many of you get scared. I know what you're thinking. "Don't machines put those terrible swirl marks in my paint?" Only if you use the wrong machine and the wrong polishes. However, Griot's Garage has developed a safe, fast and fun system that you really can't mess up. Plus you can eliminate those sore arms and elbows. The same machine can also be used to wax your car, delivering spectacular results. For detailed information as to exactly how this system works, visit http://www.griotsgarage.com/pdfs/10625.pdf.

If you don't want to go to all the trouble of removing swirl marks but choose to temporarily fill them in, use a carnauba-based wax that can handle three to six applications and not suffer from any hazing. This should hide most of the swirl marks and bring out the best in your finish. Avoid paint sealants. I'm not a big fan of paint sealants, especially on the concours show circuit. They just don't deliver the color, depth or clarity.

When hand waxing, apply your wax with a foam applicator. Cotton pads or cotton cloths work, but these are more aggressive, soak up more wax, and may actually induce small micro-scratches. As always, be sure your paint surface is dry and cool. Apply some wax to your pad and spread it evenly over the surface of the pad (a little goes a long way). Wipe it on in straight lines, back and forth and then up and down. When you apply the wax to your pad, the wax should almost begin to disappear as you wipe it on. If you have to remove a lot of product when you wipe it off (look at your cloth) you are using too much wax. Work in small areas, such as a fender or a quarter of a hood, then wipe off. Don't cover the entire car and then go back to wipe off. The wax will set-up too much and be difficult to remove, plus dirt has a chance to settle on your paint, possibly causing micro-scratches in your paint.

If you are having a problem with hazing, smearing or a dull look after removing excess wax here are some tips to help. Hazing usually happens when you've applied too much wax under a high humidity condition and the moisture is caught underneath the fast-drying carnauba wax. If the paint's temperature is cooler than the outside air, it speeds up this process, allowing the top of the wax to harden quicker. If this happens, you should let the wax fully set up more before removing it. Another way to deal with it is to keep a spray bottle of distilled water or Speed Shine handy. Spritz the surface and wipe it with a dry, clean 100% Cotton Polishing Cloth or Micro-Fiber Wax Removal Cloth. The excess wax will adhere to the droplets and be carried away with the cloth.

What brand of wax should you use? Well, mine of course! Griot's Best of Show Wax can be applied layer after layer with no hazing. You can put it on by hand, but applying it with an orbital machine is best. Imagine if your hand could make 400 passes in a particular spot, burnishing the wax into the paint; that should give you an idea about the level of color, clarity and depth I'm talking about and that the judges are looking for. We don't call it "Best of Show" for nothing!

One final thought: After you've spent so much valuable time preparing your car, the last thing you should do is to use the freebie, untested products that are given away at these events. If you need to do a touch-up on the paint to remove a smudge, it's essential to stick to the same quality product line you've been using all along. On the lawn at Pebble Beach, I once watched in horror as the owner of a beautiful black Ferrari put a big, ugly splotch right in the center of his hood using one of these freebie products. It was like watching someone finger-paint over the Mona Lisa. (Of course, I couldn't stand idly by; I ran over with a bottle of Speed Shine to help him out.) Moral of the story: Be prepared with a small (quality) product kit at the event. That way you'll be able to handle the dust, puddle splashes, and, of course, birds that seem to have a way of "awarding" their own "Best of Show" just before the judges walk by.

Now go have fun in your garage, and at the concours. I hope to see you at a future event! ◆

Price Guide

	Yrs. Built	No. Made	Price Range Low	Price Range High	Grade	Rating	Last Featured
JAGUAR							
SS I coupe	31-36	n/a	$30,000	$40,000	C	★★	
SS II coupe	31-34	n/a	$32,500	$42,500	C	★★	
SS 90	35-36	n/a	$100,000	$150,000	B	★★	
SS 100 2 1/2 Litre	36-40	190	$120,000	$160,000	B	★★★	11/94
SS 100 3 1/2 Litre	38-40	118	$160,000	$200,000	A	★★★	10/00
SS Jaguar saloon	35-40	n/a	$18,000	$25,000	D	★	
SS Jaguar DHC	38-40	n/a	$35,000	$45,000	B	★★	
Mk IV saloon	45-49	n/a	$22,000	$30,000	D	★	
Mk IV DHC	47-49	n/a	$45,000	$65,000	B	★★	
Mark V saloon	49-51	n/a	$15,000	$20,000	D	★	
Mark V DHC	49-51	n/a	$40,000	$55,000	B	★★	
XK 120 roadster (alloy)	49-50	240	$95,000	$135,000	A	★★★★	
XK 120 roadster	51-54	7,391	$40,000	$65,000	B	★★★★	4/00
XK 120 coupe	51-54	2,678	$25,000	$40,000	C	★★★	1/97
XK 120 DHC	53-54	1,769	$40,000	$60,000	B	★★★	
(SE option: dual exhausts, spoke wheels, cams, etc., add $5,000.)							
XK 140 roadster	54-57	3,347	$40,000	$60,000	B	★★★★	
XK 140 DHC	54-57	2,740	$37,500	$57,500	B	★★★	
XK 140 coupe	54-57	2,797	$25,000	$35,000	C	★★	4/95
(MC option: C-type head, cams, suspension, spoke wheels, add $5,000.)							
XK 150 roadster 3.4/3.8	58-61	1,339	$32,500	$45,000	B	★★★	
XK 150 DHC 3.4/3.8	58-61	2,489	$32,500	$47,500	B	★★	3/02
XK 150 FHC 3.4/3.8	58-61	4,101	$25,000	$30,000	C	★★	
(Add $5,000 for 3.8L engine.)							
XK 150S 3.4 roadster	59-61	1,466	$50,000	$75,000	A	★★★★	
XK 150S 3.4 DHC	59-61	inc.	$45,000	$65,000	B	★★★	
XK 150S 3.4 FHC	59-61	inc.	$35,000	$45,000	B	★★★	8/96
(Add $10,000 for 3.8L 150S FHC and DHC. Add $25,000 for 3.8L 150S roadster.)							
Mark VII saloon	51-56	n/a	$12,500	$15,000	F	★	
Mark VIII saloon	57-58	n/a	$11,500	$14,000	F	★	
Mark IX saloon	59-69	n/a	$16,000	$19,000	F	★	
Mark X/420G	62-64	n/a	$8,000	$10,000	F	★	
Mk II saloon 2.4	56-59	83,000	$7,000	$9,000	D	★	
Mk II saloon 3.4	60-66	inc.	$9,000	$13,000	D	★★	
Mk II saloon 3.8	60-67	inc.	$20,000	$30,000	B	★★★★	
(Deduct $2,000 for disc wheels, $2,000 for automatic, $1,500 for no overdrive.)							
XK C-type	50-53	54	$750,000	$900,000	A		
XK D-type	53-55	77	$800,000	$1,200,000	A		
XK-SS	56-57	18	$850,000	$1,100,000	A		
(Price ranges for XK C, D and SS Jaguars are determined by provenance, completeness and originality. A car with all of its original parts and no stories will bring three to four times what a "bitsa" that has only a few authentic parts will.)							
XKE factory lightweight	61-62	16	$900,000	$1,100,000	A	★★★	
XKE convertible 3.8 flat-floor	61-62	7,827	$35,000	$60,000	B	★★★★	
XKE coupe 3.8 flat-floor	61-62	7,669	$25,000	$35,000	B	★★★	
XKE convertible 3.8	62-64	inc.	$35,000	$55,000	B	★★★★	
XKE coupe 3.8	62-64	inc.	$25,000	$35,000	B	★★★	11/04
XKE convertible 4.2 (SI)	64-67	9,548	$35,000	$60,000	B	★★★	
XKE coupe 2+2	66-67	4,220	$14,000	$16,000	D	★★	
(Deduct $3,000 for automatic transmission.)							
XKE coupe 4.2 (SI)	64-67	7,770	$30,000	$45,000	B	★★★	
XKE convertible 4.2 (SII)	68-71	8,627	$30,000	$45,000	C	★★★	
XKE coupe 2+2 (SII)	68-71	5,326	$13,000	$18,000	D	★★	
(Add $1,000 for air conditioning. Deduct $3,000 for automatic transmission.)							
XKE coupe 4.2 (SII)	68-71	4,855	$18,000	$27,000	C	★★★	
XKE convertible V12 (SIII)	71-74	7,990	$32,500	$50,000	B	★★★	2/03
XKE coupe V12 (SIII)	71-74	7,297	$20,000	$27,000	C	★★	
(For SIII, deduct $3,000 for automatic, $2,000 for disc wheels, $1,000 for no air conditioning. Add $3,000 for factory hardtop.)							
XJ 220	91-93	300	$125,000	$150,000	B	★★	9/01
(Due to changes in US DOT laws, XJ 220s can now be brought into the US.)							
XK-8 coupe	97-03	n/a	$20,000	$65,000	C	★	
XK-8 convertible	97-03	n/a	$23,000	$70,000	C	★★	
XKR coupe	00-03	n/a	$35,000	$80,000	C	★★	
XKR convertible	00-03	n/a	$38,000	$85,000	C	★★	

Advertisers

FOR SALE
1973 JAGUAR V-12 RDSTR.
BOTH TOPS • LOW MILES
$55,000/OFFER

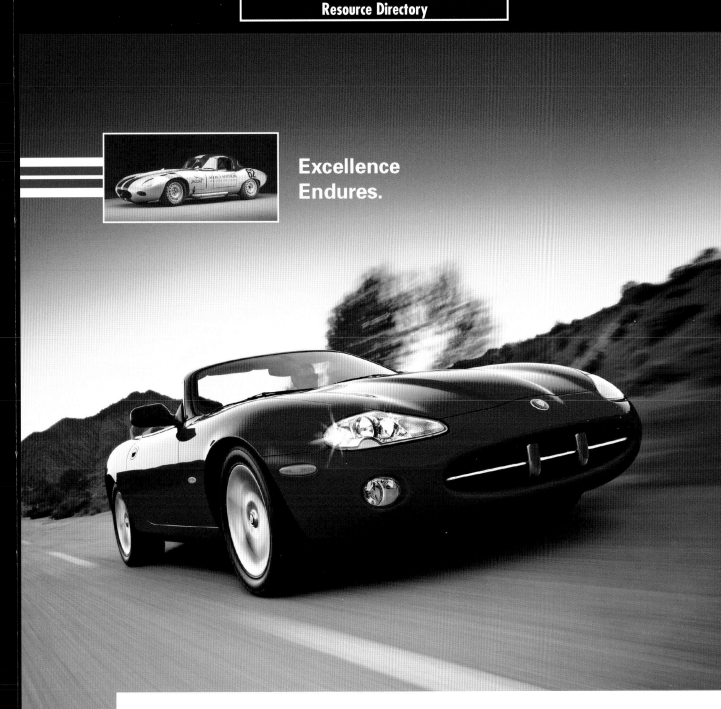

**Excellence
Endures.**

Celebrating 30 Years of Sales, Service and Stewardship.

503.224.3232
1638 W. Burnside
www.monteshelton.com   Portland, OR 97209

MONTE SHELTON
JAGUAR

INFINITE LOVE

INFINITE RESULTS

www.zymol.com
800.999.5563

XJR

born with: revolutionary alloy body

As you lead the 390-hp XJR into each successive curve, it all makes sense. An incredible amount of horsepower pulling an incredibly light and rigid body leads to an array of rewards from the laws of nature. Hairs standing on end, for example.

Bauer Jaguar • 1455 South Auto Mall Drive • Santa Ana, CA • (714) 953-4800 • www.bauerjaguar.com

JAGUAR
Born to perform

lives for: driving 100 miles to travel 30

© 2004 Jaguar Cars

Classic.

1962 E-TYPE

2003 XK

Future Classic.

Jaguar Select Edition is sponsoring a pair of legendary E-TYPEs at vintage racing events nationwide. Which is only fitting. After all, as a repeat winner of IntelliChoice's Best Pre-Owned Luxury Program award, Jaguar Select Edition has an impressive track record of its own.

| Best Pre-Owned Luxury Program* | Best Warranty in Class** 6-year/100,000-mile No deductible | Best Checklist in Class* 140-point inspection | 24-Hour Roadside Assistance | Complimentary Oil and Filter Maintenance*** |

 | SELECT EDITION RACING

Jaguar

Jaguar Specialists

Motoring, Racing, or Show, We Offer Superb Restoration & Cat Care

Automotive Restorations, Inc.
1785 Barnum Avenue
Stratford, CT 06614
203.377.6745 tel
203.386.0486 fax

WWW.AUTOMOTIVERESTORATIONS.COM

MORE MUST-READS!

Keith Martin on Collecting Ferrari collects *Sports Car Market*'s best articles **and** auction reports covering the Ferrari marque, including many articles by **renowned** Ferrari experts Mike Sheehan, John Apen and Steve Ahlgrim.

Inside you'll find information on what to buy, how to buy, what to look for and **how** to use Ferraris from 1947 to the current day, with values from $15,000 to $9 million.

Keith Martin on Collecting Ferrari is a gold mine for anyone who loves Ferraris. Full of pithy comments and straight talk about the pros and cons of Ferrari **ownership**, this book is a terrific value for Ferrari lovers and fans of *SCM*.

What SCMer Jerry Seinfeld has to say about *Keith Martin on Collecting Porsche*:

"Why anyone, other than me, would be interested in this amount of Porsche drivel I can't imagine! I, of course, read each word as if it were heart attack nitroglycerine tablet instructions."

The best of *SCM* on Porsche from the past decade. Foreword by Hurley Haywood. Profiles, market reports, 356/911 Q&A, more. 112 pages, full color.

Order your copy today!

Just $19.95 each plus shipping. To order, call 800.289.2819 (outside US 503.243.1281), fax 503.253.2234, or order online at www.sportscarmarket.com.

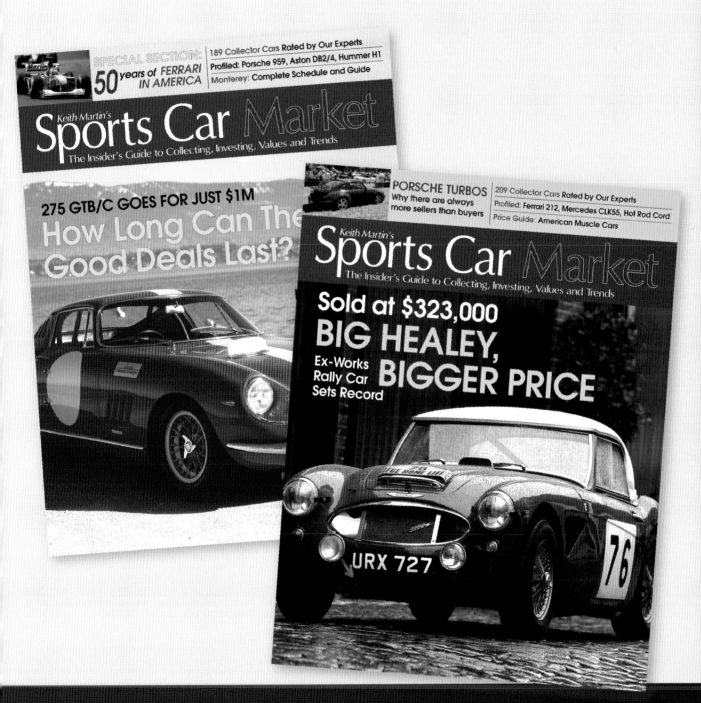

AUCTION COMPANIES

Artcurial-Briest-Poulain-Le Fur. +33.1.42992020, fax +33.1.42992021. Maison de vente aux enchères, 7, Rond-Point des Champs Elysées, 75008 Paris. artcurial@auction.fr. www.artcurial.com. (FR)

Barrett-Jackson Auction. 480.421.6694, fax 480.421.6697. 3020 North Scottsdale Rd, Scottsdale, AZ 85251. info@barrett-jackson.com. www.barrett-jackson.com. (AZ)

Bonhams & Butterfields. 415.391.4000, fax 415.391.4040. 220 San Bruno Avenue, San Francisco, CA 94103. www.butterfields.com. (CA)

Bonhams. +44.207.228.8000, fax +44.207.585.0830. Montpelier St., Knightsbridge, London, SW7 1HH. www.bonhams.com. (UK)

Branson Collector Car Auction. 800.335.3063, Jim Cox, fax 417.336.5616, 1316 W. Hwy. 76, Suite 199, Branson, MO, 65616. www.bransonauction.com. (MO)

Christie's. 310.385.2699, fax 310.385.0246. 360 N. Camden Dr., Beverly Hills, CA 90210. www.christies.com. (CA)

Dana Mecum Auction Company. 815.568.8888, fax 815.568.6615. P.O. Box 422, Marengo, IL 60152. www.mecumauction.com. (IL)

eBay Motors. List your car for sale for only $40 and pay $40 more when it sells. Visit the "Services" section on www.ebaymotors.com for more details.

H&H Classic Auctions. +44.1925.730630, fax +44.1925.730830. Whitegate Farm, Hatton Lane, Hatton, Cheshire, UK. WA4 4BZ info@classic-auctions.co.uk, www.classic-auctions.com. (UK)

Kensington Motor Group, Inc. 631.537.1868, fax 631.537.2641. P.O.Box 2277, Sag Harbor, NY 11963. KenMotor@aol.com. (NY)

Palm Springs Auctions Inc. Keith McCormick, 760.320.3290, fax 760.323.7031. 244 N. Indian Canyon Dr., Palm Springs, CA 92262. www.classic-carauction.com. (CA)

RM Auctions, Inc. 800.211.4371, fax 519.351.1337 One Classic Car Dr., Blenheim, ON NOP 1A0. www.rmauctions.com. (CAN)

Russo and Steele. 480.517.4005, fax 480.517.9112. 4117 N. 16th St, Phoenix, AZ 85016. russoandsteele@qwest.net, www.russoandsteele.com. (AZ)

AUTOMOBILIA

Spyder Enterprises. 831.659.5335, fax 831.659.5335. Since 1980, providing serious collectors with the finest selection of authentic, original vintage posters, pre-war thru mid-1960s; mainly focused on Porsche, Ferrari, Mercedes, and racing. Producer of "Automobilia Monterey" August 10-12, 2004. 38-page list of memorabilia available. singer356@aol.com or www.vintageautoposters.com. (CA)

www.arteauto.com. 631.329.8580. l'art et l'automobile gallery and auction house Web site, featuring drawings, paintings, prints, vintage posters, photos, sculptures, objects, toys, models, books, literature, memorabilia, and more from the beginning of the automobile to date. View online and mail order automobilia auction lots. info@arteauto.com. (NY)

BUY/SELL/GENERAL

Cosmopolitan Motors LLC. 206.467.6531, fax 206.467.6532. 2030 8th Ave., Seattle, WA 98121. Experts in collector cars worldwide. Whether buying, selling, evaluating, consigning or appraising, we cut the edge on the current market. Over 1 billion dollars in worldwide experience. Top prices paid; from one car to entire collections, condition and location are no obstacles. sales@cosmopolitanmotors.com. (WA)

eBay Motors. Everyday drivers, collector cars, auto parts and accessories, motorcycles and automobilia. List your car for sale for only $40 and pay $40 more when it sells. Every vehicle transaction is covered by $20,000 in free insurance. www.ebaymotors.com.

Fantasy Junction. 510.653.7555, fax 510.653.9754. 1145 Park Ave., Emeryville, CA 94608. Specializing in European collectible autos and racing cars from the 1920s to the 1970s, with over 50 cars in stock. Bruce Trenery has over 25 years exprience in this business, based in the East Bay area. sales@fantasy-junction.com, www.fantasyjunction.com. (CA)

Grand Prix Classics. 858.459.3500, fax 858.459.3512. 7456 La Jolla Blvd., La Jolla, CA 92037. Specialize in the buying, selling trading and consignment of historic sports and racing cars. Been in business for 25 years and maintain an inventory of 15 to 20 historic cars. www.grandprix-classics.com; info@grandprix-classics.com. (CA)

Hyman Ltd. 314.524.6000. One of the largest dealers of quality collector cars in the US with over 100 cars in stock. We act as principal in the acquisition of collector cars and are aggressive buyers for complete collections. Our specialties include European sports cars and full classics. www.hymanltd.com. (MO)

Oldtimer Garage. +41.31.8190000, fax +41.31.8195191. Gurbestrasse 3, CH-3125, Toffen, Bern, Switzerland. www.oldtimergarage.com. (CH)

www.historicalcars.com We buy, we sell, we find. Europe/US/Asia/Far East. If you are looking to buy or sell a vehicle with historic or collector appeal, try us. 30 years of experience, your satisfaction our priority. Any time, any place. www.historicalcars.com.

CLASSIC CAR TRANSPORT

Cosdel International. 415.777.2000, fax 415.543.5112. Now in its 33rd year of international transport. Complete service, including import, export, customs clearances, DOT and EPA, air/ocean, loading and unloading of containers. Contact Martin Button, info@cosdel.com, www.cosdel.com. (CA)

Passport Transport. 800.325.4267, fax 314.878.7295. Classic and specialty cars delivered anywhere in the USA. Special event services, including Pebble Beach, Monterey Historics, Barrett-Jackson, and Auburn. Standard-of-the-industry service since 1970. www.passporttransport.com. (MO)

Intercity Lines, Inc. 800.221.3936, fax 413.436.9422. Rapid, hassle-free, coast-to-coast service. Insured, enclosed transport for your valuable car at affordable prices. State-of-the-art satellite transport tracking. Complete service for vintage races, auctions, relocations. www.intercitylines.com. (MA)

PC BEAR Auto Transport. 717.859.1585, 135 Broad St., Akron, PA 17501. Specializing in all types: hobby, collector vehicles, toys, neat old stuff, regular cars, parts, and winching. Life-long car nut. Clean driving record since 1959 in all states. I sleep in my truck while transporting. Door to door delivery. Talk to me anytime. (PA)

Concours Transport Systems. 702.361.1928, 253.973.3987, fax 702.269.0382. Enclosed auto transport nationwide. Liftgateloading, experienced personnel. Classic and exotic cars. Special events. Fully insured. All major credit cards accepted. Fred Koller, owner. fredkoller@concourstransport.com, www.concourstransport.com. (WA)

COLLECTOR CAR FINANCING

J.J. Best Banc & Company. 800.USA.1965, fax 508.945.6006. The largest national leader on Antique, Classic, Exotic, Rod, and Sports Cars with low rates and long terms. Call, fax or e-mail your application today for quick 10-minute approval. www.jjbest.com. (MA)

Woodside Credit. 800.717.5180, fax 800.717.5177. Founded on more than 40 years of consumer lending experience, we are dedicated to providing our dealers and customers with attractive financing options. Competitive rates, flexible terms, and consumer lending expertise. Contact us directly, apply online, or ask your dealer. Open 7 days a week. www.woodside-credit.com.

COLLECTOR CAR INSURANCE

Hagerty Collector Car Insurance. 800.922.4050. Collector cars aren't like their late-model counterparts. These classics actually appreciate in value so standard market policies that cost significantly more won't do the job. We'll agree on a fair value and cover you for the full amount. No prorated claims, no hassles, no games. www.hagerty.com. (MI)

Parish Heacock Classic Car Insurance. 800.678.5173. We understand the needs of the classic car owner—agreed value, one liability charge, 24-hour claim service and the ease of paying for your premium by credit card. Available in 44 states throughout the US. Get an instant quote at www.parishheacock.com. (FL)

COLLECTOR CAR LEASING

Premier Financial Services. 203.267.7700, fax 203.267.7773. With over 20 years of experience specializing in exotic, classic and vintage autos, our Lease Purchase plan is ideal for those who wish to own their vehicle at the end of the term as well as those who like to change cars frequently. Our Simple Interest Early Termination plan allows you the flexibility of financing with the tax advantages of leasing. www.whynotlease.com. (CT)

Putnam Leasing. 866.905.3273, Never get in a car with strangers. Custom-tailored, lease-to-own financing for your dream car. Easy, fast, and dependable. Exclusive leasing agent for Barrett-Jackson, Cavallino, and Ferrari Club of America 2004 International Meet. www.putnamleasing.com. (CT)

PHOTOGRAPHY

Bob Dunsmore Racing Photography. PO Box 80008, Multnomah, OR 97280. 503.244.4646. photoraces@aol.com. (OR)

RESTORATION – GENERAL

CARS of Pittsburgh, Inc. 866.877.8866, fax 412.653.3798. 1147 Cochran's Mill Rd., Pittsburgh, PA 15236. Complete classic and custom auto restoration/fabrication. Metal repair, polishing, and plating. Pre-purchase inspection, appraisals and title services. The most customer friendly restoration company in the world. davidsteffan@carsofpgh.com, www.carsofpgh.com. (PA)

Performance Restoration. 440.968.3655, fax 440.968.3263. 17444 US Route 6, Montville, OH 44064. Metal fabrication, prep and paint work experts. Knowledgeable mechanics for running gear, suspension, electrical, and carburetion issues. As mentioned in The Wrenching Truth, *SCM*, March 2002. We finish your projects! supercharged@alltel.net. (OH)

Guy's Interior Restorations. 503.224.8657, fax 503.223.6953. Award-winning interior restoration. Leather dyeing and color matching. 431 NW 9th, Portland, OR 97209. (OR)

SPORTS AND COMPETITION

Vintage Racing Services, Inc. (ARI/VRS), 203.377.6745, fax 203.386.0486, 1785 Barnum Ave., Stratford, CT 06614. Vintage race car restoration, preparation and race track support at events throughout North America; in Europe and South America by arrangement. Historic Rally Support. www.vintageracing-services.com. (CT)

VINTAGE EVENTS

The Colorado Grand. 970.926.7810, fax 970.926.7835. Frank Barrett. 1,000-mile tour of western Colorado. Pre-1961 sports cars. (CO)

CLUB

Jaguar Clubs of North America. 888.CLUBJAG, JCNA, 100 Glenbrook Rd, Anchorage, KY 40223. The primary organization of Jaguar enthusiasts in the US and Canada. 52 local clubs provide social and other activities. JCNA sponsors championships in concours, rally, slalom. Members receive bi-monthly Jaguar Journal magazine. www.jcna.com. (KY)

This 1952 XK 120 was driven by Sterling Moss in the 1953 Scunthorpe Grand Prix. Pictured here on the 2004 Colorado Grand.